# Remarkable Birds

# Remarkable Birds
## of South Africa

Dr Peter le Sueur Milstein

BRIZA

Published by
BRIZA PUBLICATIONS
CK 1990/011690/23

PO Box 56569
Arcadia 0007
Pretoria
South Africa
www.briza.co.za

First edition, first impression 2010

Copyright © in text: Dr Peter le Sueur Milstein
Copyright © in photographs: Individual photographers
Copyright © in published edition: Briza Publications

All rights reserved. No part of this publication may be reproduced or transmitted in any form or by any means without written permission of the copyright holders.

ISBN 978 1 875093 58 8

Project manager: Reneé Ferreira
Cover design: Sally Whines, The Departure Lounge
Inside design and typesetting: Alicia Arntzen, Purple Turtle Publishing Services
Printed and bound by Craft Print International Ltd., 9 Joo Koon Circle, Singapore

While every effort has been made to trace copyright holders, this did not always prove possible. Please contact the publisher with queries in this regard.

**Front cover:** *Lesser Jacana* (Microparra capensis), *the world's smallest jacana species, about to settle on its magnificent glossy eggs.* (Photo: Alan Weaving)
**Back cover – top to bottom:** *Ostrich* (Struthio camelus) *eggs hatching.* (Photo: Eliot Lyons); *Green Twinspot* (Mandingoa nitidula) *male.* (Photo: Cyril Laubscher); *Great White Pelican* (Pelecanus onocrotalus) *group.* (Photo: Sharon Heald); *Half-collared Kingfisher* (Alcedo semitorquata). (Photo: Geoff McIlleron)
**Half title page:** *A trio of Wattled Cranes* (Bugeranus carunculatus) *resembling a line of chorus girls.* (Photo: Clem Haagner)
**Title page:** *Alert Lilac-breasted Roller* (Coracias caudatus) *on the lookout for small vertebrate and invertebrate prey.* (Photo: John Wesson)
**Acknowledgements page:** *Pair of Blue Cranes* (Anthropoides paradiseus) *with their large chicks.* (Photo: Clem Haagner)
**Contents page:** *Southern Double-collared Sunbird* (Cinnyris chalybeus). (Photo: Nico Myburgh)
**Endpapers:** *African Skimmer hunting in its normal spectacular way at dusk.* (Photo: Tony Heald)

*Dedicated to the wonder of God's great plan,
as we increasingly unravel more about its infinite wisdom bit by bit*

## Acknowledgements

I would like to acknowledge first and foremost the loving help and support of my family during the lengthy gestation of this book, particularly during the trying periods of my recent illnesses. Then I would like to thank the many friends and acquaintances as far as England and Australia who have been kind enough to supply the brilliant bird photographs which illustrate it and who are named in each case, as well as various other friends who assisted me when I struggled. Sonja van der Berg kindly did the typing of the great majority of my hieroglyphics willingly. My grateful thanks are also due to the Matron of Rusoord (Centurion), Mrs Magda Labuschagne, and her able staff for the facilities provided to me.

Obviously I would like to thank Briza for all the essential assistance they have given me, particularly Christo Reitz, who had the vision and commissioned the book through Briza, and Reneé Ferreira and her team who cheerfully provided the absolute essential support and assistance without which nothing would have eventuated.

Finally I would like to thank Bets for inspiration to keep going and complete the task when I faltered.

# Contents

Introduction ........................................................... 8

## ORDER STRUTHIONIFORMES ............. 10
Family Struthionidae: Ostrich ............................. 10

## ORDER GALLIFORMES ........................ 12
Family Phasianidae: Francolins, Partridges and
    Quails ............................................................ 12
Family Numididae: Guineafowls ....................... 14

## ORDER ANSERIFORMES ...................... 15
Family Dendrocygnidae: Whistling Ducks ........ 15
Family Anatidae: Ducks and Geese .................... 17

## ORDER TURNICIFORMES .................... 19
Family Turnicidae: Buttonquails ........................ 19

## ORDER PICIFORMES ............................. 21
Family Indicatoridae: Honeyguides and
    Honeybirds ................................................... 21
Family Picidae: Woodpeckers and Wrynecks ... 23
Family Lybiidae: African Barbets ...................... 25

## ORDER BUCEROTIFORMES ................. 27
Family Bucerotidae: Typical Hornbills .............. 27
Family Bucorvidae: Ground-hornbills ............... 29

## ORDER UPUPIFORMES ......................... 31
Family Upupidae: African Hoopoe .................... 31
Family Phoeniculidae: Wood-hoopoes ............... 33
Family Rhinopomastidae: Scimitarbills ............. 35

## ORDER TROGONIFORMES .................. 36
Family Trogonidae: Trogons ............................... 36

## ORDER CORACIIFORMES .................... 38
Family Coraciidae: Typical Rollers .................... 38
Family Alcedinidae: Alcedinid Kingfishers ....... 40
Family Dacelonidae: Dacelonid Kingfishers ..... 42
Family Cerylidae: Cerylid Kingfishers .............. 44
Family Meropidae: Bee-eaters ............................ 46

## ORDER COLIIFORMES .......................... 48
Family Coliidae: Mousebirds .............................. 48

## ORDER CUCULIFORMES ...................... 50
Family Cuculidae: Old World Cuckoos ............. 50
Family Centropodidae: Coucals .......................... 53

## ORDER PSITTACIFORMES .................... 55
Family Psittacidae: Parrots .................................. 55

## ORDER APODIFORMES ......................... 58
Family Apodidae: Swifts and Spinetails ............ 58

## ORDER MUSOPHAGIFORMES ............. 60
Family Musophagidae: Turacos (Louries) ......... 60

## ORDER STRIGIFORMES ........................ 63
Family Tytonidae: Barn Owls and Bay Owls .... 63
Family Strigidae: True Owls ............................... 64

## ORDER CAPRIMULGIFORMES ............ 67
Family Caprimulgidae: Nightjars ........................ 67

## ORDER COLUMBIFORMES ................... 69
Family Columbidae: Pigeons and Doves ........... 69

## ORDER GRUIFORMES ........................... 71
Family Otidae: Bustards and Korhaans .............. 71
Family Gruidae: Cranes ...................................... 74
Family Heliornithidae: Finfoots ......................... 76
Family Rallidae: Crakes, Rails, Gallinules, Flufftails
    and Coots ...................................................... 78

## ORDER CHARADRIIFORMES ............... 81
Family Pteroclidae: Sandgrouse .......................... 81
Family Scolopacidae: Waders ............................. 83
Family Rostratulidae: Painted-snipes ................. 85
Family Jacanidae: Jacanas ................................... 87
Family Chionidae: Sheathbills ............................ 89
Family Burhinidae: Dikkops (Thick-knees) ....... 91
Family Haematopodidae: Oystercatchers ........... 93
Family Recurvirostridae: Avocets and Stilts ..... 95

Family Charadriidae: Plovers ................................. 96
Family Dromadidae: Crab Plover ........................ 100
Family Glareolidae: Coursers and Pratincoles ......... 103
Family Laridae: Skuas, Skimmers, Gulls and Terns 105

## ORDER FALCONIFORMES ........................ 108
Family Accipitridae: Hawks, Kites, Vultures,
  Buzzards and Eagles .................................... 108
Family Sagittariidae: Secretarybird ....................... 112
Family Falconidae: True Falcons ......................... 114

## ORDER CICONIIFORMES ........................ 117
Family Podicipedidae: Grebes ............................. 117
Family Phaethontidae: Tropicbirds ....................... 118
Family Sulidae: Gannets and Boobies .................. 120
Family Anhingidae: Darters ................................ 122
Family Phalacrocoracidae: Cormorants ................. 123
Family Ardeidae: Herons, Egrets and Bitterns ........ 125
Family Scopidae: Hamerkop .............................. 129
Family Phoenicopteridae: Flamingoes .................. 132
Family Threskiornithidae: Ibises and Spoonbills ..... 135
Family Pelicanidae: Pelicans .............................. 137
Family Ciconiidae: Storks .................................. 139
Family Fregatidae: Frigatebirds ........................... 142
Family Spheniscidae: Penguins ........................... 144

## ORDER PROCELLARIIFORMES ............. 147
Family Hydrobatidae: Storm-petrels ..................... 147
Family Diomedeidae: Albatrosses ........................ 149
Family Procellariidae: Petrels and Shearwaters ....... 151

## ORDER PASSERIFORMES ....................... 153
Family Pittidae: Pittas ....................................... 153
Family Eurylaimidae: Broadbills .......................... 154
Family Oriolidae: Old World Orioles ................... 155
Family Dicruridae: Drongos ...................... 156
Family Monarchidae: Monarch
  Flycatchers ................................................. 157
Family Malaconotidae: Bush-shrikes,
  Puffbacks, Tchagras, Boubous, Helmet-shrikes,
  Batises and Wattle-eyes ................................ 159
Family Corvidae: Crows and Ravens ..................... 161
Family Laniidae: True Shrikes ............................. 162
Family Campephagidae: Cuckooshrikes .................. 163
Family Chaetopidae: Rockjumpers ...................... 165
Family Paridae: Tits and Penduline-Tits ................ 166
Family Hirundinidae: Swallows and Martins .......... 167
Family Pycnonotidae: Bulbuls and Nicators ........... 169
Family Sylviidae: Leaf-warblers, Babblers and
  Warblers .................................................... 170
Family Zosteropidae: White-eyes ......................... 172
Family Cisticolidae: African Warblers ................... 173
Family Alaudidae: Larks and Sparrowlarks ............. 175
Family Salpornithidae: Spotted Creeper ................. 176
Family Muscicapidae: Thrushes, Robins, Chats
  and Old World Flycatchers ............................ 177
Family Sturnidae: Starlings, Mynas and Oxpeckers 182
Family Nectariniidae: Sunbirds ........................... 184
Family Promeropidae: Sugarbirds ........................ 185
Family Ploceidae: Weavers, Queleas and Widows ... 186
Family Estrildidae: Waxbills, Firefinches and
  Twinspots .................................................. 189
Family Viduidae: Whydahs, Widow-finches and
  Cuckoo-finch .............................................. 192
Family Passeridae: Sparrows and Petronias ............. 194
Family Motacillidae: Wagtails, Longclaws and
  Pipits ......................................................... 195
Family Fringillidae: Canaries, Buntings and
  Chaffinches ................................................ 196

Epilogue ....................................................... 198

Bibliography ................................................ 199

Index ........................................................... 202

# Introduction

For aeons, birds have been of great fascination to humans. From the earliest of times, humans have admired and envied the ability of birds to fly. Apart from providing a considerable source of food, people have always found the great variety of sizes, colours and shapes of birds, together with their fascinating habits and often hauntingly beautiful birdsong, most appealing. This interest in birds continues unabated today. Birdwatching for recreation, or simply 'birding' as it has come to be known, has grown incredibly to become the largest-scale outdoor activity in the world.

This book is not a field guide to our country's avifauna. The aims of field guides are twofold. First they are well illustrated to enable birders to identify the birds they encounter, and have become a specialized industry with an art form of their own. The second aim of a field guide is to indicate on accompanying maps the natural distribution of each bird species, preferably indicating seasonality and as accurately as feasible. The objective of this book is to introduce the reader to a wider understanding of our birds by discussing bird families and their inter-relationships, highlighted by aspects of our most interesting and intriguing species. Field guides, due to their more limited scope and concentration on identification for birders, are simply unable to supply the mass of data contained in a handbook.

This book was largely written prior to publication of the latest 'Roberts', and has not drawn on it for material apart from the systematic order, for which permission was granted. Consequently it has neither drawn on the latest 'Roberts', nor simply rehashed earlier editions. The latter have been the basis of general birder knowledge over decades. The latest 'Roberts' is a first-class handbook, though many of the name-changes are most regrettable and even plain undesirable in a number of cases. I am one of many birders who will not use some of the more ridiculous proposed names like 'swamphen' for one particular gallinule only.

## What is a bird?

Birds belong to the advanced group of animals that have backbones and are called vertebrates. Among the vertebrates, birds are second only to fish when it comes to diversity of species, with about 9 000 bird species worldwide, of which over 900 occur in South Africa. It is a sobering statistic that there are as many species of birds on earth as all the reptiles, amphibians and mammals combined. While not all people know clearly by definition what a reptile or a mammal is, almost everyone, whether uneducated or ultra-sophisticated, knows what a bird is. In a nutshell, the main reason for this is that all birds have feathers, but only birds have feathers. Furthermore, with a few rare flightless exceptions, most birds can fly, even though some species have limited powers of flight.

Unlike the early heavily boned proto-dinosaurs and even recently extinct mammals like the Woolly Mammoth with still-edible meat found frozen in glaciers, very little fossilized evidence for the origin and ancestry of birds exists. This is due to the fragility of their bones. This rarity of avian fossils led one scientist to describe the discovery in 1877 of the best-preserved complete fossil of the first known bird, as possibly the most important natural history specimen in existence. He considered it to be the 'missing link' between reptiles and birds. It is scientific fact that birds originated from reptiles. Birds have been flippantly described as 'glorified reptiles'. It is interesting to note here that birds did not develop from the flying reptiles known to us as the pterodactyls and pterosaurs, but from cotylosaurs, the first primitive reptiles, which later gave rise to advanced reptiles called thecodonts. A branch of thecodonts, the pseudosuchians, gave rise to dinosaurs, dating from the Jurassic Period about 140 million years ago.

The first discovery was of a single asymmetrical flight feather, indistinguishable from those of modern birds, adapted for flying. The second was of a complete skeleton of the animal from which the feather was presumed to have come, a bird similar in size to the Knysna Lourie or Turaco, and showing many reptilian characteristics like teeth. It was named *Archaeopteryx lithographica*. Another specimen was discovered in 1956, and subsequently two additional less-perfect specimens, previously considered to be small coelurosaurian dinosaurs, have also been assigned to *Archaeopteryx*. Although all these specimens have minor differences between them, these can probably be ascribed to intra-specific variation in age and sex.

Many features of *Archaeopteryx* resemble modern birds rather than modern reptiles. These include the backward-directed pubis that facilitates egg-laying, the unique feature of fused clavicles to form the wishbone or furcula, and the fusion of foot-bones for added strength with an opposite hind-toe which aided in gripping branches when climbing trees. Both the evidence and modern theory suggest that early bird ancestors were tree-dwellers before they developed the ability to fly. *Archaeopteryx* had prominent wing-claws that would have aided it in scrambling around in trees. Interestingly, similar wing-claws are still found in the nestlings of a modern bird, the Hoatzin of South America. A number of birds still have rudimentary wing-claws, and one of them is our African Finfoot.

As pointed out, *Archaeopteryx* was similar in size and shape to the Knysna Lourie, and it therefore is very likely that its locomotory behaviour was also similar. It has been suggested by a leading expert on bird anatomy that *Archaeopteryx*, like the Knysna Lourie, also ran along branches, leaping from one to another, and swooping from tree to tree in an early form of flight by gliding and limited flapping. From the anatomy of fossils and modern birds, we have learnt much of the evolution and development of birds, including many interesting facts about their biology. Because of overriding demands for the development of flight and the limitations which this places on design, the morphological structure of all flying birds is essentially the same.

An intriguing discovery was that the feather developed from the reptilian scale. The composition is precisely the same, and they even share the same early developmental stages. Feathers are very light but remarkably strong, and the honeycomb-like structure of the bones of the master flyers among birds is in some species so well developed that the bird's skeleton is lighter overall than its feathers. Only the left ovary in the female is functional, with the right redundant and seasonal growth adequate. The proportionally heavy eggs are understandably laid soon after they have been formed. Unlike mammals but similar to reptiles, birds do not have sweat glands other than only one gland on the skin, the preen or uropygial gland situated above the tail.

A number of delicate bird fossils have relatively recently been discovered principally in China, where suitable geological formations occur. Such fossils have been carefully excavated, and find a ready commercial market. Clearly we still have much to learn from such gradual accumulations concerning the background of birds.

*A cast of the fossil remains of the first known bird,* Archaeopteryx lithographica, *found in Bavarian limestone deposits, and dated to the Jurassic Period about 140 million years ago.*
(Photo: Geoff McIlleron)

ORDER STRUTHIONIFORMES
# Ostrich
## Family Struthionidae

Ostriches are exceptional birds that differ so much from other birds that they are classified in their own monotypic family, a family with a single living species. Five to eight extinct ostrich species, up to 60 million years old, are known. Robinson & Matthee (1999) confirm that the Somali subspecies is the most genetically distinct, probably due to partial Rift Valley isolation as pointed out by Freitag & Robinson (1993), with superficial differences like a bluer neck. This should be regarded as an incipient species, but certainly lacks evidence of full species status. When introduced into the Nairobi National Park it interbred with another subspecies (*massaicus*) in the wild, producing fertile hybrids, and this, together with the evidence of various other instances of interbreeding between races, led Brown *et al*. (1982) to conclude that specific rank for any race was doubtful.

Easily the world's largest living bird, although some extinct birds were larger, it also lays the world's largest egg. This hard-shelled egg weighs 1–1,5% of the female's mass, about 1,3 kg as against about 120 kg, whereas the Kiwi of New Zealand lays an egg weighing about 25% of the female's mass. The ostrich is the only African representative of the five families of flightless birds, which include the Rheidae of South America, the Casuariidae of Australia and New Guinea, the Dromadidae of Australia, and the Apterygidae of New Zealand. It must be stressed that the anatomy of all these birds shows without any doubt that they are all derived from ancestors which could fly, and not, as sometimes stated, that they never had powers of flight.

In its adaptation to totally terrestrial life, the Ostrich has progressed further than any other bird. Most birds

*A pair of Ostriches* (Struthio camelus) *in Kalahari calcrete. The black-and-white male on the left, brown female on the right. Note the large toe has a claw but the reduced other toe not.* (Photo: Alan Weaving)

have four toes; the Ostrich alone has two. Even then, it normally runs on one toe only. The second toe is mainly used to balance, and already lacks a claw. With its considerable height of about 2,5 metres and its large eyes, the Ostrich can see long distances over the flats and make a timely escape from its enemies. Brown *et al.* (1982) emphasize that the ostrich eye, with a diameter of 50 mm, is the largest of any terrestrial vertebrate. Ostrich speed is little more than 60 kph, and reports are often exaggerated.

Females may lay their eggs together in one nest, but the dominant female then chases off the younger females and incubates all the eggs without their help. For obvious reasons the brownish female broods mainly during the day, and the black male at night, but this is not invariable. Elaborate greeting ceremonies between male and female take place at change-over time. However, the male's 'war-dancing' threat display is much more remarkable. Chicks hatch at an advanced stage with open eyes and a hairy down-coat, and soon run with their parents, which can become very aggressive during the breeding season, when the hollow booming of males is often confused with lion roars. An ostrich kick can rip a standing man wide open, but someone wisely lying down may be bruised black and blue yet survive, for ostriches can only kick downwards and not backwards.

Today ostriches are found naturally only in Africa, usually with declining ranges, but they were found in Arabia and even Syria, where the last were eradicated during the Second World War. Wild ostrich flocks suffered greatly under the ostrich feather fashions of a century ago, and many flocks were exterminated. Feather prices reached R450 per kilogram. If domesticated flocks largely in South Africa had not supplied the feather trade in time, the species may even have been brought to the brink of extinction or become extinct over most of its range.

Ostrich egg drinking-vessels have been found in Syrian graves dating from 3000 BC, and there are many legends about this exceptional bird. The nonsense that ostriches seek concealment by burying their heads in the sand presumably has its origin in the completely logical habit of chicks and incubating adults hiding from danger by laying their heads and necks flat on the ground to avoid detection. The legend even quoted by Shakespeare, that ostriches can digest metal, has its origin in their habit of swallowing shiny objects together with food and digestion-aiding stones. In time, even metal may be finely ground-up in its stomach.

**Far left:** *Ostrich eggs hatching in a Kalahari nest scrape: largest eggs in the world.* (Photo: Eliot Lyons)
**Below left:** *Newly hatched brood of Ostrich chicks, accompanied by the black-plumaged male.* (Photo: John Wesson)
**Left:** *Note only two toes per foot. Reddish pigment indicates development of breeding condition.* (Photo: Eliot Lyons)

ORDER GALLIFORMES

# Francolins, Partridges and Quails
## Family Phasianidae

In southern Africa, only two of the six families of this well-known order are indigenous. Justifiably described as the most important birds in the world, this order has provided our domestic fowls and turkeys as well as the most important gamebirds. The 183 species of the Phasianidae also include some of the most beautiful and spectacular birds in existence, some so unbelievably colourful that one wonders how they can survive in nature. The two lovely central tail-feathers of the Crested Argus Pheasant are the longest feathers known in nature: longer than 1,5 metres and 15 cm broad. The well-known Blue and Green Peacocks would probably never even reach the final round in a beauty contest held among the Phasianidae. Regrettably, most of these gorgeous but shy species occur in the forests of Asia. With Africa's wealth of predators, only representatives with relatively dowdy plumage and short tails have survived here. They resemble poultry, with short strong curved bills, sturdy feet with three fore-toes and one hind-toe, and short rounded wings which fit snugly around the body. They fly well and fast over short distances, run well, but swim poorly.

Traditionally in South Africa the 'francolin' group was divided into francolins ('fisante') and partridges ('patryse') on obvious characteristics. A well-meant British study (Hall 1963) based on inadequate evidence has regrettably had a serious harmful effect on the latter group's conservation. She tentatively placed all 41 species into a single genus, *Francolinus*, with seven loose groups all named 'francolins', both illogical and unsatisfactory. Regrettably many bird books prematurely followed this lead.

Our six *Pternistis* francolins consist of 'runner' species, mainly dark brown in colour, sometimes with red legs and bills or bare throats. All have loud harsh calls, very different (e.g. Milstein & Wolff 1987) to our four *Scleroptila* cryptically coloured 'squatter' partridges with their pleasant whistles, although the aberrant *Dendroperdix* Crested Partridge differs somewhat in its call. This species always roosts in trees, but was wrongly stated to never do so. Even the 'squatter' chicks show clear differences in calls, together with other ancestral aspects like differently patterned down-coats at hatching. The little *Peliperdix* Coqui Partridge has sexually dimorphic plumage, with golden-headed males but females resembling other

**Left:** *Shelley's Partridge* (Scleroptila shelleyi), *an attractive Lowveld species.* (Photo: Fanie Hendriks) **Middle:** *Coqui Partridge* (Peliperdix coqui), *this is a dimorphic male with golden head and hind-spur.* (Photo: John Wesson) **Right:** *Roosting Crested Partridges* (Dendroperdix sephaena), *a supposedly non-roosting species.* (Photo: Peter Ginn)

'squatters'. The Coqui will even suicidally squat to hide on a bare tarred road, alternatively crawling down earth burrows when available. The Hartlaub's Francolin, found isolated on higher ground in Namibia, is also sexually dimorphic and probably merits different classification than *Pternistis*.

'Partridge' is a term used world-wide for similar-appearing gamebirds. Conservation-minded mainly Afrikaans-speaking landowners have had friction with mainly urban-based English-speaking gamebird hunters talking at cross-purposes ever since this regrettable and ill-considered name-change. They wish to conserve their vulnerable partridges, but to permit hunting of crop-damaging *Pternistis* francolins. However, many hunters shoot what they consider to be all 'francolins'. The newest fad is quite unjustifiably to call the former francolins 'spurfowl' and the former partridges 'francolins'. Chaos can only increase while partridge conservation declines.

Our smallest true quail, the rare but beautiful Blue Quail, is confined to higher rainfall areas in eastern South Africa, and is apparently also increasingly threatened. The other two larger true quails migrate, with a pattern not yet really understood. They simply appear and immediately commence large-scale egg-laying. The Harlequin Quail is much more handsome than the Common Quail, which is the same species that fed the Israelites in Sinai during the exodus from Egypt. These northern quail populations have now been largely eradicated through greed. From the early twentieth century the Egyptians marketed up to 2 million quails per year, but after a peak of more than 3 million in 1920, the great flocks crashed and had disappeared permanently by the thirties. In contrast with such over-exploitation, the Japanese improved this quail by selective breeding as poultry, so that they lay more than 200 eggs per year. However, this modification has resulted in a marked compensatory tendency for these domesticated quails not to brood their own eggs, requiring the use of artificial incubators.

**1:** *Natal Francolin* (Pternistis natalensis) *female, sheltering small chicks from rain, larger chicks nearby.* (Photo: Peter Williams)
**2:** *Male Swainson's Francolin* (Pternistis swainsonii), *a popular gamebird.* (Photo: Fanie Hendriks)
**3:** *Red-billed Francolin* (Pternistis adspersus) *male at his calling post.* (Photo: Eliot Lyons)
**4:** *Male Blue Quail* (Coturnix adansonii), *not to be confused with the similar male Painted Quail.* (Photo: Peter Ginn)
**5:** *Harlequin Quail* (Coturnix delegorguei) *male and female, our most attractive large quail.* (Photo: Fanie Hendriks)

# GUINEAFOWLS
## FAMILY NUMIDIDAE

This family of Africa south of the Sahara and in Madagascar is known mainly because of our Helmeted Guineafowl. It has been domesticated for centuries, and today even forms a major part of commercial broiler production, particularly in France. It was known to the ancient Greeks and Romans, who kept it as poultry. This origin was probably North Africa, as indicated by the family name. Somehow it disappeared from Europe early in the Christian era, and was unknown until re-introduced from Guinea in the fifteenth century by the early Portuguese navigators.

At least six species of guineafowl exist, with considerable geographical variation contributing to the problem of identification. One 'species' in north-eastern Africa is unlikely to be valid: the main difference is bristles at its nostrils. There are two rare and shy smaller species in the forests of West Africa that few would consider guineafowls, the White-breasted Guineafowl and the Black Guineafowl. Neither species has a single spot, and both have primitive spurs indicating their relationship to the Phasianidae. The Black Guineafowl in particular was doubted, but investigation of its metacarpal bone indicated that it was indeed a guineafowl. Another aberrant species is the Vulturine Guineafowl from arid areas in East Africa. It is the largest of the guineafowls, and its head, which is mostly bare, resembles that of a vulture.

Our Crested Guineafowl has a curly crest of soft black feathers on its head. This immediately distinguishes it from the Helmeted Guineafowl with its hard bare casque. The wing-feathers also differ in having white outer webs, forming a white wing-panel in flight. Even a single feather with its pale blue spots instead of white spots can indicate its presence. Its distribution is largely limited to the hotter tree-covered eastern parts of the country like Zululand and the Lowveld, but it also extends along the whole length of the Zoutpansberg, and can continue over the flats to Langjan Nature Reserve. Its patchy distribution and geographical colour variation further north in Africa have not been properly studied. People knowing our Crested Guineafowl, with its bare slate-grey facial and neck skin

**Left:** *Crested Guineafowl* (Guttera edouardi), *white panel visible in wing, soft-feathered crest. Blue dots, not white, on feathers.* (Photo: Will Nichol) **Right:** *Helmeted Guineafowl* (Numida meleagris). *No blue feather dots anywhere on feathers, hard casque on head.* (Photo: Martin Goetz)

and whitish skin-fold from nape to gape above a broad black-feathered neck-collar, can certainly be forgiven if they encounter Kenyan guineafowl with bare red face and blue neck above continuous spotted feathers without any broad black collar, and believe that they have encountered another species. Perhaps they have. Baboon and monkey troops have a feeding association with Crested Guineafowl under tall riverine trees, and it is amusing to see the guineafowl scurrying along below to pick up fallen fruit.

The well-known Helmeted Guineafowl is a favourite with farmers due to its value in combating harmful insects, and became very plentiful on the Highveld. This resulted from the rapid replacement of trek-oxen with large-scale tractor ploughing after the Second World War. Unlike the Red-billed Quelea, which became an agricultural pest, the guineafowl were a definite asset. They became our most important gamebird, although they have one undesirable trait from the hunter's viewpoint, which precluded their export as a gamebird world-wide. This is for an entire flock to run on ahead of pointing dogs, rather than taking cover like almost all other gamebirds. Such strong flocking instincts resulted in an incident near Pietersburg when an inexperienced young Martial Eagle which had caught one of a flock was surrounded, attacked and nearly killed by the aggressive flock-mates.

Flocks sleep communally in selected tree roosts, but in treeless areas will amusingly sleep scattered on successive telephone poles. Sadly, the large guineafowl flocks have recently largely disappeared. They have ruthlessly and deliberately been poisoned mainly by organophosphate agricultural poisons on grain bait, and their carcasses eaten after intestine-removal. The worst case involved over 1 500 simultaneous guineafowl deaths near Rustenburg in spring 2002, followed in midsummer on the same farm by the poisoning of 45 White Storks and five Abdim's Storks (Verdoorn & Van Zyl 2003). Changes in farming practices, such as carelessly leaving inadequate cover or destroying roosts, have also contributed.

Large clutches of hard-shelled eggs, hardiness and temperament enabled the upgrading improvement of the Helmeted Guineafowl as a domestic animal. Various colour phases including sex-linked indicator plumages were bred, and a broad-breasted variety with short legs, short casque, increased egg-production and a tendency not to become broody resulted. These characteristics are precisely what one does not want to see in wild guineafowl. This must be emphasized, because well-meaning people release such tame guineafowl to 'help' nature. They then hybridize freely with wild guineafowls. Without any doubt, this is a most undesirable practice which seriously reduces the genetic fitness of wild guineafowls to survive in nature. It should be immediately stopped.

ORDER ANSERIFORMES

# WHISTLING DUCKS
## FAMILY DENDROCYGNIDAE

The whistling ducks are a most attractive and, with one exception, remarkably similar group of small ducks. Despite the Greek prefix derived from 'dendron' or tree, it is misleading to call them 'tree ducks' since they hardly ever perch in trees. They are clearly related through the Coscoroba Swan of southernmost South America to the true swans, which they resemble in structure and shape. The whistling ducks have long necks of 17 vertebrae, which they hold erect and straight like geese, also when swimming. They stand erect, walk gracefully and easily, and are described as deliberate and dainty, very different to the ducks in general. Their voices are also unlike other waterfowl, being high-pitched shrill whistles, either clear or squeaky.

They are gregarious and noisy, and can occur in vast congregations of a quarter million or more. Yet they tend to keep to themselves, and not one of the whistling ducks has ever been recorded as hybridizing with other anatids, which as a group have hybridized more than any group of birds. However, interspecific hybrids with other whistling ducks are recorded. They pair for life, and whistling ducks show considerable similarity in attitude, voice and display in both male and female. They have one moult per year, like the swans and true geese. Both male and female share in the incubation of the eggs as well as parental duties. The pair bond is unusually strong, and is maintained by regular interactions such as allopreening each other's faces.

The broad rounded wings of the whistling ducks have the primaries and secondaries approximately equal in length, with the primaries notched or emarginate. Although the wings are flapped at a relatively slow flying rate, they make a whirring sound due to the edge-modification of the primaries. The long neck is stretched out in flight, and the legs are stretched out past the shortish tail. Both male and female have elaborate though identical plumage patterns, with longer flank feathers a feature. Juvenile plumage is similar to that of adults but duller, and only worn for a few weeks.

The ancestral duckling down pattern of the eight typical *Dendrocygna* species is distinct and peculiar to them. However, the related Coscoroba Swan cygnet partly possesses this duckling pattern on its head. Unique among waterfowl, a diagonal white or pale yellow line extends over the occiput and then back down under the eyes to the bill. A dark line extends from the bill through the eye, with a light line above this. Underparts are light, upperparts dark, with three or four pairs of large light blotches on the back, except in two species. These have a light line down either side of the back, and have been considered more primitive because this pattern is found in some other duck species. Although whistling ducks sometimes build substantial nests, they do not in general line these nests with down. Scant quantities of down are rarely found in their nests. Their eggs are shorter and rounder than those of other waterfowl, with both eggs and ducklings considered remarkably small.

In southern Africa, we only have two *Dendrocygna* representatives of the whistling ducks, but these are the two most widespread of the genus: the Fulvous Duck and the White-faced Duck. The amazing distribution of the

**Top right:** *White-faced ducklings* (D. viduata) *accompanied by both parents.* (Photo: Fanie Hendriks)
**Bottom right:** *White-backed Duck* (Thalassornis leuconotus), *only realized recently to be a whistling duck (see text).* (Photo: Fanie Hendriks)
**Below:** *Fulvous Duck* (Dendrocygna bicolor) *group, swimming low in the water, showing erectile flank feathers.* (Photo: Peter Ginn)

Fulvous has been described as 'without parallel among birds', since it occurs in at least six widely separated areas in the Americas, Africa, Madagascar and Asia, with no geographic variation in size or colour. The White-faced Duck is also abundantly represented throughout tropical South America, Africa and Madagascar.

However, relatively recently another remarkable duck has to universal surprise been discovered to be a whistling duck. Its original formal description was part of the first comprehensive classification of the Anatidae, by Eyton (1838). Quite astoundingly, Eyton's classification of this species among the diving stiff-tailed ducks (later tribe Oxyurini) was accepted from 1838 to 1967. Then Johnsgard (1967) provided strong evidence that the White-backed Duck *Thalassornis leuconotus* was clearly an aberrant whistling duck, and not an oxyurid though convergent evolution had made it appear so. Recognition of that family itself involves a new approach on an even more solid foundation. It was formerly treated as a tribe of a subfamily in the classic waterfowl classification of Delacour & Mayr (1945). This had received wide acceptance ever since. Johnsgard (1967) emphasized that this species had been one of the most inadequately studied species of waterfowl. Its eggs weighed a mean of 82,5 g, which was a substantial 11,2% of the female's mass. The large pale brown eggs were smooth in texture, and this was one of the clues overlooked. The specialized diving adaptations of the White-backed ducklings had closely resembled the equally specialized diving ducklings of the Maccoa Duck and other stiff-tails. All hatching from unusually large eggs laid in floating nests without down had enabled the equally advanced White-backed ducklings to escape notice among the advanced diving ducklings of the stiff-tails. However, the stiff-tail eggs were white with a chalky texture.

Various other whistling duck affinities clinched the radical classification change. These included the dark cap and occiput stripe of downy whistling ducklings, similar distress calls of downy ducklings, aggressive displays like whistling ducks, both White-backed parents escorting ducklings, male White-backed sharing incubation, White-backed post-copulatory 'step-dance' display like whistling ducks, as well as similar pre-flight behaviour, post-copulatory wing-raising on side away from mate, reticulated tarsal pattern, and adult calls similar to whistling ducks rather than to any other anatids. Johnsgard's (1967) evidence was simply incontrovertible.

# Ducks and Geese
## Family Anatidae

This family with its world-wide distribution is exceptionally well known, and has existed in our literature for 2 500 years. Its fossil record is 80 million years old. This creates classification problems with aberrant species, and an excellent example involving the White-backed Duck was discussed in the previous family.

In general, all the 146 species of waterfowl have a relatively uniform appearance. All are water-associated, with relatively short legs and webs between the three front toes, relatively long necks and flattened broad bills with concealed surrounding grooves to filter food. Their food is mainly vegetable matter. They have dense plumage and in general can fly well. They normally lay large clutches of uniform-coloured largish eggs which are oval or roundish. Down plucked from the female's breast is used for lining the nest, a unique feature. Babies are hatched with a down coat and open eyes, and can soon accompany their parents. After breeding, this family drops all its flight feathers simultaneously, like grebes and cormorants, so that they are flightless for about a month. Enormous concentrations of these species can occur, particularly during migrations: on one photo 174 740 geese of a single species were counted.

The classification of this family is more advanced than that of most birds because of the vast amount of available information that could be utilized. It was formerly divided into two subfamilies, and then a number of tribes, loose groups with communal likenesses. Due to the variety of our ducks and geese, it is on balance still desirable to discuss them more or less in this broad framework. The strange Magpie Goose of Australia, which looks superficially like a Spur-winged Goose, is a classification problem which probably merits recognition in its own monotypic family. Apart from that, two tribes were recognized in the subfamily Anserinae, which only undergo one feather moult per year: first, the former whistling duck tribe, now elevated to its own family; second the tribe Anserini of swans and true geese, which has no representative with us, except formerly the imported Mute Swan, with a romantic shipwreck origin. It first established itself on the Kromme River, and later spread to Knysna. Regrettably, it is now extinct as a breeding species in South Africa.

The majority of our ducks and geese were then incorporated in the subfamily Anatinae, with two body moults per year. In the tribe Tadornini, our South African Shelduck represents seven typical species with world-wide distribution. Also included here is our aberrant Egyptian Goose, a species which justifies its own genus. This adaptable bird breeds in a remarkable variety of nest-sites, including church towers and high nests of other birds. Even from such heights, the goslings are simply called and fall to the ground, but are not carried (Milstein 1975a).

In the tribe Anatini nine of our duck species are classified, including three rare migrants from the northern hemisphere: the Northern Pintail, Garganey and Northern Shoveler. These are the most typical ducks, and include our commonest species, the Yellow-billed Duck, as well as our most plentiful, the Red-billed Teal. In these species the male usually deserts the female when she commences incubation, and she carries on alone. Correlated with its arid habitat and the likelihood of potential brood failure, our Cape Teal male tends to be more constant. The tribe Aythini consists of 12 broad-billed species and three narrow-billed species. We have one representative of the latter, the Southern Pochard, also found in South America.

The tribe Cairini consists of quite a mixture, and here our African Pygmy Goose, Knob-billed (or Comb) Duck, and Spur-winged Goose are classified. This pygmy goose and two other closely related species in Asia and Australia are regarded as the smallest of the family. The Knob-billed Duck also occurs in South America and Asia. The males, which are much larger than the females, keep a harem and show no finesse in mating. The

*Egyptian Goose* (Alopochen aegyptiaca) *in flight, an aberrant shelduck, highly successful and even urban in South Africa.* (Photo: Fanie Hendriks)

Spur-winged Goose's relationships are not clear, but the dangerous spurs on its wings are well known. Of the Somateriini tribe, which includes the well-known Eider Duck with its famous down, and the Mergini, a strange group of ducks which feed on fish, we have no representatives.

Of the last tribe, Oxyurini, we have the Maccoa Duck as representative, probably the last endemic duck species to reach Africa south of the Sahara. All our other breeding ducks were obliged to abandon what turned out to be the luxury of both breeding plumage and non-breeding plumage. This was due to our considerable climatic vagaries in the southern hemisphere. There was simply no time to waste, when the irregular rains took place, to enable moulting into the striking alternative duck breeding plumages so prevalent in the northern hemisphere. The controlling mechanism for this secondary plumage loss was the advantage on balance of a relatively simple hormonal plumage suppression. Different to these other adapted waterfowl, the Maccoa Duck still has both breeding and non-breeding plumages present (Siegfried 1968). The most reasonable hypothesis is its relatively late colonization, and that it has not yet adapted to the secondary single plumage found generally in the ducks of the southern hemisphere (Milstein 1979, 2000).

**1:** *African Pygmy Goose* (Nettapus auritus), *closely associated with waterlilies* (Photo: Fanie Hendriks)
**2:** *The scarlet iris of the male Southern Pochard* (Netta erythrophthalma), *when kept in darkness and then suddenly exposed to light, temporarily turns pale yellow in colour.* (Photo: Eliot Lyons)
**3:** *Knob-billed Duck* (Sarkidiornis melanotos). *The erectile bill-knob increases in total area and thickens with the start of the breeding season.* (Photo: Eliot Lyons)
**4:** *A Maccoa Duck* (Oxyura maccoa) *male in a breeding display with dimorphic plumage, indicative of it being the last waterfowl species to colonize southern Africa from the north.* (Photo: Charles Barrett)

## ORDER TURNICIFORMES

# BUTTONQUAILS
## FAMILY TURNICIDAE

Superficially similar to the true quails is a most interesting little family of 14 or 15 quail-like birds called buttonquails or hemipodes, also bustardquails. They even merit their own order. In addition, two aberrant species are often placed in this family. One certainly does not belong here, but rather in its own monotypic family. This is the little Plains Wanderer of Australia's central deserts, which has paired instead of a single carotid artery, lays sharply-pointed eggs, and has four toes. The other aberrant species is an odd bird found immediately south of the Sahara, known as Quail Plover or Lark Quail, which reminds one of a tiny courser or a long-legged lark except for its boldly pied wings. Although it shows links to the buttonquails, the Plains Wanderer does not belong here in an exclusively three-toed family, a buttonquail characteristic. All the other buttonquails are classified in the genus *Turnix*, decidedly similar and obviously close relatives. The best Afrikaans group-name is undoubtedly Prozesky's 'drietoonkwartel', referring to the three toes, instead of the relatively meaningless diminutive of 'kwarteltjie', or little quail.

Buttonquails are not found in flocks like true quails, but instead singly or in pairs. When flushed, they fly whirring off with rapid wingbeats and sometimes dangling legs. They often initially jink away at speed in different directions in the best elusive gamebird tradition. On landing, they may pause instantaneously and then immediately scurry off, almost always in a different direction. This ensures that they are seldom flushed a second time, because they are not where they are expected to be. Their size ranges from 10 to 18 cm long, but they appear smaller in flight due to their rounded wings and ridiculous little remnant tails of only a few soft feathers. Buttonquails are found in grasslands from southern Europe and Africa to the Far East and Australia, and even some large islands. Although they feed mainly on fine seeds, tender shoots and small insects, they do not possess a crop.

One of the most interesting buttonquail aspects is their reversed sexual roles, relatively uncommon in birds. The female is not only more attractively coloured, but also larger than the male, and much more aggressive. She displays around the male while calling loudly. His sound apparatus is much less developed. After mating, which is initiated by her taking up a prone position, she apparently selects the nest-site, scratches a nest-bowl, and lays 3–5 speckled eggs. She then promptly leaves to find her next male

**Top:** *Male Black-rumped Buttonquail* (Turnix nanus), *more attractively and more distinctly marked than the Kurrichane Buttonquail.*
**Above:** *Male Kurrichane Buttonquail* (T. sylvaticus) *at the nest, taking complete charge after clutch completion, when the female leaves to seek out other males.* (Photos: Peter Ginn)

of possibly several in a breeding season, always smaller and duller than herself. Her former mate is simply left to undertake the domestic chores: incubating the eggs and raising the chicks. Nests are sometimes reported on the bare ground, but are generally hidden in vegetation at the base of a grass-tuft. I have even found them cleverly hidden actually inside a grass-tuft. These small eggs are marketed in paper containers in Thailand on a considerable scale.

The buttonquails have an exceptionally rapid rate of development. The incubation period is only 12–13 days, rapid for any bird group, but exceptional in one where the chicks hatch at such an advanced stage. Their eyes are open, they are covered by a down-coat, and can leave the nest almost immediately. They begin to flutter after a week, and can fly as early as 10 days old with us, but two weeks appears more usual. At 6–7 weeks of age they are as large and heavy as adults. They can achieve adult plumage at 10 weeks, and may breed themselves at 4–5 months old, possibly even at three months. These adaptations strongly remind one of the Galliformes, but the development of the flight feathers is a little less efficient.

We have two species of buttonquails with a possible third recently resurrected. The first is our widespread Kurrichane Buttonquail, which extends to Europe and Asia. It is a pale bird with a paler eye, bluish-grey bill and pink legs. Characteristic heart-shaped blackish markings are found down both sides of the breast. The Black-rumped Buttonquail is much more rufous with a diagnostic dark brown eye and dark brown back and rump. It prefers moist soils in eastern South Africa. The third species, known as the Hottentot Buttonquail, is a little problematical. An isolated population from the extreme southern Cape, which may have achieved species status, it is supposed to resemble the Black-rumped Buttonquail closely, as illustrated by Sinclair, Hockey & Tarboton (2002). However, Sinclair & Ryan (2003) illustrate what strongly resembles a Kurrichane Buttonquail with the most buttonquail-like bill, diagnostic bright yellow legs in the female, and spots on the belly, also diagnostic. More clarity is needed here.

## ORDER PICIFORMES

# HONEYGUIDES AND HONEYBIRDS

## FAMILY INDICATORIDAE

A small family of birds less than 20 cm long and in general of a dull brownish-grey colour would be surprising candidates to be regarded as among the most interesting birds in the world. Yet this is the case with the honeyguides – because of their exceptional habits. Most are found in Africa, with only two species of the largest genus, *Indicator*, in Asia. Four genera of probably 16 species are currently recognized: one in *Melichneutes*, one or two in *Melignomon*, two or three in *Prodotiscus*, and the rest in *Indicator*. The latter genus is the source of most of our information on honeyguides. The breeding habits of *Melichneutes*, for example, are unknown. What we do know is that it displays over the forest, using its lyre-shaped tail to make a series of mechanical noises in the same way that a snipe drums with its vibrating outer tail-feathers.

Some experts believe that our Sharp-billed Honeybird with its brown back and our Slender-billed Honeybird with its green back, together with Cassin's Honeybird forming the genus *Prodotiscus*, justify their own family. Recognition of the Prodotiscidae as not merely a primitive genus of the Indicatoridae is a more realistic approach, and with more knowledge will probably be globally accepted. Their fine bills differ from the stubby strong bills of the honeyguides, they do not eat wax but waxy scale-insects, and they parasitize birds with open nests like the white-eyes. It is uncertain where the monotypic genera fit in.

Honeyguides and honeybirds all have white panels in their graduated tails, as well as two toes forward and two toes backward. Honeyguide bills are short, sturdy and blunt, with raised funnel-like rims around their nostrils. Their skins are notably thick, with a protective membrane over the eye. Clearly some of these adaptations are useful as protection against bee-stings. Aiding their unique habit of eating wax is the presence of at least one bacterium, *Micrococcus cerolyticus*, in their digestive systems to break down the wax. This was only discovered in 1956, yet the wax-eating habit was first noted in the sixteenth century, when a Dominican missionary in Mozambique described how little birds flew into his church to steal wax from the altar candles. Although only the Greater and Scaly-throated Honeyguides are proven as definite guides to bee-hives, part of this association is also indicated in various others.

The habit of guiding humans to bee-hives is unique in the entire animal kingdom. Honeyguides flirt their white tail-panels directly in front of people, and utter their guiding call. My guiding experience involves only the Greater Honeyguide, and the call has been well-likened to a half-empty box of matches being shaken lengthwise. Tease the honeyguide by turning off slightly, and it becomes very excited until one follows again. At the hive it sits still and waits for action, or flies in little circles. Honey is highly rated as a delicacy in Africa, and tribes like the Wandorobo regard hive-robbing as their duty, or they will displease the gods that sent the honeyguide. It is said that, in the Congo, people who kill honeyguides have their ears cut off. This guiding of humans is clearly a centuries-old adaptation of a still older relationship developed by the honeyguides with the Honey Badger, the most effective known extractor of honey. It is alleged that as the tribesmen become more sophisticated and neglect their 'duty', the honeyguides have gradually commenced losing the habit. Another superstition is that, unless the honeyguide's portion of the raid is left out for it, the next person will be guided to a leopard or a mamba. Honeyguides not only eat the larvae, but they are extremely fond of the wax. By putting old combs out, one can readily determine whether or not there are honeyguides in the vicinity.

As far as is known, all honeyguides and honeybirds are obligatory nest-parasites that can (within reason) retain their eggs in oviducts until a suitable host nest is located. I obtained one of the few authentic honeyguide eggs when I was extracting a female Greater Honeyguide from a mist-net, and she laid an egg (Milstein, 1967). Unlike honeybirds, the white eggs of honeyguides are always laid in a dark nest.

The indications are that honeyguide females destroy host eggs, but it is alleged that female Lesser Honeyguides may carry off such eggs. The eggs can be laid with remarkable speed. A friend once showed me a Black-collared Barbet nest with a honeyguide chick, after detailing how the Greater Honeyguide repeatedly enticed the barbet parents away from their nest before streaking back to it. The problem was that I could

**1:** *The Lesser Honeyguide* (Indicator minor) *is much overlooked but relatively easy to identify in the field.*
**2:** *Scaly-throated Honeyguides* (I. variegatus) *are forest-dwellers and not easy to see. Their distinctive, trilling call is a considerable aid.*
**3:** *Greater Honeyguide* (I. indicator) *female, best-known of the honeyguides, lacks the male's darker head-markings. Territories are occupied by individual males for years.* (Photos: Geoff McIlleron)

clearly see that the chick was a Lesser Honeyguide! While I tried to resolve this impasse without losing an insistent friend, he remembered that during the marathon battle a small bird had once flown into the nest literally for seconds. Problem solved!

Again unique, the honeyguide chick hatches with the aid of exceptional egg-teeth: sharp hooks on both mandibles. Like other egg-teeth, they fall off after 7–10 days, but in the interim are used to murder the host's chicks or puncture other eggs. Honeyguide chicks stay an exceptionally long time in the host nest: 39–40 days. Unlike cuckoos, emergent young honeyguides are apparently independent, and may even be attacked by the formerly fond foster-parents when seen. In contrast, honeybird babies are fed by their foster-parents after nest-leaving. Honeyguide fledglings instinctively search out wax, although otherwise adults and fledglings feed mainly on insects captured in flight.

# WOODPECKERS AND WRYNECKS
## FAMILY PICIDAE

The woodpeckers are a well-known group, and consist of between 206 and 210 species. They have a worldwide distribution in treed regions except for the large islands of Australia and Madagascar. The two species of wrynecks are sometimes classified in their own family, but are really the prototypes of the woodpeckers, and better regarded as primitive woodpeckers. The Northern Wryneck is found in the Palaearctic and Oriental regions, while our Red-breasted Wryneck is endemic, found only in Africa. Their strange name is derived from the nearly unbelievable twisting of their necks, particularly when excited. Both species are cryptically coloured, but with soft tail-feathers compared to the hard prop-feathers of the woodpeckers. Their bills cannot compare with the chisel-bills of the woodpeckers, and they are therefore unable to excavate their own nest-holes, but must make do with natural holes or the old nests of woodpeckers and

**Left:** *Red-breasted Wryneck* (Jynx ruficollis) *at its nest with a beakful of ant eggs and larvae.* (Photo: Cyril Laubscher)
**Below:** *Ground Woodpecker* (Geocolaptes olivaceus) *on a flat rock surface near the nest.* (Photo: Nico Myburgh)

**Left:** *Female Bennett's Woodpecker* (Campethera bennettii); *note clear cheek-patch and posture: propped-up position supported by stiff tail.* (Photo: Garth Batchelor)
**Right:** *Male Bennett's Woodpecker at his nest feeding chicks; note heavy red moustachial streak.* (Photo: Cyril Laubscher)

barbets. The wrynecks can also not drill after insects like woodpeckers, but feed chiefly on ground-dwelling ants, using their long tongues.

Woodpeckers differ in size from small to a few species as large as crows. They are often black, white and red in colour, but our nine species are more camouflaged like the wrynecks and are also smaller, possibly reflecting selection by our wealth of birds of prey. The woodpecker is nature's percussion drill. Because of the exceptionally strong bill, used like a chisel against the hardest wood, they have various other adaptations. Their skull is thick to protect the brain against shocks, and the slim neck has powerful muscles. There are again two toes forward and two backward, but in three genera the first toe is absent. The third point of the woodpecker's power triangle is the propping-up tail. To emphasize its importance, the central pair of tail-feathers are only moulted after the others have all grown out, so that a propping support is always available. Furthermore, the nostrils are protected by fine hairy feathers against wood-chips.

Woodpeckers' tongues are incredibly long, often as long as the bird's body. The tongue roots can extend right around the skull to in front of the eye, or even further to near the point of the upper mandible! This wonderful tongue is seldom seen. The woodpecker drills for example into a wood-boring insect's gallery, and then the tongue is inserted and used to capture the insect by a variety of adaptations. These range from a spear-point, or hooks at the tip, or brush-like hairs, or excreted gum. In ant-feeding species, the gum is alkaline to counteract the ant's formic acid.

Most woodpeckers have loud penetrating calls, and that of Bennett's Woodpecker is the strangest of our nine species. This species is almost invariably the one that will be seen flying up into trees from the ground, where it was feeding on ants. During the breeding season, some woodpeckers like our Cardinal and Bearded call to proclaim territories and also drum with their exceptional bills on a stump or branch which has been specially selected for resonance. Even corrugated iron roofs and stovepipes are sometimes selected to serve as drums. Unlike barbets, with their lesser drilling ability, woodpeckers are not restricted to dead wood to excavate their nests. They also drill into living trees which can be incredibly hard. Also unlike barbets, their chicks are fed solely on insects. Even under unfavourable environmental conditions, these insects are to be found behind bark or extracted from wood.

Woodpeckers commence foraging at the base of trees, work upwards, and then fly with their characteristic dipping flight to the base of the next tree. It appears usual for them to raise up to two broods per season in a fresh nest, then abandon it. They therefore do not appear to indulge in the regular nest sanitation of barbets, which fling soiled chips from nests or even carry them some distance away, or to have the problem that barbets regularly encounter, of eventually digging through the bottom of the favoured nest-boxes unless hard bases are utilized.

Finally, apart from two similarly adapted South American species, we can boast the only other woodpecker in the world that spurns trees and nests in earthen banks, or rarely termite mounds and the adobe walls of derelict buildings. Conventional wisdom regards such major changes as having taken place gradually over long periods. However, in a recent popular article (Oatley 2003), the expert on Ground Woodpeckers (who is also the leading expert on our robins) highlighted some of the most interesting aspects of his doctoral thesis. He indicated strong evidence that the puzzling change in Ground Woodpecker nesting habits was forced on the birds in an 'all-or-nothing' desperate adaptation. This was due to dramatically changed environmental conditions such as a major tree die-off where the woodpeckers occurred. Indications are that the change in Ground Woodpecker nesting is an excellent example of so-called 'punctuated equilibria', an exciting theory first proposed in 1972 and still gaining support world-wide. It proposes differing tempos in evolution, such as the rapid ground-nesting or extinction alternative in Ground Woodpeckers. These woodpeckers appear to be susceptible to heat stress, regularly sitting facing the sun to present minimal body area to it, and also often panting. This suggests physiological adaptation to a cooler climate than that which prevails now. Equally fascinating is their efficient selection of the protein-rich eggs and cocoons moved by ants to unseen warm temporary positions under surface stones. Discovery of such delectable hoards by experience then requires rapid gobbling by the woodpecker group before the alarmed ants can move their treasures out of tongue reach. Such gobbling close to the ground makes the birds vulnerable to aerial predators, so the Ground Woodpecker has developed a sentry system unique in the woodpecker family, with regular relief of sentries by others of the group.

**Left:** *The scarlet crest of the male Olive Woodpecker* (Dendropicos griseocephalus) *distinguishes it from the female.*
**Below:** *The Bearded Woodpecker* (D. namaquus), *our largest woodpecker, has no difficulty constructing nest-holes even upside-down!* (Photos: Fanie Hendriks)

# African Barbets

## Family Lybiidae

The barbets (Afrikaans: 'houtkapper') are often confused with the closely related woodpeckers (Afrikaans: 'speg') in South Africa due to similarity in group-name meaning, but there are clear differences between these distinct families. Prominent bristles are found around barbet bills, and one group even has strange feather tufts over the nostrils. Together these give rise to the 'barbet' name. Barbets show clear affinities with some coraciiform families like the kingfishers and rollers. Both families make similar-shaped holes, but only the woodpecker is capable of excavating hard or living wood. Both have two toes forward and two toes backward. However, the soft tail-feathers of barbets are a fundamental difference. Furthermore, barbets tend to have thick, heavy and shorter bills, not as strong as the finer, longer and straight bills of woodpeckers.

The barbets have a wide distribution across the world tropics, probably indicating a common forest origin. Of the approximately 72 species, over half are in Africa, mainly in the tropics. Some 23 are found from India to the East Indies, and another 12 or 13 from Costa Rica to Brazil. The African barbets have now been split off from the Capitoniidae, and of these we have 10 species of five genera. These include three large colourful barbets, one per genus, which are among our favourite garden birds; three dull species of one genus, relatively little-known, which are found in our indigenous forests; and four little tinkers, all from the same genus. All our barbets are resident species, and none show migratory tendencies.

Our well-known Crested Barbet, with its attractive but monotonous trilling call, nests in normal tree nest-holes. However, close relatives in East Africa nest in burrows in earth-banks or termite mounds. I once found an extremely well-hidden Crested Barbet nest in a willow tree that had been snapped off by the wind. Presumably

*Back view of the Crested Barbet* (Trachyphonus vaillantii) *perched near its nest-hole.* (Photo: John Wesson)

*The heavy bill of the Black-collared Barbet* (Lybius torquatus) *is formidable as many bird-ringers have found to their cost.* (Photo: Geoff McIlleron)

*An adult Acacia Pied Barbet* (Tricholaema leucomelas) *feeding a full-grown chick at the nest.* (Photo: Fanie Hendriks)

*Red-fronted Tinker* (Pogoniulus pusillus) *feeding a full-grown chick at the nest.* (Photo: Geoff McIlleron)

*Yellow-fronted Tinker* (P. chrysoconus) *about to alight at its nest entrance hole.* (Photo: Geoff McIlleron)

trees. However, the Crested Barbet often walks around on the ground, obtaining insects. All naturally join in the termite feasts with so many other bird species, when the termite alates fly off to start new colonies after their brief aerial mating.

the owners of a nest which had been snapped off halfway-down with the trunk, the barbet pair had then dug straight through the first chamber's floor, and from there completed a normal nest with second chamber, although its two vertical entrance shafts had no shelter from rain.

The Black-collared Barbet's ringing duet call caused much argument among birders as to precisely how it was uttered. Then Gordon Maclean solved it by careful observation, establishing that the male and female uttered precisely the same call at the same tempo as they bowed to each other. The Acacia Pied Barbet (to separate it from two similar species further north) has two general calls: one a donkey-like braying. It is generally found in drier habitat. Surprisingly it has nested in holes in grape-vines and candelabra-type *Euphorbia* trees. Our larger barbets and our little tinkers both subsist mainly on fruit, but also eat insects which they usually obtain in

Four species of tinkers complete our spectrum of barbets. The well-known Yellow-fronted Tinker is probably our main spreader of mistletoe, regurgitating the sticky seeds and wiping them off its bill on a branch. While I was working at Mariepskop on the short calls of the Yellow-rumped Tinker (with its diagnostic black crown) in a new range extension up the Drakensberg, I found the tinks to be an irregular series of 2–12 with a mean of 6,0 over 731 series (Milstein 1995). I wanted a numeric comparison with the decidedly monotonous Yellow-fronted Tinker, so asked Siegel Godschalk, who had studied them spreading mistletoe at Loskop Dam, for the maximum continuous number of tinks he had recorded. It was a surprising 530 tinks in 5 minutes and 5 seconds! The Red-fronted Tinker gives short series of tinks, but this has not been precisely determined, while the Green Tinker is almost unknown.

I have never understood why the attractive, neat and apt name of 'tinker' has the redundant 'barbet' or even worse 'bird' forced on to it as a suffix. Most people realize that they are birds, and many that they are barbets. Perhaps, in the fullness of time, they will revert formally to plain 'tinker'. We now all call 'bishops' plain bishops again, but few seem to know that for a

**Left:** *The Yellow-rumped Tinker* (Pogoniulus bilineatus), *easily identified by its diagnostic black crown.* (Photo: Fanie Hendriks)
**Right:** *Rarely seen in tinkers, two Yellow-rumped Tinkers displaying, the ardent male on the left.* (Photo: Cyril Laubscher)

long time they were similarly all called bishopbirds. Fewer realize that this was by an arbitrary decision of the fuddy-duddy editor of the British journal *Ibis*, who considered the title of a submitted paper by Dr David Lack as quite unacceptable: 'Territory and polygamy in a bishop'. Perhaps commonsense rather than dictatorship will yet prevail. Finally, one of the most interesting observations on the Yellow-rumped Tinker was made in East Africa. Barbets are known to be regularly parasitized by honeyguides, and in this case the host tinker actually enlarged the nest-hole to provide sufficient room for the outsized adoptee!

ORDER BUCEROTIFORMES

# Typical Hornbills

## Family Bucerotidae

The hornbills are a well-known ancient group with a long fossil history, probably since pre-Tertiary time. A primitive hornbill found in Eocene deposits in Europe indicates this lengthy period, and also that it formerly occurred in areas outside its present range. However, hornbills are limited to the Old World, and have no link to the superficially similar toucan family (Ramphastidae) of the New World, with their equally enormous bills. Hornbills comprise about 50 species, with some of uncertain status, and occur from Africa through southern Asia to southern Pacific islands, but are absent from Madagascar and Australia. As befits such an old family,

they have some unique features in common, like the fusion of the first and second neck vertebrae. More obvious is that they are among the very few bird species to have long eye-lashes like the Ostrich. The second, third and fourth toes are joined at their bases, like other closely related families.

The hornbills include some large birds, with the longest the Helmeted Hornbill of Malaysia, which has a body length of 1,6 m. While other hornbills have bills that are either hollow or filled with a light honeycomb support structure, this hornbill provides the unique hornbill ivory, or 'ho-ting'. It comes from the casque at the base of the upper mandible, a block of about 60 cc of a hard substance with a consistency like ivory, deep red on the outside but golden yellow within. This was valued by weight at far more than gold, jade or ivory by the Chinese. Only the finest craftsmen were allowed to carve it, mainly for the belt-buckles of high-ranking mandarins. The prized red colour can be maintained by applying secretions from this hornbill's uropygial gland. Hornbill ivory has been used to carve ornaments and fetishes in Borneo since at least the fourteenth century.

Hornbills have now been classified in their own order, rather than the separate suborder of former classifications. The typical hornbills, which form the great majority, are placed in the family presently under discussion. The two strange ground-hornbills are now placed in their own family, which will receive attention next. The characteristic large bills are usually augmented by a ridge along the top of the bill called a casque, much larger and longer in males than females. The wattled hornbills have the most excessive casque of any hornbill. In colour the hornbills are basically black, dark brown or grey with contrasting white or cream patches. The bills are sometimes brightly coloured: red or yellow or combinations, though most bills are horn-coloured. Bare facial skin is also characteristic, particularly in the smaller hornbills, and may be similarly brightly coloured.

The hornbills lack underwing covert feathers, and for this reason have a distinctly noisy flight with the wind whistling through the bare feather-shafts. Their calls vary considerably, often increasing in tempo and volume until a climax is reached, possibly correlated with breeding display peaks. Our noisiest is probably the Trumpeter Hornbill, which brays like a donkey. Some hornbills are arboreal, spending most of their time in trees, but others spend much time foraging on the ground, running or hopping. However, all these hornbills have relatively short legs.

As a family the hornbills are omnivorous, but hornbill species seem to specialize in different food resources.

**1:** *Climax to Yellow-billed Hornbill* (Tockus leucomelas) *display: head down with wings spread to add to the call climax.* (Photo: Peter Williams)
**2:** *The Yellow-billed Hornbill male.* (Photo: Geoff McIlleron)
**3:** *The relatively delicate head and bill denote a female Yellow-billed Hornbill.* (Photo: John Wesson)
**4:** *A male Trumpeter Hornbill* (Bycanistes bucinator) *bringing fruit to feed his mate in a nest-hole.* (Photo: Martin Goetz)

**Left:** *African Grey Hornbill* (Tockus nasutus): *dull coloured, the male is distinguished by a casque on his bill.*
**Right:** *Red-billed Hornbills* (T. erythrorhynchus) *are easily distinguished from the Southern Yellow-billed Hornbill by their more delicate reddish bills.* (Photos: Fanie Hendriks)

The attractive White-crested Hornbill, found in forests north of our limits, has a definite feeding association with monkey troops. They feed mostly on large insects disturbed by the monkeys. Some hornbills specialize in various fruits, others in insects and similar organisms like termites, while some are reported to feed substantially on the eggs and chicks of other birds. Indigestible portions like fruit pips and the hard chitinous insect remnants are regurgitated later after the food items have been swallowed whole. I once watched a Southern Yellow-billed Hornbill systematically smash the shell of a giant land-snail *Achatina immaculata*, until it later swallowed only an unrecognizable lump of jelly.

However, it is the unique breeding system of this family that has caught the imagination of people ever since the Roman historian Pliny described it. The female builds up fat reserves, and is then walled into a suitable nest-hole except for a small slit enabling the male to feed her bill-tip to bill-tip. Although males moult normally in the smaller *Tockus* hornbills, the females moult all their feathers almost immediately, while the larger hornbills only moult their flight and tail-feathers at this stage. *Tockus* females are then like plucked poultry, with only the wispy filoplumes remaining. She lays her eggs and incubates them. When the chicks are about half-grown, she breaks out to help feed them. The chicks instinctively use whatever material is available, including their own droppings and apparently regurgitations, to seal up the nest again. The parents also help from the outside due to the urgency of possible predation. Originally it was thought that the male brought material while the female built the hard wall, but males may also help build. In *Tockus* hornbills the incubation period is about 30 days and fledging 50 days, while in the larger *Bycanistes* hornbills they are about 50 days and 45 days respectively. Two Silvery-cheeked Hornbill females of the latter genus are known to have been incarcerated for 108 and 112 days in total respectively. When the chicks are ready to fledge, they break out, and the nest-hole is left open until the next breeding season. Defecation out through the feeding slit involves acrobatics, but regurgitated material is disposed of by bill through the slit.

# Ground-hornbills
## Family Bucorvidae

The ground-hornbills were originally described as two different species, then they were considered to be one species with two allopatric subspecies, until it became accepted that they were in fact two good species. They were first placed in the same family with the other hornbills, then elevated to their own subfamily. Now it has been realized that they merit a family of their own, and that there are a number of differences between them and the typical hornbills. Certainly the long-legged, black-coloured family groups appear very different to the arboreal hornbills as they walk through the veld. They have a peculiar way of walking, and are possibly the only birds to walk so to speak on tip-toe, on the terminal phalanges of their toes. This gives them a most unusual gait for a largely terrestrial bird. They only fly up into trees to roost, to reach their nests, or when they are frightened.

Up close one is immediately struck by two impressive features. The first is their long eye-lashes, strongly reminiscent of the Ostrich, and most rare in birds. The second is their unusual casque, smaller in our Southern

Ground-Hornbill than in the Northern Ground-Hornbill. The front of the casque is not closed, so that one can actually look into it. In the Northern Ground-Hornbill, the casque is also tilted up in front. There are additional differences in the facial skin: basically blue in the northern species, and red in the southern. The southern female has a small blue patch on the red throat adjacent to extensive red throat pouches, while the northern female is totally blue. The northern male has red throat pouches adjacent to a blue throat, while the southern male is totally red. The Southern Ground-Hornbill has a heavier plain black bill, whereas the northern species has a longer decurved bill with orange-yellow patches at the base of the upper mandible. Both species have conspicuous white primaries and primary coverts, which are only visible in flight.

A major difference between the typical hornbills and the ground-hornbills is that the latter female is not walled-up and is free to leave the nest at will. She also moults gradually in the normal bird mode like the typical hornbill males, and not in the specialized hornbill female mode. Ground-hornbills also have a strong family group structure, and the group together defends a permanent territory which often exceeds 100 ha around the chosen nest. Intruders from another group of ground-hornbills are sometimes chased off in an aerial skirmish. Nests are normally large tree-holes lined with grass and leaves, about 6 m off the ground. Holes in a rock face or donga have also been utilized. A cliff nest 120 m from the ground has been recorded.

Breeding is in response to rainfall, and most eggs are laid between September and December. The alpha female, who undertakes the incubation, is fed in the nest by various ground-hornbill males and also occasionally immatures. After an incubation period of 40 days and a nestling period of about 85 days, the brownish immature with yellowish facial skin is fed collectively by the group for a period which may exceed six months, and increasingly forms part of the family group. According to Kemp & Kemp (1980), who have been responsible for most hornbill research, including that carried out on ground-hornbills, the mean group size for 290 groups was 3,6, varying from 2 to 11. Part of the territorial defence involves calling in the early morning and possibly in the late afternoon as well. The call of 4–5 syllables may be a duet or a chorus but involves an extremely low-pitched booming which carries some distance. This call is often likened to that of lions, and Dr Dick Harwin can vouch for that. Nonchalantly approaching what he thought was a Southern Ground-Hornbill calling in Zimbabwe, he discovered in time that the source was a concealed lioness less than 50 m away.

A group of ground-hornbills mincing through the veld on tip-toe are ready to eat whatever they encounter

**Far left:** *In Ground-Hornbill* (Bucorvus leadbeateri) *adults, there is only a slight difference between the sexes.*
(Photo: John Wesson)
**Left:** *A Ground-Hornbill calling from a perch, with throat distended.*
(Photo: Martin Goetz)

of reasonable size. Snakes are surrounded and attacked in turn from the vulnerable rear with competent teamwork, tortoises are a regular prey item, lizards and chameleons are welcomed as are frogs and toads, birds' nests receive short shrift, mammals up to the size of a hare are in danger, and various invertebrates like snails serve merely to whet the appetites. With such a wide-ranging diet and few enemies except efficient predators like leopards taking the occasional chick or brooding adult, the general decline in this species is hard to understand. Suitable nest-sites may be a limiting factor, and this is currently being addressed through conservation efforts by the Ground-Hornbill Project sponsored by the Green Trust in Limpopo Lowveld. Harvesting and rearing the rarely-raised second chick without imprinting makes good sense for future releases.

Particularly in the Sudan, actual mounted heads or accurate carvings of ground-hornbill heads and necks are used to aid hunters and delude game in close stalks through long grass, but cannot be a significant problem. The easy smashing of reflective picture windows by the powerful bills of territorial ground-hornbills have resulted in these birds being occasionally shot by the odd short-sighted and unenlightened landowners who could easily utilize other proven ways to eliminate the 'threatening' reflections. Ground-hornbills prefer woodland and savanna habitats, and only utilize forest and grassland to a limited degree. Marc Herremans has pointed out that even in Botswana with its limited crop-farming, low human population density and large conservation areas, atlas reporting rates were over 20% lower in unprotected areas compared to the protected areas. The gradual decline due to human development of the environment continues. It is sincerely hoped that current research efforts will solve the problem of this surprisingly sensitive species with its apparent low reproductive success.

ORDER UPUPIFORMES

# African Hoopoe

## Family Upupidae

Recent classification regarded the hoopoe as a single species divided into nine or more widely separated populations, all differing somewhat from each other, from Europe and northern Africa to the Middle East, southern Africa, Madagascar, India, Sri Lanka, Malaysia and Sumatra. However, the most distinctive and richest-coloured population, that found in the southern half of Africa, has been recognized as a full species, the African Hoopoe. There are a number of other constant differences apart from the much richer dark cinnamon colour. Examples are all-black primaries but much more extensively white secondaries, no white sub-terminal bar on the crest feathers, and a differing call.

The African Hoopoe is a spectacular bird with its red-brown crest tipped with black, and its head, neck and body of the same colour, augmented by the striking black-and-white wings and the black tail with white bar. The crest is usually kept closed while the hoopoe walks

*African Hoopoe* (Upupa africana) *feeding young in flight, an unusual but spectacular method. Usually the prey is passed directly to the most insistent chick, normal bill to bill.* (Photo: Cyril Laubscher)

in its characteristic way, probing with its graceful slightly decurved bill vertically into the ground in search of insects. Then the crest looks like a second narrow bill in the opposite direction. However, when the hoopoe becomes excited, gets a fright, or even perches, then the beautiful crest may be spread wide open like an old-fashioned fan. Much more spectacular is a rare display apparently triggered by the appearance of a raptor overhead. Lying back on the ground, the hoopoe spreads its spectacular pied wings so wide that the tips nearly touch. At the same time it spreads its tail open, throws its head back, and points its bill up at the sky.

Although the undulating flight of the hoopoe may not seem impressive, the African Hoopoe is a partial migrant. However, one must remember that the closely related Eurasian Hoopoe in the unfavourable northern parts of its range is a proper migrant. This is mainly at night, but flocks of over 100 have been counted. It has been recorded up to 6400 m in the Himalayas. In India, when trained falcons have been set on it, the hoopoe has shown remarkable ability to evade them, including by out-climbing the falcons in the sky. Normally hoopoes prefer to walk around in a stately way, but they can run. They seldom search for insects in trees, but this has been observed. They flick over cow-pats with sideways and upward bill movements. Their diet is mainly insects, but also spiders, centipedes, millipedes, earthworms, snails and slugs, lizards up to 16 cm long, frogs and toads, and exceptionally birds' eggs. The hoopoe's tameness where not persecuted has enabled it to become an urban bird, feeding contentedly on lawns and grassy pavements. They love sandbaths, but are apparently not interested in water, not even to drink.

Nests are usually in a natural hole, often in a tree or termite mound, but also in a cliff or a hole in the ground, more recently under roofs or sites like chimneys. Some nests are deliberately lined with soft vegetation, but others are unlined. The eggs are a most attractive pale blue when fresh, but soon become a khaki-brown colour. This is usually ascribed to dirty parental feet, but may involve a physiological process. The reason is that the pores also appear to change colour, and shortly before hatching are a clear white. Nests are often described as dirty and stinking, but this criticism is unfair as attempts are made to clean them. The real reason is the remarkable chemical warfare waged by the female to protect her chicks, and the chicks to protect themselves.

There is a double-barrelled strategy. The first is a remarkably modified oil-gland which from the fourth day after hatching starts to exude a special liquid with an 'intolerable stink'. This temporarily enlarged gland reaches its maximum size at 12 days, and then gradually shrinks. The smell is well-likened to rotten meat. From the sixth day, 'copious and forceful' stinking faeces is shot from the cloaca to provide the second 'barrel'. At first the chicks are inaccurate with both 'barrels', but their accuracy improves rapidly. Older chicks all hit what they aim at, simultaneously if possible. They can spray up to about 60 cm. The female is reluctant to abandon her chicks to an attack, and undergoes the same temporary weapon development of both barrels to provide effective

*African Hoopoe carrying prey to a burrow nest.* (Photo: John Wesson)

*Peculiar posture taken up by African Hoopoe when a raptor passes overhead.* (Photo: Frank Douwes)

support in the nest-hole. Together this is a formidable arsenal in the truest sense.

This disgusting but most valuable habit is presumably the reason why the hoopoe is classified in the Old Testament as a proscribed impure bird species. However, in the Authorized Version there was an erroneous translation from the Hebrew as 'lapwing' instead of 'hoopoe'. It is regarded as a delicacy in some Eastern regions, but strictly protected by superstitions in others. During the Middle Ages, authors associated the hoopoe with magic and the supernatural. Soothsayers recommended various hoopoe organs in their concoctions, particularly to stimulate vision and memory. Probably the painting of hoopoes in ancient Egyptian and Cretan tombs and temples also had a magical connotation. However, possibly the artists were simply motivated by the striking beauty of the hoopoes.

# WOOD-HOOPOES
## FAMILY PHOENICULIDAE

Few birders overlook a group of wood-hoopoes in their vicinity because of their noisiness and peculiar antics as they work their way through the trees. Far more than mere chattering, these birds readily exhibit almost hysterical group-cackling and bowing. They are among the most sociable of our birds. The similarity to our fairer sex chattering gaily and volubly has of course not been lost on our chauvinistic tribesmen. Various African-language names have been given to the wood-hoopoes on the lines of 'old women laughing together', and I have never heard the aptness of this description being challenged by our ladies.

The decision to split the wood-hoopoes as a family off from the largely ground-feeding Eurasian and African Hoopoes was a wise one. A major difference is that the wood-hoopoes spend virtually all their time foraging in trees. The group even sleeps together in a necessarily large enough tree-hole. Clearly ignorant of the better-known chemical defences of the *Upupa* hoopoes, Wanless (2001) made exaggerated claims of 'unique' chemical protection of these nest cavities by wood-hoopoes. Territories are defended not only by vigorous calling, but also includes a habit called 'flag-waving', where objecting wood-hoopoes pick up a bit of lichen or bark, and wave it! Much more radically different, the group of usually 6–8 wood-hoopoes stay together and all help raise the progeny of the alpha or dominant pair. Groups of up to 16 have been recorded.

*Seldom encountered singly, the Red-billed or Green Wood-Hoopoes* (Phoeniculus purpureus) *are normally part of a restless raucous group hunting for insects and other invertebrates.* (Photo: Peter Ginn)

*The metallic sheen of the Green Wood-Hoopoes is clearly seen here. Note also the much heavier bill found in males.*
(Photo: Geoff McIlleron)

Wood-hoopoes also differ dramatically from hoopoes in appearance: dark blue or green in colour with a metallic gloss, and lacking the spectacular crest. At a distance they appear black. They have longer decurved red bills, and also possess much longer tails, which develop damaged feather-tips because they are not stiff. White patches near the tips are present in the graduated tails, with a white bar usually present in the wings. The best-known species was formerly known as the 'Red-billed' Wood-Hoopoe but this name was changed to 'Green' due to its green metallic gloss. Another very similar species – almost the only real difference is its clear violet gloss – in Namibia was apparently recognized as occurring together, the Violet Wood-Hoopoe. However, some hybrization has recently been reported here.

A third species in a limited area of East Africa is known as Grant's Wood-Hoopoe. However, although allopatric in distribution, this wood-hoopoe is doubtfully distinct, and probably only a subspecies. A fourth apparent species, the Black-billed Wood-Hoopoe, is found further north and has a black bill, but sometimes this has a red base. There is also a fair amount of racial variation found in the Green Wood-Hoopoe, which complicates the issue further. However, there are additionally two smaller forest wood-hoopoes, dark glossy green in colour, and which differ clearly in size, the Forest Wood-Hoopoe and the White-headed Wood-Hoopoe in Central and West Africa. These two show no white plumage other than whitish or buffy heads in a colour phase present in both species. The nominate form of Forest Wood-Hoopoe is chestnut-headed, black-billed and black-legged, but also has dark-headed males. The White-headed species has a more decurved red bill and red legs.

Best known in the Green Wood-Hoopoe, the social organization of the group dominates their lives. Seldom indeed do observers see only one or two wood-hoopoes together, and the explanation for this is probably the initial stages of the formation of a new group. Strongly exclusive in the defence of their territory, even a tiny group goes through the same noisy and excited display procedure as a large group when groups meet. Such break-away groups are probably siblings which have broken away from a large group together. Ongoing research by Radford (2003) of the Percy Fitzpatrick Institute is continuing to throw new light on the species with remarkable findings. Sexual dimorphism in the species has long been known, with the longer-tailed males 10% heavier than females, but males have bills 40% longer than females so that there is no overlap.

The larger wood-hoopoe male bill is used for probing after prey on larger branches, rather than pecking as does the female. Bill size and shape play a role here. This differentiation takes place from about six months of age, when male bills approach adult size. Fascinatingly a male will forage happily next to a female with their differing techniques, but quarrel with another male. Single birds follow the rule of feeding more successfully than a competing group does, but run a higher risk from potential predation. However, sex is not the only factor, and the males and females have their usual dominance hierarchies. Dominant males probe for longer periods into cavities than do subordinate males, and dominants seem to exclude subordinates from prime feeding areas. The alpha female stays in the nest-hole throughout incubation and the early nestling period, and is fed by other members of the group. She stimulates them to feed her by uttering a distinctive begging call. It is easy to see how such a situation could progressively lead to the far more advanced system of hornbill females being protectively incarcerated in their nests, and assiduously fed by their mates.

# Scimitarbills
## Family Rhinopomastidae

Separating the wood-hoopoes from the *Upupa* hoopoes of the Upupidae was a wise decision, and erection of the family Phoeniculidae certainly appears to be justified. However, to further split the scimitarbills off into their own family Rhinopomastidae has doubtful validity. Differences between the Phoeniculidae and Rhinopomastidae, as proposed, do exist, but it is doubtful that they are sufficiently distinct to justify a family split. Treatment of the scimitarbills as a separate genus *Rhinopomastus* of the Phoeniculidae has been widely accepted world-wide. On balance, unless there is far more evidence than appears to be the case, this familial split appears to be exaggerated and unjustified. The hoopoes, wood-hoopoes and scimitarbills have in common that only their inner two front toes are fused at the bases, indicative but certainly not overwhelming acceptable evidence.

Three species of scimitarbill are now currently recognized. In north-eastern Africa there is the Abyssinian Scimitarbill, a small black species with a single white wing-bar and no white in the tail, but with a strongly decurved red-orange bill and black legs. Then there is our Common Scimitarbill in south-central Africa, with a black bill, black legs and white-tipped tail-feathers. There is one white wing-bar across the primaries per wing, and also a patch of white primary coverts. In between we have the Black Scimitarbill, with a shortish fairly straight bill, little or no white in its short tail, but otherwise like the Common Scimitarbill. The latter two intergrade all the way from southern Angola to the Democratic Republic of the Congo, and the Black Scimitarbill seems most unlikely to be a valid species.

The scimitarbills are not found in large gregarious groups like the Green Wood-Hoopoe, but usually solitarily or in pairs. Occasionally a small family party is encountered. Scimitarbills are also not noisy like this wood-hoopoe, but usually utter a monotonous single-note repeated call. Rendered variously in the case of the best-known species, our Common Scimitarbill, as 'sweep', 'wheep' or 'wha' in up to 25 repetitions, it is a soft, moderately-pitched call, but one which carries well and is readily recognized. There are several other calls described, including a rolling alarm call. Although they tend to be silent when foraging, the male scimitarbill will pause from time to time and call to the female, to remain in contact with her.

Occasionally scimitarbills forage on the ground, but much more on peripheral branches and also on tree-trunks. Here they excel in probing into bark crevices and behind loose bark with their fine, sharply decurved bills. They do not seem to carry quantities of food simultaneously at all, rather bringing a rapid succession

*Common Scimitarbill* (Rhinopomastus cyanomelas) *females have a brown head, not uniformly coloured head matching the body. Usually only one prey item at a time is carried to the nest.* (Photo: Peter Ginn)

*A male Scimitarbill searching among* Aloe excelsa *florets for insects.* (Photo: Darrel Plowes)

of single prey items like grubs. Decidedly acrobatic in foraging, they readily hang upside-down while probing. Scimitarbills often join bird-parties. In miombo woodlands, they can be seen in direct competition with the Spotted Creeper, even working their way up the same tree in the same manner at the same time (Ginn 1979). Characteristically, the scimitarbill flies to the base of the next tree before again working its way to the top.

Scimitarbills will readily nest in old woodpecker or barbet holes, but will also readily use natural holes including those which are definitely larger than their body-size, unlike most hole-nesting birds. Remarkably the female sleeps in the nest, while the male prefers to roost separately in a crack or crevice in a large tree at dusk. He may apparently use this same roost all year if not disturbed there, simply hanging unobtrusively asleep through the night. At a scimitarbill nest, I was unexpectedly faced with one of the classic dilemmas which conservationists face. Most are committed to letting nature take its course without interference, versus active sentimental interference. Male Common Scimitarbills can be clearly distinguished by their glossy blue-black heads compared to the dull brown heads of the females. I was showing a group of birders a male repeatedly carrying prey items to his nest in a large marula tree with several holes visible. Then a Banded Gymnogene arrived, and commenced investigating the holes for potential prey. As it approached the scimitarbill nest, thrusting talons into each hole in succession, I was subjected to a barrage of cajoling by the ladies in the group. I was about to accede to their importuning when loud squeals rang out. Like a conjuror, the hawk with a flourish produced a firmly grasped Bush Squirrel from a hole. Dropping immediately to the ground below with such a large prey item, the gymnogene commenced jumping on it to assist penetration of its claws. Interestingly the poor squirrel received scant sympathy in its death throes, the ladies were so relieved that the baby scimitarbills were safe!

## ORDER TROGONIFORMES

# TROGONS

## FAMILY TROGONIDAE

The trogon family includes some of the world's most beautiful birds, and they are also known for possessing the world's relatively thinnest and most fragile skins. They have a peculiar distribution, but resemble each other closely, so much so that one wonders about the validity of the subdivision into various genera. In Central and South America 22 species of five genera are found, with one species extending as far north as Arizona. Three species of an endemic genus occur in Africa, including our Narina Trogon, the so-called Bare-cheeked Trogon of Central Africa, and the more widely distributed Bar-tailed Trogon, found in disjunct montane forests in Central Africa. Then in the Oriental Region another 11 species occur, all classified in another endemic genus. The key to this once pan-tropical forest distribution lies in the Oligocene deposits of France, where the remains of a fossil ancestral trogon have been discovered. All our trogons clearly have a common origin, probably in the forests of the Neotropical region.

Together with this divided distribution, we also find differences in diet. In the Oriental region, the trogons are almost totally insectivorous. Our trogons are largely insectivorous, but also eat some berries. In the Neotropical region, however, fruits form a considerable part of the trogon diet. These trogons also have their bills more notched and serrated than those of the Old World trogons. There is probably some correlation between this and the remarkable way in which they take fruit, actually on the wing like hawking insects in flight. Flying or perched insects are hawked like a flycatcher or bee-eater from a perch with a surprisingly fast, twisting flight of short duration. This is launched when the almost motionless trogon, with only its head moving, has decided that they are within range.

Most South Africans regard the Narina Trogon as our most beautiful bird species. However, trogons are exceptionally attractive as a family. One of them in particular is a strong candidate for the title of the most beautiful bird in the world. This truly magnificent trogon, metallic green and scarlet with white under the tail, is basically coloured like a Narina Trogon male. So breathtaking is this Resplendent Quetzal that it was worshipped by the well-known Aztec and Mayan tribes of South America as their god of the air. It is about 35 cm in length, but four already lengthened upper tail-covert feathers extend for a further 60 cm past the tip of the tail! These particular feathers were much sought-after by these cultured tribes for ceremonial purposes, but the birds were never killed for them. Instead the quetzals were captured, the special feathers removed, and these trogons then carefully released to grow more.

Like most trogons, our Narina Trogon nests in a natural hole in a tree, where the three or four pure white eggs are laid without a lining. Despite their typically weak but broad and flattened trogon bills, some of the New World trogons prefer to dig their own nests in rotten wood. Some even take over large aerial termite or wasp nests built in trees, and hollow them out. The defending termite soldiers or adult wasps and their larvae are simply eaten first, and the trogons appear to be immune to these previous inhabitants. Trogons have one other anatomical peculiarity. Of the various zygodactylous birds with the two-forward two-backward toe arrangement, they are the only birds in the world to have the second or inner toe moved backward, instead of the fourth or outer toe.

Courting or territorial Narina Trogons utter a soft series of rather ventriloquial hoots, and at each hoot the long tail is wagged slightly forward. This call is fortunately easy to imitate, and the shy but beautiful forest bird can be readily attracted. If one is close enough, one can see the exposed bright blue-pigmented skin at the eyes and near the bill where the Bare-cheeked Trogon shows more obvious yellow skin. When the trogon hoots with a distended throat, the throat skin can also be seen to

*Most South Africans consider the Narina Trogon* (Apaloderma narina) *to be our most beautiful bird species.* (Photo: Nico Myburgh)
**Inset:** *Female Narina Trogon.* (Photo: Cyril Laubscher)

be bright blue, but usually concealed by feathers. Despite their individually bright colours, this combination of disruptive patterning of bright colour blends into the broken light of the forest, and makes the trogons more difficult to see. Narina Trogons are also content to sit typically hunched for lengthy periods with only slight surveillance movements of their heads. This species was named by the well-known early French explorer, François le Vaillant, among other noteworthy achievements the last artist to paint the now extinct Blue Buck from a freshly-shot specimen. Le Vaillant named the trogon after Narina, an attractive Hottentot girl whom he admired.

ORDER CORACIIFORMES

# Typical Rollers

## Family Coraciidae

The roller family is now restricted to the 11 'true' rollers of the genera *Coracias* and *Eurystomus* by omitting the five ground-rollers (formerly subfamily Brachypteraciinae) and the single cuckoo-roller (formerly subfamily Leptosomatinae) to classify them separately. All six of these aberrant species are endemic to Madagascar, and this wise omission is clearly a considerable improvement. These 11 rollers differ from all other coraciiformes in basic foot structure. Their two inner front toes are connected for much of their length, but the outer toe moves freely. They are sturdy birds, but with noticeably short legs and weak feet. The sexes are alike, tending to be brightly coloured: dominant colours are blue, green and chestnut. Several species have attractive elongated outer tail-feathers. Although bills are blackish in the eight species of *Coracias*, they are yellow or red and broader in the three species of *Eurystomus*. Rollers are undoubtedly attractive birds, but in general have harsh screeching calls which do not match their beauty. Eight species are found in Africa south of the Sahara. The Blue-bellied Roller, recently recorded from Pilansberg, is a new addition to the South African list. Four roller species extend across the warmer temperate areas of Europe and Asia, southward to northern Australia and eastward to the Solomon Islands.

All the rollers are masters of flight, cannot walk, and are reluctant to hop on the ground. They also tend to fly from perch to perch in trees, rather than clamber around. The *Coracias* rollers have a basic hunting strategy of swooping down from a perch to snatch prey from the ground below, and returning

*The Lilac-breasted Roller* (Coracias caudatus) *swoops down with spectacular spread wings to snatch a millipede.* (Photo: Eliot Lyons)

**1:** *The European (Eurasian) Roller* (Coracias garrulus) *is the only true migrant among our rollers and has the longest wings.* (Photo: AfriPics)
**2:** *A Broad-billed Roller* (Eurystomus glaucurus) *feeding its chicks in a nest-hole in a tree.* (Photo: Peter Barichievy)
**3:** *Blue-bellied Roller* (Coracias cyanogaster) *recently recorded several times during September 2004, first by Bryan Groom and then by several others, is a spectacular addition to the South African bird list.* (Photo: Cyril Laubscher)
**4:** *The Purple Roller* (C. naevius) *has a spectacular white eye-stripe and breast heavily streaked with white.* (Photo: Warwick Tarboton)
**5:** *The rather obvious racket-ended outer tail-feathers distinguish the Racket-tailed Roller* (C. spatulatus) *from our other roller species.* (Photo: Cyril Laubscher)

to a perch. Should they miss, they are usually reluctant to continue the pursuit on foot. The three smaller *Eurystomus* rollers are even better flyers (although they do not 'roll'), proportionately longer-winged, and prefer to drink from the surface of water by swooping down like swallows and swifts. Here their broader bills with much wider gapes are better adapted, but naturally also for capturing the aerial prey they depend on. Rollers get their name from the spectacular display flights that they undertake during the breeding season and particularly courtship. These include rapid rolling tilts from side to side at speed, barrel-rolls, somersaulting and looping the loop, calling while they do so.

Both genera of rollers prey mainly on insects, though flying termite alates when swarming provide a major food source. However, the *Coracias* rollers incorporate many other small non-insect items in their diets. Examples are millipedes, centipedes, spiders, scorpions, solifuges, snails and slugs, mussels, earthworms, frogs, lizards, rodents, even birds and their nestlings. They readily attend veld-fires to feed on the small animals attempting to flee the flames. Their strong slightly hooked bills enable them if necessary to smash and batter insect prey well-protected by chitinous 'armour-plating'. Normally they select less difficult prey. As a young girl at Messina, my mother was greatly privileged to have a hand-raised Lilac-breasted Roller as a pet. When she walked in the veld, the stunningly beautiful roller would sit on her shoulder like a falcon, and fly off to catch any insect, mainly grasshoppers, that it fancied. One can empathize with Moselekatse, the famous founding chief of the Matabele tribe, who considered this species so beautiful that he forbade anyone else of his subjects to wear its feathers under unequivocal threat of instant death.

We have six roller species in southern Africa, one of which is the European Roller, a true migrant from the northern hemisphere, with longer wings than our other four species of *Coracias* rollers. One mass migration observed in Somalia involved an estimated 40 000 to 50 000 European Rollers. Our only *Eurystomus* roller, the Broad-billed Roller, is also a migrant but with two completely distinct patterns. One is from Madagascar, where it breeds and is the only true roller, moving to East Africa as a non-breeding visitor. The other is another subspecies which moves from central Africa both north and south into the respective woodland belts to breed, reaching as far south as the Limpopo and Mpumalanga Lowveld and even further to KwaZulu-Natal. Our other two rollers with extended tail-feathers, the Lilac-breasted and Racket-tailed Rollers, nest like the foregoing two usually in natural tree-holes, or woodpecker nests if they are large enough. Our largest roller in terms of body-size, the Purple Roller, extends further west into Namibian desert habitat than any other of our rollers. Here, where there are no trees available, they are obliged to nest in rock-holes or holes in cliffs. Remarkably, they have also commenced nesting in large-diameter vertical pipes.

In Europe, particularly as migration time approaches for their journey south, European Rollers have been recorded as roosting communally. Although this does not seem to be recorded in southern Africa, I have observed European Rollers flying in the late afternoon to such a communal roost in the Limpopo Lowveld near Hoedspruit. Roller movements in South Africa appear to be irregular and not necessarily repeated from year to year. In one particular year a number of European Rollers left their hunting perches on roadside telephone lines almost simultaneously to migrate north. They were so rapidly replaced by Lilac-breasted Rollers appearing from apparently nowhere to take their places that I felt like rubbing my eyes in disbelief. Yet with their attenuated tail-feathers and clear colour differences there could be no mistake.

# ALCEDINID KINGFISHERS
## FAMILY ALCEDINIDAE

The kingfishers are a large and familiar group of birds which show a cosmopolitan distribution, being absent only from extreme habitats such as the polar regions. For a number of years the approximately 90 species were divided in two subfamilies, basically the 'fishing' kingfishers and the 'forest' kingfishers. However, this did not prove a satisfactory classification, and the present three basic groups were then recognized by various authorities like Fry on morphological grounds. An independent study of kingfisher primary moulting modes by the Stresemanns confirmed the validity of these three groups, which are now regarded as families. The eleventh primary is much reduced in kingfishers, and absent in the alcedinids.

The first family of about 25 species fittingly includes the well-known Common Kingfisher *Alcedo atthis*, which has a wide distribution over almost all the Palaearctic Region (except the far north) and through the Oriental Region as far as the Solomon Islands. A brightly coloured little bird, it exemplifies this basically long-billed short-tailed family, and is beloved in the northern hemisphere. The ancient Greeks called them *alkuōn* (*alcyon* in Latin), and believed that they nested on the open sea. The relatively calm fortnight before the winter solstice was supposedly decreed by the gods to enable the kingfishers to breed, and this is why periods of calm and peace have been described as 'halcyon days' ever since. According to Greek mythology, Alcyone was the daughter of Aeolus and one of the Pleiades who married the son of Hesperus named Ceyx. When he was drowned in a storm, the grieving Alcyone threw herself into the sea, and the sympathetic gods changed them both into kingfishers. The names of the lovers have been subsequently immortalized in the scientific names of kingfishers.

This genus includes another six species in Africa and Asia. All these are 'fishers', dependent on fish prey, and burrow into earth banks to nest. However, others in the family are almost solely insectivorous, though they also excavate earth burrows. Examples are our tiny Pygmy Kingfisher, only 12 cm long, and the even smaller Dwarf Kingfisher of Central and West Africa at 10 cm long.

The Pygmy Kingfisher is an inter-African migrant which migrates at night. It always gives me a thrill when one of these incredibly beautiful little feathered jewels comes gently knocking on our lighted windows at night. To ensure the survival of such bewildered birds, it is best to carefully capture them at the window from the dark before one of the predators does so. They should then be kept overnight in a suitable container, for release in the morning. Their extremely short little tarsi require the application of special narrow bird-rings. Our Pygmy Kingfisher has a close relative endemic to Madagascar, which is totally rufous-coloured above.

The kingfishers show their coraciiform links in their front toes being joined for more than one-third of their length. There is also a tendency in this family to reduction in the number of toes, for example in the genus *Ceyx*. This comprises 10 species found in the Oriental tropics and as far as Australia. These small brightly coloured kingfishers have only two remaining toes in the forward position, with the usual one backward. This genus is also remarkable for the degree of colour differentiation found in it. Here major secondary integration of kingfishers that appeared to have clearly become definite species has taken place, with the supposed species 'hybridizing' on a large scale (Sims 1959). This proved beyond any doubt that the extensive plumage differentiation was deceptive, and that development of biological isolating mechanisms enabling them to become true species in terms of the Biological Species Concept had not taken place.

Finally, two of our familiar little kingfishers also in this family deserve a special mention. The first is an obvious close relative of the Common Kingfisher, our attractive Half-collared Kingfisher. Although obviously a good species, it looks a lot like the Common Kingfisher, is classified in the same genus, nests in exactly the same manner, flies and calls like its Palaearctic relative, and feeds on a similar fish diet which it catches in the same way. What is noteworthy is that it seems to have a low tolerance of water pollution, and its presence on our streams and some dams like the Blyde Dam is an indication of pure clean water. Secondly, our little Malachite Kingfisher is a widely distributed favourite bird, which sometimes burrows into ridiculously low

**1:** *A Half-collared Kingfisher* (Alcedo semitorquata), *closely related to the widespread Common Kingfisher.* (Photo: Peter Barichievy) **2:** *The tiny Pygmy Kingfisher* (Ispidina picta) *is a feathered jewel catching insects nearly as large as itself.* (Photo: Geoff McIlleron) **3:** *In contrast, the larger Malachite Kingfisher* (Alcedo cristata) *is a true fisherman. Note the slightly raised crest (see text), usually a sign of excitement.* (Photo: Fanie Hendriks)

earth banks to nest. As in many kingfishers, the adult with its scarlet bill is readily distinguished from the juvenile with its blackish bill. It was formerly known as the Malachite Crested Kingfisher to acknowledge the additional crest of turquoise blue barred with fine black lines. Although I have never seen this phenomenon published, I had removed a Malachite Kingfisher from a mist-net for ringing purposes, and was holding it carefully in my hand. Suddenly, as if in protest at the liberties which I was taking with it, the kingfisher erected its crest and continued lifting until the entire crest lay flat along its bright bill.

# DACELONID KINGFISHERS
## FAMILY DACELONIDAE

Crossword-puzzle fanatics will immediately recognize that *Dacelo* is an anagram of *Alcedo*, which has its roots in Greek mythology. This is the nominate genus of the Alcedinidae family of both fishing and insectivorous kingfishers. *Dacelo* is also the genus of the well-known Kookaburra or Laughing Jackass of Australia, with three other congeneric relatives in the Australo-Papuan area. Although the large Kookaburra is not a particularly attractive kingfisher, it is famous for its loud weird calls. Kookaburras combine to emit a wild chorus of what has been described as crazy laughter when they go to roost at dusk. Just as dawn breaks, they again wake everyone in earshot with such precision that Australians call them the 'bushman's clock'. Australians also appreciate their killing of even fairly large snakes, either apparently by dropping them from sufficient height to stun or kill them, or by simply bashing them with their large heavy bills. However, their farmyard raids to eat chicks or ducklings are not appreciated. Another fascinating kingfisher in this family is the very large Shovel-billed or Earthworm-eating Kingfisher from New Guinea, which actually digs out earthworms with its large flattened bill. One final group in this family deserving mention is also from the Australo-Papuan area. These are the seven *Tanysiptera* paradise kingfishers, which unlike all other kingfishers have much elongated tail-feathers with racket-shaped tips.

Compared to these strange birds, our five representatives of the approximately 60 dacelonid kingfishers seem so normal as to be comparatively humdrum. The so-called 'forest', 'tree' or 'bush' kingfishers have no need

**Left:** *A Brown-hooded Kingfisher* (Halcyon albiventris) *with a large Holub's Sandveld Lizard* (Nucras holubi).
(Photo: Peter Barichievy)
**Below:** *The Grey-hooded Kingfisher* (H. leucocephala) *has a widespread distribution including north of the Sahara.*
(Photo: Martin Goetz)

to seek out aquatic habitat, but simply hunt large insects, amphibians, reptiles and even other birds and small mammals. Again, in keeping with other kingfishers, they all nest in holes. Some excavate their earth burrows themselves, others are tree-hole nesters, and a number dig their burrows into aerial termite nests.

Our first dacelonid kingfisher is the attractive medium-sized Grey-hooded (Grey-headed) Kingfisher, an insectivorous species which is a long-distance inter-African migrant, and extends north as far as the Cape Verde islands. Most regrettably, it is the least known of our five representatives, with its movements the least understood here. Most breeding records of this species are from areas to the north of us, and it replaces the much commoner Brown-hooded Kingfisher in northern Namibia and Botswana. Superficially similar to the Grey-hooded Kingfisher, the Brown-hooded Kingfisher is larger, plainer and less attractive. It has a much wider distribution though, and is also better known due to its habit of sitting out on fences and telephone wires. Like the Grey-hooded Kingfisher, it is largely insectivorous, but excavates an earth burrow. It appears to be resident and definitely non-migratory, but there may be some local post-breeding movements.

Next is one of our favourite and most attractive birds, even regarded as the harbinger of summer to some people: the beautiful Woodland Kingfisher. Recently Tarboton (2004) has pointed out that this species seems to have been a much rarer bird in southern Africa in the first half of the twentieth century. Having studied the species in the early sixties (Milstein 1962) when it was undoubtedly considered a rather rare bird, I am in full agreement with him. This species does not excavate earth burrows, but always uses the old nests of woodpeckers or barbets or similar natural tree-holes, never supplying a lining other than the accumulating remnants of insects. Although largely insectivorous, it does not hesitate to include small vertebrates like fish (rarely), amphibians, lizards, small snakes, small birds and mammals in its diet when the opportunity offers itself. The Woodland Kingfisher is also a long-distance inter-African migrant, and the Sudan is indicated as its main winter quarters (Milstein 1962).

**1:** *The beauty of the well-known Woodland Kingfisher* (Halcyon senegalensis) *is brilliantly captured in this photograph as it flies to its nest to feed chicks.* (Photo: Cyril Laubscher)
**2:** *The Mangrove Kingfisher* (H. senegaloides), *which penetrates inland in winters up rivers on the coastal plain, has a heavier, all-red bill and a small black underwing bar.* (Photo: Geoff McIlleron)
**3:** *Less attractive than its congeneric relatives, the Striped Kingfisher* (H. chelicuti) *is duller, but also has a two-tone coloured bill though exactly opposite to the Woodland Kingfisher in coloration.* (Photo: Geoff McIlleron)

Almost identical to the Woodland Kingfisher in appearance is the Mangrove Kingfisher, of much restricted habitat in our limited mangrove swamps. However, it has a heavier and completely red bill, rather than a black mandible like the Woodland. Furthermore, it also has a small black underwing-covert bar. It also lacks the black post-orbital stripe of most Woodlands, and has a grey head and breast rather than a continuous blue head and a white breast. (This post-orbital stripe is lacking in the sedentary forest form of the Woodland Kingfisher with its brown crown, which has once been recorded within our limits on the Cunene River.) It is alleged that the Mangrove Kingfisher nests both in earth burrows and in old woodpecker nests, but the former is unlikely to say the least. It is probably a local migrant. Its diet resembles that of the Woodland Kingfisher, but obviously includes more crabs. Greg Theron (2001) amusingly describes the smallest Mangrove Kingfisher territory on earth, a mere four square metres in an open mangrove swamp tank at the Durban Aquarium, which the free-flying kingfisher left every evening to roost elsewhere.

Lastly, our fifth dacelonid kingfisher is the dullish but still attractive Striped Kingfisher, which is apparently sedentary, strongly insectivorous, and also nests in old woodpecker and barbet nest-holes in trees. The Striped Kingfisher has a black maxilla and a red mandible, where the Woodland Kingfisher almost always has a red maxilla and a black mandible. However, beware late-maturing Woodland immatures which exceptionally and temporarily may have red bills!

# CERYLID KINGFISHERS
## FAMILY CERYLIDAE

Formerly classified as the first group of kingfishers in systematic order, the small family of the cerylid kingfishers is now classified last. Although it comprises only nine species, it is important for various reasons. Probably the first is that it includes the only kingfishers to have colonized the New World. Another is that one of the world's most widespread kingfishers, our Pied Kingfisher, is included. This is comparable in distribution only to the Common Kingfisher of the family Alcedinidae. Yet another is that it includes easily the best hovering kingfishers in the world. This attribute appears to involve an important basic adaptation not found throughout the family. Like the other kingfishers, there is no sexual differentiation in size found in this family. However, there is regular sexual dimorphism in plumage patterns, so that the males and females can be clearly differentiated in the field. Although the other two kingfisher families contain brilliantly coloured species, the Cerylidae are relatively simply coloured. All have black bills and blackish legs and feet. They are generally black-and-white in colour, with limited rufous areas, although the black may be substituted in the New World for either slate blue or dark green.

There is not yet unanimity in the classification of the genera in this family. There do not seem to be any problems with the genus *Chloroceryle* with its four species and distribution mainly in South America. This is the only genus in the entire kingfisher family which is endemic to the New World. The problem arises with the other two cerylid genera, *Megaceryle* and *Ceryle*, on which there is not yet clarity. There seem to be two schools of thought. The first is to place all five species in *Ceryle*, which simplifies the entire issue and has much to recommend it. The other is the classification supported by Fry and others, which involves recognizing the considerable deviation of our Pied Kingfisher in *Ceryle* as a monotypic genus, wisely classifying only the other four cerylid kingfishers in the genus *Megaceryle*. These would include the Belted Kingfisher as the only fisher found in most of North America, and the larger Ringed Kingfisher, which just enters the United States, and is resident in the Rio Grande Valley. The slightly larger Crested Kingfisher, found from Kashmir to China and Japan, would also be included. Lastly, the genus would also include our Giant Kingfisher, the largest of the African kingfishers. This is confined to Africa south of the Sahara, from Senegal in the west to the Ethiopian highlands.

Our Pied Kingfisher is widespread in sub-Saharan Africa, through Egypt, the Near East and the Middle East to China. Often perched quietly in groups, it is an extremely active species when hunting, flying up and down shore-lines, hovering to detect suitable fish prey. When sighted, it may drop down to hover at a lower level before diving into the water and seizing the prey. Large prey is battered into submission, and then, like all expert fish-eaters, swallowed head-first in all cases to avoid being impaled on the spines. It will fish wherever

**1:** *The Pied Kingfisher* (Ceryle rudis), *the most widespread of the kingfishers and the best hoverer.* (Photo: John Wesson)
**2:** *A Pied Kingfisher hovering – an adaptation enabled by its much lighter skeleton, almost certainly pre-adapted.* (Photo: Tony Heald)
**3:** *Male Giant Kingfisher* (Megaceryle maximus) – *a still-hunter which almost never hovers.* (Photo: Martin Goetz)

suitable fish are found, from tiny pools and ditches to large impoundments, tidal pools and the open sea behind the breakers. As evidenced by its wide distribution, it is an undoubtedly successful species.

In Lake Kariba a freshwater sardine known locally as 'kapenta' was introduced from Lake Tanganyika, and provides a local fishing industry. However, the kapentas prefer deep water well away from land. To utilize this well-suited prey, the Pied Kingfisher flies out to distances given as 3,2–5 km from the shore. Obviously such hovering prowess requires basic modification as most kingfishers merely still-hunt, diving after prey from a suitable perch. The problem has probably been pre-adapted by the Pied Kingfisher having a comparatively light skeleton for its size, which enables the extensive hovering. The North American Belted Kingfisher is also an adept hoverer, and the same basic modification must presumably apply. Our Giant Kingfisher almost never hovers, and that extremely briefly. Clearly there is no comparison between it and the two foregoing species. It is interesting that the Belted Kingfisher is an accidental visitor to western Europe, probably another indication of its adaptability. It is about 30% heavier than the lightweight Pied Kingfisher.

The sexual dimorphism found in the Giant Kingfisher has an amusing result. The male has a rufous breast, but a white belly and vent, while the female has a rufous belly and vent as well as underwing coverts: clearly 'wearing the pants'. In the Pied Kingfisher the male has a double breast-band, while the female has only an incomplete broad one, lacking the thin lower band entirely. One last point is that all kingfishers, like others of the coraciiforms and some of their close relatives, have 'prickly' chicks. This is presumed to be an adaptation to unhygienic nest conditions. Chicks do not rupture the sheaths of their feathers until shortly before leaving the nest. Consequently they avoid soiling their feathers with the messy nest floor.

# BEE-EATERS
## FAMILY MEROPIDAE

Closely related to the kingfishers, and also with partly-joined third and fourth toes, is the bee-eater family, comprising 25 species. As a family they can be regarded as among the most beautiful of all birds, with their graceful shapes and glowing colours. Unlike the long straight bills, short necks and short tails of the kingfishers, they all have long delicate decurved bills well balanced by long tails, often with the central tail-feathers elongated. They are alert and vivacious by nature, sociable and friendly towards each other. Apart from three less elegant species classified in two small genera found mostly in Asia, 22 species are classified in the main genus *Merops*. They are remarkably similar, and there is no difficulty in identifying them as bee-eaters. They nest singly, in small groups, or in enormous colonies, making earth burrows into sandbanks. Some are long-distance migrants, others inter-African migrants, and some are sedentary. Their distribution tends to be tropical, from Africa and southern Europe to the Far East and Australia.

Bee-eaters have a characteristic flight of a few rapid wing-beats interspersed with graceful glides holding wings closed. They often fly around communally before roosting, and can be heard flying on moonlit nights. They are adept at catching insects on the wing, but also capable of taking them from the ground. Over their wide distributional range from rain forests to the edge of the desert, one would therefore expect them to feed on a wide variety of insects. However, this is one of the most remarkable aspects of the bee-eaters. They live up to their name indeed. The main prey of all the bee-eaters is remarkably specialized: honeybees and social wasps. They concentrate everywhere on hymenopterans: ants, bees, wasps and their allies, apart from occasional binges like a feast of termite alates on the wing, or an outbreak

*The European Bee-eater* (Merops apiaster) *breeds on a small scale in the Cape Province but is primarily a European migrant.* (Photo: Nico Myburgh)

*The Swallow-tailed Bee-eater* (M. hirundineus) *has a deeply forked tail.* (Photo: Eliot Lyons)

of locusts. Bee-eaters are among the keenest feeding participants at veld fires, and are attracted to them from a considerable distance.

The great majority of bees on which they feed are the most dangerous workers, the stinging sterile female caste. The wasps can be dangerous indeed as well. How they overcome the problem of the venom is adeptly described in detail by Fry (1984) in his excellent monograph on the bee-eaters, and there is clear differentiation in the treatment of stinging hymenopterans compared to other insects. The bee-eater returns to its perch, carrying the bee or wasp in the tip of its mandibles. It changes its grip to just behind the thorax, and bending one way hits the head hard against the perch. Almost too quick for the eye to see, it then changes its grip to the tip of the abdomen. Bending the other way, it rapidly rubs the bee against the perch, crushing both abdomen and sting. Closing its eyes to avoid the venom and bowel water, the bee-eater then rapidly rubs the bee several times to devenom it. Then the grip is switched again for head-blows, and the 'processed' bee is swallowed. The devenoming process takes up to 10 seconds. All other insects receive only head-blows, as the rubbing is unnecessary. Fry (1984) indicates that the largest bee-eater, our Southern Carmine Bee-eater, has apparently succeeded in sometimes carrying out this devenoming process while continuing to fly high. However, he is uncertain how this is done.

With such efficient predation on bees, conflict with bee-farmers is inevitable. Paintings in caves and rock shelters indicate that in Spain bee-farming is at least 8 000 years old, while such paintings are found widespread also in Africa, Asia and Australia. Fortunately it is generally realized in enlightened countries at least that bee-eaters also prey extensively on honeybee predators or parasites – various wasps in particular, robber-flies and dragonflies. Investigations have clearly shown that, on balance, bee-eaters are beneficial. Fry (1984) indicates

**1:** *Spectacular Southern Carmine Bee-eaters* (Merops nubicoides) *outside a nest colony.* (Photo: Alan Weaving)
**2:** *A Little Bee-eater* (M. pusillus) *having captured a honeybee.* (Photo: Alan Weaving)
**3:** *The Blue-cheeked Bee-eater* (M. persicus) *is a migrant to Africa, and an important prey species of the Sooty Falcon when passing through.* (Photo: Geoff McIlleron)
**4:** *White-fronted Bee-eaters* (M. bullockoides) *are a handsome species, usually nesting in smallish colonies.* (Photo: Fanie Hendriks)

that bee-eaters eat as many as one predator for every four honeybees. The slaughter of bee-eaters in places like Cyprus, Malta and the Nile Delta is for 'sport' and food, not to protect bee-hives.

Africa has about two-thirds of the world's bee-eaters, and in South Africa we have nine species present. These range from the small and solitary Little Bee-eater and Swallow-tailed Bee-eater to the enormous colonies of the Southern Carmine Bee-eater and other more sociable bee-eaters. Some species extend the parental pair to helpers at the nest. Long-distance Palaearctic migrants like the European and Blue-cheeked Bee-eater augment our bee-eater numbers as non-breeding migrants. However, the European Bee-eater also has a much smaller breeding population in South Africa (mainly the Cape) and Namibia. It is uncertain where their non-breeding quarters are – probably Central Africa, as it is most unlikely that they fly to the northern hemisphere.

The confusion over the status of the Olive (Madagascar) Bee-eater is gradually being resolved. Moreau and others had correctly doubted a postulated annual migration from Madagascar to the continent of Africa. There appears to be another population of the nominate race breeding from Somalia to Mozambique, not the Madagascar birds, and another subspecies (*alternans*) breeding in Angola and across into Namibia. Drab juveniles and moulting adults of the Blue-cheeked Bee-eater have been misidentified as Olive Bee-eaters, but it is certainly not conspecific. For obvious reasons, the confusing name of Madagascar Bee-eater should be abandoned for Olive Bee-eater as in the Atlas (Harrison et al. 1997).

Our Southern Carmine Bee-eater hitches rides on the placid Kori Bustard, from which it pursues insects, but its sibling species, the Northern Carmine Bee-eater, is far more of a hitch-hiker. Fry (1984) records it utilizing camels and other livestock, ostriches, two bustards (including Kori), five species of storks, one heron, one egret (momentarily), Sacred Ibis, two cranes, Secretarybird, zebra, at least four antelopes, warthogs, and once a dog.

*A Southern Carmine Bee-eater hitching a ride on the back of a Kori Bustard.* (Photo: Clem Haagner)

ORDER COLIIFORMES

# Mousebirds

## Family Coliidae

The mousebirds are a small family of six species endemic to Africa south of the Sahara. Superficially they do not appear to be remarkable birds, yet they differ so much from other birds that they are classified in their own order as well as family. Two genera, *Colius* and *Urocolius*, are recognized, apparently mainly on skull characteristics. Small slender-bodied birds with the sexes indistinguishable, their tails are twice as long as their bodies. They all have an obvious crest, which they raise when excited. Although links to the turacos or louries have been proposed, they are more likely to be related to parrots, or rather derived from the same basic stock. Their short, sturdy and decurved bills are not hinged to the skull for leverage like parrots, nor do they have the strange leg-scales of parrots. However, there are resemblances to parrots with regard to the palate, heart, pelvis, intestines and the oil-gland. They are also agile like parrots, readily hanging upside-down and in other unusual positions when foraging for fruit.

Mousebirds sleep tightly packed together in remarkable tight bundles, head up and tail down as a general rule, but there are allegations that some sleep upside-down. Their basic coloration is brownish or greyish, and the feathers are remarkably soft. Unlike most other birds, the hair-like contour feathers grow all over the body, and are not confined to specific feather tracts. Feathers are loosely attached to the skin. The ten-feathered tails are up to 25 cm long, with the tail-feathers clearly graduated into obvious pairs. The general impression is of a tail which tends to a sharp point, clearly visible in flight. The short rounded wings make a whirring sound in flight, followed by long glides. Mousebirds seem to fly directly into a bush or tree at speed, rather than perch on the perimeter first. Mousebird toes may also not look unusual at first glance, but they are remarkable indeed. Both the first and fourth toes are reversible. This enables them to easily hang from a twig by all four toes with their sharp claws forward, as a swift does. Alternatively they can clamber around like a woodpecker, with two toes forward and two toes backwards.

Mousebirds are exceptional fruit-eaters, to such an extent that they often become the arch-enemies of the gardener and fruit-farmer. They begin on the side of a ripe fruit, and simply hollow it out. Alternatively, they may just 'spoil' a fruit by pecking a hole in it, and then not finding it to their liking. They also consume large quantities of green garden plants, sometimes causing considerable damage by completely consuming cherished flowers. This occurs particularly during dry periods or real droughts, when mousebirds require green feed like buds or tender shoots. They also consume insects, and are especially fond of aphids.

Unexpectedly, there is one case on record where a mousebird ripped open a sunbird nest and devoured the babies. This appears to have been exceptional, and to state that they are therefore mobbed by small birds may be somewhat exaggerated pending further evidence.

**1:** *The Red-faced Mousebird* (Urocolius indicus) *with its red mask flies well, and is probably the most mobile of our three mousebirds.*
(Photo: Alan Weaving)
**2:** *In contrast, the White-backed Mousebird* (Colius colius) *with its distinct back pattern is probably the least mobile mousebird.*
(Photo: Peter Ginn)
**3:** *Speckled Mousebirds* (C. striatus) *perched sociably on a stick. They prefer the hotter regions with high rainfall.*
(Photo: Fanie Hendriks)

Despite being decidedly sociable and allopreening each other readily, creeping around on branches like mice enables mousebirds to be far less conspicuous than one would expect. Early in the morning they are particularly fond of sunbathing together, often lying back and amusingly exposing their bellies to the rays of the sun. They are also particularly fond of sandbathing, apparently much in preference to utilizing water for this purpose. Mousebirds drink by lowering their bills in water and sucking it up into their mouths. They then drink without lifting their heads.

The large sociable flocks break up into pairs to nest. Nests are sometimes well-concealed but sometimes fairly obvious. Some are cups of fibrous material lined with soft grasses. Others have a platform of sticks, sometimes with thorns on, below an impressive nest-cup made largely of vegetable down. Eggs usually number up to four, and larger clutches seem to be the result of more than one female laying. Both sexes share the incubation duties, and both feed the chicks by regurgitating partially digested food. The strange-looking chicks leave the nest early to clamber in the surrounding branches using beak, wings and feet. However, they return to the nest to be brooded at night. The parents eat the faeces of their chicks.

Of the six species of mousebirds, three occur with us. Bare facial skin and fleshy ceres seem to be characteristics of the mousebirds, including red or black coloration. Legs and feet are usually shades of red in colour. The white back bordered with black of the White-backed Mousebird is a unique feature in the mousebirds, and diagnostic for this species. The Red-faced Mousebird has a uniform light pale-grey back which also helps to identify it. With its cheery three-noted whistle characteristically falling in pitch, the Red-faced flies particularly well. It is found all over southern Africa except a section of the Namib littoral and high-altitude Lesotho. However, there are indications that it has been recently partly replaced along the lower Vaal River by the White-backed Mousebird, also with a whistled call, and found mainly in the arid western part of the country. It has a pied underwing compared to the rufous of our other two species, and a whitish bill with a black tip. Arguably it is the poorest flyer of our three species. In the eastern part of southern Africa with its higher rainfall, the faintly barred browner Speckled Mousebird, with its two-tone bill – black maxilla and white mandible – predominates. It has an almost strident harsh call, which also serves as a relayed alarm call to alert the flock to a potential danger in dense vegetation. However, in the centre of South Africa, all three species may occur together at the same locality at the same time, without apparent friction. There are clear indications that all three of our mousebird species have utilized gardens and fruit production in general to extend their respective geographical ranges.

## ORDER CUCULIFORMES

# OLD WORLD CUCKOOS

## FAMILY CUCULIDAE

Everyone knows what a cuckoo is, from the charming cuckoo-clocks even if they have never seen the bird themselves. Most people know that cuckoos evade the problems of parenthood, and induce other birds to incubate their eggs and raise their progeny for them. The word 'cuckold' has been used for centuries to describe a man who unwittingly raises a child which is not his own. With the latest classifications, we have now upgraded the coucals or 'rainbirds' with their bubbling calls to their own family. This still leaves approximately 100 species in this family which includes the majority of parasitic cuckoos, although such research-based changes continue. Of these 100 species, it is important to realize that only about half are obligatory nest-parasites on other birds. The others make their own nests and raise their own babies, like the Green Malkoha. This is a strange name previously used for one species in East Africa, but now extended here for a bird that birders knew for convenience (though incorrectly) as the Green Coucal. It builds its own platform nest, incubates its own eggs and raises its own chicks.

Including that one, we have 14 cuckoo species here of five genera, and aspects of them and their main hosts will be briefly discussed. To operate successfully, a biological system like that of these parasitic cuckoos must be complicated. Not only must the cuckoo species have an adequate supply of hosts for fostering, but the hosts must not be so misused that there are insufficient to raise the foster-children. Just as natural selection for 'clever' cuckoos continually takes place, this must be balanced against 'clever' hosts that are not fooled. It has been estimated that fewer than 3% of hosts in South Africa are parasitized.

In *Clamator* we have first the Jacobin Cuckoo, which parasitizes mainly bulbuls and the Fiscal Shrike. It lays decidedly obvious large white eggs which the hosts appear to generally accept. Then the Striped (Levaillant's) Cuckoo lays a reasonably accurate blue egg to match the main host Arrow-marked Babbler's lovely blue eggs. Finally the Great Spotted Cuckoo parasitizes crows and some other hosts like the Pied and Burchell's Starlings. Cuckoo chicks in nests of the host species tend to overwhelm the host babies, but in the crow group cuckoo chicks are often reared with the bigger crow chicks as these cannot be outperformed. Then in *Pachycoccyx* we have a remarkable size difference between the Thick-billed Cuckoo and the much smaller Retz's Helmet-shrike, its only host. Seen so far by researcher Carl Vernon and his assistant only, the big cuckoo

**1**: *The African Cuckoo* (Cuculus gularis) *is distinguished with difficulty from the world-famous Common (European) Cuckoo but there are a number of slight differences in the call and certain markings. Apparently parasitizes mainly the Fork-tailed Drongo.*
**2**: *An adult Great Spotted Cuckoo* (Clamator glandarius). *Easily identified, it parasitizes crows and a few larger starlings.*
**3**: *Best known from the ringing 'Piet-my-Vrou' call, the Red-chested Cuckoo* (Cuculus solitarius) *parasitizes robins in particular. Far more often heard than seen.*
**4**: *The Diderick Cuckoo* (Chrysococcyx caprius) *parasitizes weavers, bishops and sparrows.*
**5**: *Klaas's Cuckoo* (Chrysococcyx klaas) *parasitizes sunbirds and small warblers mainly, often such small nests that the eggs have to be dropped in.*
**6**: *The African Emerald Cuckoo* (Chrysococcyx cupreus) *apparently parasitizes mainly the Green-backed Bleating Warbler, but is little known.*
(Photos 1–5: Geoff McIlleron; Photo 6: Graham Kearney)

literally knocks or frightens the screaming helmet-shrike female off the nest in the absence of her supporting clan. By the time the helmet-shrike has picked herself up, the cuckoo has straddled the nest preparatory to laying the precisely matching parasite egg. Then away she flies with a host egg in her bill. No room for host babies as the big whitish cuckoo chick develops. In Vernon's study area, half the sparsely distributed host nests were parasitized by this cuckoo.

In *Cuculus* the best-known of our six cuckoos are found. The Red-chested Cuckoo is much more heard than seen, but the female keeps close tabs on various robins in particular. The Black Cuckoo is also relatively shy, and parasitizes Crimson-breasted Shrike, Southern and Tropical Boubous with well-matching eggs – so well-matching that they were only discovered at last in a Crimson-breasted nest as late as 1970. The Common (European) Cuckoo is the best-studied cuckoo, but only visits us as a non-breeding migrant. In the United Kingdom one exceptional female laid in 50 days a record number of 25 eggs in 25 Meadow Pipit nests. This is a perfect example of how a biological race has developed there with a specific Common Cuckoo line selecting only Meadow Pipit hosts. Our African Cuckoo, with a different call (equal accent on both syllables), so closely resembles the Common Cuckoo that for many years they were erroneously lumped together. It parasitizes the Fork-tailed Drongo, but up to 70% of poorly matching eggs are detected and rejected by this wide-awake host.

These four species of cuckoo chicks have a stimulatory sensitive itch associated with their hollow backs for the first few days after hatching. This itch stimulates the naked blind cuckoo chick with unbelievable determination to carry other nest contents on its back. The result is throwing the host eggs and babies, or those of another cuckoo, out of the nest with remarkable strength. It uses bill, wings and feet to feel for its goal of the edge of the nest. Thereafter the itch disappears, proven by survival of simultaneously-hatched cuckoo chicks which could not succeed initially in evicting the other. The average time to dispose of an egg is 3,5 minutes, sometimes as little as 20 seconds.

The Lesser and Madagascar Cuckoos are smaller editions of the Common and African, but almost nothing is known about them. In *Cercococcyx*, the Barred Long-tailed Cuckoo, only one authentic egg is known, laid in captivity. The host is unknown, but is suspected to be the African Broadbill, where similar eggs were found in two nests. *Sheppardia* robins are also likely hosts. Again, almost nothing is known about this cuckoo.

In *Chrysococcyx*, the Klaas's Cuckoo tends to parasitize hosts much smaller than itself, like sunbirds and prinias. The female cuckoo cannot enter some such nests to lay, and she is obliged to deposit her egg in from the entrance. Some such 'dropped' eggs crack or break badly. The cuckoo chick often becomes so large that the nest actually splits at the figurative seams. The Emerald Cuckoo is only known to have three hosts: the Starred Robin, Blue-grey Flycatcher and Bleating Warbler. The two first-mentioned may well have been 'dumped' eggs. Clearly further investigation is required.

Most is known about the Diderick Cuckoo, where gentes or biological races are in the process of development. The problem faced was that if a male established a territory and protected it by aerial patrolling, he mated within it with any female raised by the main hosts: Red Bishop, Masked Weaver and Cape Sparrow. How was it then that these biological races were maintained and improved? Obviously the male could not be allowed, whatever his host origin was, to disrupt the development of the genes favouring a matching egg-colour. Jensen (1996) correctly postulated that the gene(s) governing egg-colour inheritance had to be found on the female sex chromosome. Females returned to parasitize the host species nest in which they had been raised, and the matching egg-colours could then continue to develop by selection, as the male had no genetic influence on them. Parasitized Red Bishop nests with considerable egg visibility have a surprisingly good colour match with the blue host eggs. The darker Masked Weaver nests have eggs which match one of the 10 egg colours involved rather well, and were not usually rejected. Finally the much darker Cape Sparrow nests have the poorest egg colour match.

# Coucals
## Family Centropodidae

The coucals are close relatives of the cuckoos, and until recently were classified as a subfamily of the Cuculidae. The couas of Madagascar were formerly classified in the same subfamily, but this has been long rectified. The 29 true coucals are now classified in their own family. Although this family is mainly encountered in the Oriental Region, we have eight species in Africa. These are all endemic except one that barely extends into Arabia. All our African species are decidedly similar, and the problem for birders is not so much to identify one of them as a coucal as to distinguish between them. The general impression given by a coucal is of a largish clumsy bird with a long, broad, dark, graduated tail. The bills are strong and decurved in shape, often with a slight hook, and generally black or blackish in colour. The wings are short, rounded, and usually rufous in colour. In general they are not strong flyers, and spend much time foraging on the ground. After a short flight, they usually flop clumsily into cover. One coucal observed trying to fly across a river could not reach the opposite bank, and flopped into the water. It rested, swam to the bank, clambered ashore and walked off.

The eyes have red irises, and also have well-developed eye-lashes. The heads usually have black hoods. The underparts are much paler, white or whitish in most cases. This is emphasized by the chicks, which are sparsely covered with coarse, straggly and stiff white down. Yet the pattern of black skin above and pink skin below is obvious in nestlings except in the Black Coucal *Centropus grillii*, which is black-skinned. The plumage in general is coarse, with the feathers of head, neck and breast stiff and bristly. Even the nests are similar, a large round untidy ball of grass with a side entrance, usually placed low in vegetation. However, one nest is recorded 22 metres high in a palm tree. The eggs are rounded and white. Rather like some raptors, fresh green leaves are added regularly to the nest-lining. The calls are even like each other's, deep hollow dove-like vocalizations. The usual call for all our coucals is termed the 'dove' call, often given

**1:** *The Black Coucal* (Centropus grilli) *is our best-studied species and is proven to be polyandrous.*
(Photo: Alan Weaving)
**2:** *The most familiar species is the Burchell's Coucal* (C. burchellii)*, with its well-known 'glugging' call.*
(Photo: Fanie Hendriks)
**3:** *Our largest coucal is the Coppery-tailed Coucal* (C. cupreicaudus)*, rather a rapacious species.*
(Photo: Fanie Hendriks)

in duet. It falls and rises in cadence with minor variations. Another common call is the 'water-bottle' call, a glugging series of sounds like water being poured from a bottle.

In southern Africa we have five of the eight African coucal species. Despite the difficulty of their similarities rather than differences, aspects will be briefly discussed. Even their diets are similar, varying more with the size of the coucal and its habitat, but still small vertebrates and invertebrates like snails and insects. The best study so far on an African coucal (Vernon 1971) was on the Black Coucal. The indications of possible reversed sexual roles in our coucals had always been there with sexual dimorphism in favour of larger females. Furthermore males of other coucal species were known to build nests and feed the chicks. The Black Coucal is our smallest species, and it clearly takes part in wet-season influxes to suitable areas. This is probably vagrancy rather than migration, which is defined as a regular seasonal movement to another locality and back again.

During such an influx, this study proved that one female had a monogamous relationship with one mate, but another female was clearly polyandrous. Over four days this same female was carefully observed to consort with two males, and three days with all three males. Over a period of less than 2,5 hours, she was observed to copulate with all three males. She also laid a replacement clutch for one of the males, which was then successful. This second female would summon one of her males by calling, and would be presented with insect food by him. Copulation would then take place, and immediately afterwards she would swallow the food she had been presented with. The first female kept giving the advertising call, but did not succeed in attracting a second male. In this study the Black Coucal males did all the incubation and feeding of the chicks. As far as could be determined, the females only went to the nests to lay eggs, and only took a cursory interest in the chicks. With other African coucals, polyandry is not yet proved or disproved, and there may be different patterns within the genus.

The Black Coucal is also our only coucal to have distinct breeding and non-breeding plumages. The breeding plumage is mainly black upperparts with prominent black feather shafts. There is a blue gloss on the head, mantle and neck. The underparts are also black with a blue gloss on the chest, while the rump has a green gloss. Non-breeding plumage has the upperpart feathers dark brown with a central cream streak on each feather, and the underparts pale with pronounced cream feather shafts on the chest. Vernon (1971) also details the misconceived taxonomic lumping of the Black Coucal *C. grillii* with the Madagascan *C. toulou* and Asiatic *C. benghalensis*. This was because of general similarities, and because all three had distinctive seasonal plumage dimorphism. However, the inconclusive methodology was rejected, and the three widely separated species fully accepted again. In southern Africa, the Black Coucal's strongholds appear to be on the Mashonaland Plateau and in the Okavango Delta. However, seasonal movements in wet years also take place from Mozambique into suitable habitat in Zimbabwe, the Limpopo and Mpumalanga Lowveld, and as far as KwaZulu-Natal.

The large Coppery-tailed Coucal inhabits permanent swamplands and the thickets of riparian vegetation which fringe them. It barely enters southern Africa in the extensive swamp area of northern Botswana, extending further north into the enormous swamps lying to the north of the Zambezi River. The White-browed Coucal, once again split off from the Burchell's Coucal, is sympatric here with the Coppery-tailed. Burchell's and the Senegal Coucal actually resemble the Coppery-tailed much more than the same-size White-browed does. However, the considerable size difference of these three compared to the Coppery-tailed is clear. The bill of the Coppery-tailed is also proportionally much heavier, and this large species is recorded as swallowing a Blue Quail whole at one gulp. The Senegal Coucal was unrecorded in South Africa during the atlas fieldwork (Harrison *et al.* 1997) despite its wide distribution in Zimbabwe. This emphasizes again the apparent complementary distribution of the Senegal and Burchell's Coucals, indicating that more than merely a barred rump versus an unbarred rump is involved. This apparent barrier, where the Limpopo River is not normally considered a zoogeographical boundary, was effective during the Pleistocene interglacials (Clancey 1994).

An interesting old observation from Uganda, when a Burchell's Coucal nest was threatened by fire, allegedly involved the coucal carrying the chicks singly between its thighs in the unusual way that a woodcock does. For many years this unusual woodcock method was not believed. Finally, coucal chicks employ two defensive stratagems when they are threatened. The first is a vigorous snake-like hissing when the nest is touched. The second is for the chicks to spray foul-smelling excrement when they are threatened. This is precisely what a hoopoe chick does for the same reason, except that hoopoes also use the uropygial gland in their chemical warfare.

## ORDER PSITTACIFORMES

# PARROTS

## FAMILY PSITTACIDAE

Although related on slight evidence to the cuckoos of the Cuculiformes on one side, and to the pigeons of the Columbiformes on stronger evidence on the other, parrots are so distinct that any relationship to other birds remains unresolved. About 320 species of about 80 genera are involved, mainly tropical, some subtropical, and a few temperate (including some recently extinct). Their main centres of distribution are South America and Australia. Compared to the 18 parrot species in Africa, Brazil alone has 70, and Australia 52. Various subdivisions have been proposed, and a reasonable one is one family with four subfamilies. Here most of our parrots would be classified in the Psittacinae, with our endemic lovebirds in the Loriinae. However, Africa also has one species of the large Oriental genus *Psittacula*. This is our African Ringneck or Rose-ringed Parakeet *P. krameri*, found from Ethiopia to Senegal. We also have another feral subspecies of this from India, introduced to the East Coast of Africa by man.

Parrots include aberrant species which can barely fly and are nocturnal. Examples are the Ground Parrot of Australia, the Owl Parrot of New Zealand, and the probably not extinct Night Parrot of Australia. One of the few parrots with a temperate distribution, the Carolina Parakeet, was eradicated by the end of the First World War in the central United States due to fruit and grain damage. A few isolated island species also became extinct.

Despite the great variation in size (length 10–100 cm, weight 15–3 000 g), parrots are all rather similar in appearance and uniform in structure, with plumage all the shades of the rainbow, and sexes usually alike. Bills are short, strong and decidedly hooked, with a cere enclosing the nostrils. In our African parrots the cere is bare, but others may be feathered. The upper mandible is not fixed to the skull, but hinged, which enables greater leverage. The power that can be exerted by the bill of a large parrot should be seen to be appreciated.

*Rosy-faced Lovebirds* (Agapornis roseicollis), *our commonest lovebird, found in arid regions and with the unique habit of carrying grass-stems stuck into its rump-feathers up to its nest.* (Photo: Cyril Laubscher)

Macadamia nuts are notorious for their hard shells, and I always find it awesome to watch a Hyacinth Macaw effortlessly open one. At a length of nearly one metre, it is one of the largest parrots in the world. The powerful bill slices effortlessly and neatly through the hard shell of the nut, the strong tongue wiggles the kernel into the macaw's mouth, and both halves of the shell fall discarded to the ground.

Parrot necks are short, bodies compact and legs short. Toe pattern involves two forward and two back. The feet and legs are covered with unique tiny granular scales. In clambering around in a tree, parrots do not hesitate to use their bill as a third foot. Parrot wings are short and rounded, designed for rapid flight rather than for long distances. For people who know parrots in untrammelled nature, where they fly around like rowdy rockets, it is a sadness to see these extremely active and intelligent birds kept sometimes in such small cages that they can barely turn around. Although in nature their calls are harsh and loud with little variety, in the frustration of captivity their imitative ability is almost unequalled. Only the Hill Myna, an Indian starling, is considered a better 'talker'. As a result of this high level of mimicry, coupled to their most attractive appearance and intelligence, they were kept as pets at least 2 400 years ago by the ancient Greeks and Romans and probably well before then.

In southern Africa are found only five of the 10 *Poicephalus* parrot species. The olive-headed Cape Parrot *P. robustus*, encountered in the montane forests approximately from the east to the south of Lesotho at about 1 000–1 500 m, has been long-isolated and is now recognized as a separate species. The grey-headed populations from about 24°N northwards, mostly in mopane and miombo woodlands usually below 1 000 m, reach Tanzania and Uganda. They were lumped together, but became incorrectly prematurely recognized as the Grey-headed Parrot *P. suahelicus*, with another

**1:** *The Meyer's Parrot* (Poicephalus meyeri) *is the same size as the Brown-headed Parrot but has more extensive yellow coloration. Despite their similarities and ready hybridization in captivity, they do not mix in nature and no true hybrids are known from the wild.* (Photo: Peter Ginn)
**2:** *The Brown-headed Parrot* (P. cryptoxanthus) *has with us a more Lowveld distribution, with the Meyer's Parrot more Bushveld.* (Photo: Fanie Hendriks)
**3:** *The Cape Parrot* (P. robustus) *and its sibling species, the Grey-headed Parrot, are our largest indigenous parrots. The Cape Parrot has a much smaller home-range, and probably because of this and the felling of mature trees, is endangered.* (Photo: John Wesson)

isolated subspecies in West Africa. This subspecies is *P. r. fuscicollis*, which formerly occurred from Angola through West Africa, but is now only common in The Gambia. In an able taxonomic review, Wirminghaus *et al*. (2002) confirmed the specific status of the smaller Cape Parrot as *P. robustus* and recognized *suahelicus* and *fuscicollis* as similar subspecies. The problem is that *fuscicollis* pre-dates *suahelicus*, and must therefore receive normal precedence over *suahelicus* as the species name for the Grey-headed Parrot. This then becomes *Poicephalus fuscicollis* (Kuhl), with the nominate race and *P. f. suahelicus* as subspecies.

Then we have three smaller parrot species, also of the genus *Poicephalus*. The Brown-headed Parrot is found from northern KwaZulu-Natal in a more or less Lowveld distribution and reaches Kenya. Brown-headed and green-breasted, with a greenish-yellow iris, it does not show a yellow shoulder patch but has an extensive yellow underwing. Adjacent to this parrot's distribution, we have the Meyer's Parrot in the Bushveld and most of Zimbabwe, with green to turquoise underparts. It has a red-orange iris with irregular yellow markings on the shoulder and often on the head, together with only limited yellow on the underwing. The irregularity of these dorsal yellow markings was misconstrued on museum specimens to claim extensive hybridization between these two species. However, they do not really associate in nature. As pointed out by Rowan (1983) and basically confirmed by Wirminghaus (1995), this 'hybridization' is a misconception of acceptable individual yellow variation in the Meyer's Parrot in particular. In northern Namibia we have the generally similar but easily distinguishable Rüppell's Parrot, with a red iris and a grey head without yellow markings. It has a dark grey-brown chest, but a blue belly, vent and rump. It does have a yellow shoulder, and also extensive yellow underwings like the Brown-headed Parrot, but unlike Meyer's Parrot. Although the ranges of these three basically similar-sized species do come together and abut, there is no reason for concern that they do not behave as true species. Hybridization is possible with imprinted parrots of these species in captivity, but this has no bearing on their status as species.

Lovebirds got their name from the way they cuddle up to each other. Our commonest is the well-known Rosy-faced Lovebird, which apparently is the only species to stick bits of grass into the specially hooked feathers of its rump to remarkably carry these up to its nest for lining. There are generally considered to be eight species of *Agapornis* lovebirds, of which we have three. However, it appears that one of these species is not valid. There is extensive hybridization in East Africa between Fischer's Lovebird and the Masked or Yellow-collared Lovebird.

It appears that these two supposed species were brought together prematurely by large-scale crop-growing in Kenya, and that they have not met the criterion of the Biological Species Concept. In other words, they were only incipient species like so many allopatric bird populations, and will fuse to form one species. Our Black-cheeked Lovebird is a good species, unlike the foregoing case, and is found only in a tiny population, remarkably isolated physically along the Zambezi from Lilian's Lovebird, as indicated by Dodman *et al*. (2000). Extensive bird-trade trapping took place, and there is an authentic record of 16 000 Black-cheeks being trapped for export in only four weeks during 1929. However, a census by Dodman *et al*. (2000) indicates that 10 000 of this species still survive. Justifiable criticism of Black-cheeked field guide illustrations by Warburton (2002) requires rectification. There is also in one guide a gremlin indicating an erroneous possible link to the blue-rumped Rosy-faced Lovebird instead of Lilian's with its green rump.

Finally, there is the interesting problem of the Ring-necked Parakeet, which has reached northern KwaZulu-Natal in flocks of up to 60. As indicated initially, these birds are not from the indigenous African population found across Africa from Ethiopia to Senegal. These Natal birds are from the Indian subspecies originally introduced by man into Zanzibar. The African subspecies might in time have reached this far south, but it is unlikely. Possibly augmented by feral parakeets, the species's survival in South Africa is in the melting pot. Again, time will tell.

ORDER APODIFORMES

# SWIFTS AND SPINETAILS
## FAMILY APODIDAE

The name of 'swift' applied to any bird must give an indication of speed. The scientific name of the order and family means 'without feet', an interesting comment on the birds generally considered to be the world's fastest and best flyers, the most aerial of all birds. The other recognized master flyers are the hummingbirds, conventionally also placed in this order as the family Trochilidae, a New World family. There is now controversy over the actual relationship, still to be resolved. Both families have the humerus short and strong, a short ulna with secondaries, and the 'hand' with the primary feathers long. Swifts and spinetails have some difficulty in taking off directly from the ground, because their feet are short and weak, best suited to hang or sit at their nests. Two subfamilies are recognized: the true swifts of the subfamily Apodinae, and the Chaeturinae spinetails, whose feather shafts extend past the tail-feather tips to form a stiff support. Of the approximately 80 members of the family world-wide, we have here 11 true swifts and two spinetails of different genera, the Mottled Spinetail and the Batlike (Böhm's) Spinetail. These spinetails both usually nest in holes in baobab trees.

Many people have difficulty in distinguishing between a swift and a swallow (Passeriformes: Hirundinidae). One obvious difference is that swifts never sit on a thin branch or a wire: they cannot. In swifts the first toe is reversible, so that they can hang from a rock face or wall with all four toes. Swifts have narrower and more sickle-shaped wings, and their tails are generally shorter. This can readily be seen in flight. Swifts fly with a series of rapid wingbeats and glides in between. Swallows indulge in relatively more gliding. Swift wingbeats are so rapid that they are hard to see, and when turning, the wings seem to beat unevenly. High-speed photography proves it: one wing beats faster than the other to compensate for the inadequate steering of their short tails. Swallows are also more brightly coloured, while swifts are grey, brown or black, with paler areas of white or light-grey.

A far greater identification problem – given their dull colours and remarkable flight-speed – is to distinguish between swift species. However, all things are possible, and even the tiny Batlike Spinetails can be identified high over the Pafuri Bridge. This is by their almost tail-lessness, fluttering bat-like flight, and white bellies glinting like specks in the sun. A constant reminder for identification care should be the carcass of a large road-casualty swift brought to a Hoedspruit bird expert by a passer-by. Only after he had fed it to an eagle did the penny drop, too late: no white belly. It was not an Alpine Swift, but the first Mottled Swift record for South Africa, now confirmed by Rushworth (2005).

Swifts are highly specialized insectivores which capture aerial insects at speed with their wide bills. However, it is interesting that they lack or do not need the sensory guiding bill-bristles that nightjars for example utilize to make their gapes even bigger. As the fastest birds in the world, distance means little to them.

*A rare photo of the Mottled Spinetail* (Telacanthura ussheri) *at their only known nest-site in South Africa, a baobab tree in the north of the Kruger National Park.* (Photo: Geoff McIlleron)

**Far left:** *The Palm Swift* (Cypsiurus parvus) *uniquely incubates its eggs actually glued to its feather-pad nest. All chicks after hatching must hang on for dear life.*
(Photo: Peter Ginn)

**Left:** *The Common Swift* (Apus apus) *winters in huge numbers in South Africa but are not easy to identify. The larger swifts have amazing survival adaptations for their eggs and chicks during unfavourable weather for hunting. However, their sleeping adaptations are more mind-boggling (see text) and certainly not yet solved.*
(Photo: Trevor Hardaker)

Objective measurement of flying speed in birds is beset with difficulties. Yet one of our Little Swifts, which nest in white-feathered colonies on our grain silos and tall buildings, was timed in level flight at 320 km per hour. It is most unlikely that this particular species is faster than our spinetails and large swifts.

A large swift such as the Alpine Swift is a far more effective predator of honeybees (and their insect predators) than any bee-eater is. They are probably immune to the venom, and at least 234 honeybees have been found in a single swift. Swift nests have a variable saliva content, and this 'cement' or 'mortar' is provided by seasonally enlarged saliva glands. The famous nests of the *Collocalia* swifts in Far Eastern caves provide almost pure saliva nests which are 'farmed' to provide the sought-after delicacy of 'birds' nest' soup. This is without harming the nesting potential of these valued swifts. Yet our Horus Swift, named after the swift-headed ancient Egyptian god, chooses to nest in an earth burrow like a kingfisher or bee-eater. Swifts usually lay 2–3 elongated white eggs, after copulation while flying.

Our tiny Palm Swift, with one Asian relative in the same genus, provides a remarkable nest, although of the usual feathers glued with saliva. Eggs are actually glued to the little vertical nest-pad, and ornithologists assumed that the swaying of the palm leaves they were glued to was sufficient to 'turn' the eggs. (With the advent of artificial incubators for poultry, including ostriches, it had been discovered that unturned eggs had a much lower hatchability.) Then Archie van Reenen first found Palm Swift nests glued to a steel railway bridge at Tzaneen. Answer: adequate vibration to 'turn' the eggs. Next were concrete railway bridges, with answer: still adequate though less vibration. Finally, with nests glued to houses at Skukuza, no answer: these eggs apparently do not need 'turning'. Palm Swift chicks have long sharp claws, because from day one at hatching they must literally hang on for dear life.

Even more remarkable, when bad weather forces large swifts in particular to hunt far away for possibly days on end, the eggs and babies survive by amazing adaptations. Eggs can be left unattended for literally days during incubation without any harmful effects. The chicks incredibly have an ability to lower their metabolism and body temperature as much as 10° C for up to 10 days, again without any harmful effects. Swift chicks have no second chances, unlike many other birds, and stay in their nests for up to six weeks to ensure a more successful departure. This is mirrored in longevity studies, where swifts apparently evade the high mortality of most first-year birds. A surprising average of only 19% mortality results.

Possibly the most remarkable aspects are yet to be told. Swifts were relatively unknown apart from Gilbert White's outstanding observations at Selborne in the late eighteenth century. Then Dr David Lack commenced his classic swift studies in a tower at Oxford, which was provided with nest-boxes. The Common Swift winters in huge numbers in South Africa, although identification is not easy. Lack (1956) noticed to his surprise that there was a mystery arising from their absence while on migration. When the swifts returned to the tower in fresh plumage to commence egg-laying, their claws were grown out, long and sharp. After the relatively short breeding period, these same claws were worn down to blunt stumps. With the reluctance of these master flyers to even walk, there seemed to be only one explanation for this phenomenon.

The obvious answer was that they had spent at least most of their time on the wing. Improbable as it might appear, there was no alternative solution. Then R.M. Lockley (1971), one of the most experienced British bird-ringers, took the investigation further. He watched as every evening the Common Swifts flew almost vertically up into the sky till he could no longer see them with his 10x binoculars. Where were they going? Electronic surveillance proved that they did not return to their nests at night. Where could they be roosting at sea? Or even more incredibly, were they roosting? Radar surveillance proved the contrary: that the swifts kept flying in the night sky hour after hour till dawn. Airmen saw them at night when flying at heights exceeding 2 000 m. Nocturnal air-strikes took place, with dead swifts penetrating into the fuselage of aircraft (Lockley 1971). Lack (1956) and Lockley (1971) are in full agreement as to how swifts make maximal use of aerial upcurrents, thermals of warm air.

One is inclined to hypothesize that somehow long controlled glides by the dozing swifts take place, like an aircraft on auto-pilot, and that in some way the swifts realize impending doom, regaining a safe height. However, this is probably an over-simplification. No one has made a noteworthy advance on the findings of Lack and Lockley. Lack (1956) described the flight of the Common Swift 'under all conditions' as the alternation of 'short glides with rapid wing-beats', and that 'they are not sustained gliders'. He was warmly endorsed by Lockley (1971). Consequently it is difficult to propose long glides as a solution to this problem. Possibly the solution is some kind of a shallow sleep, but at present we seem no nearer to solving this incredible mystery. Equally stunning is Lockley's (1971) hypothesis that once the Common Swift chick fledges, it is never fed again outside the nest, and immediately embarks on a nine-month continuous flight!

## ORDER MUSOPHAGIFORMES

# TURACOS (LOURIES)

## FAMILY MUSOPHAGIDAE

This family combines together some really beautiful forest birds with some decidedly drab birds from arid woodlands. The classification of this family (formerly under the Cuculiformes) is by no means clear other than that it is presently an endemic sub-Saharan African family. There are fossils known from Egypt and Bavaria, indicating a wider former distribution. Even relationships to the gamebirds have been indicated. On balance it is wise to follow several authorities who support classification in an own order like the mousebirds. The number of species recognized range from 18 to as many as 23, divided into as many as eight genera.

There is even considerable dispute over the vernacular group-names. The name 'turaco' is most used, and with a slight modification (*Tauraco*) is also the name of the largest genus. It has an indigenous West African origin, and is probably onomatopoeic. Moreau (1958) indicated that the widely used 'plantain-eater' name is erroneous, and that it should be discontinued. This also means that with great regret the southern African name of 'lourie', brought by the Malay slaves of the Dutch East India Company to the Cape will be discontinued in English, but lives on in Afrikaans. A regrettable and unnecessary addition is the pompously correct three-syllabled 'go-away-bird' for the grey members of the family. Our bird and our people say clearly 'go'way' in two syllables, not three. It is said that more Grey Go'way-birds have been shot with heavy-calibre rifles by frustrated hunters than any other bird species, after warning quarry of danger.

With their long broad tails, short rounded wings and apparent poor powers of flight, the tree-dwelling turacos characteristically run, hop and flap along branches in the canopy. They have been likened as close to the first known bird, *Archaeopteryx*, in locomotion. They even still have tiny hooks on the allula of the wing, though too small to be a functional aid in clambering around. They are all obligated frugivores, or fruit-eaters, eating a wide range of tree and other fruits, but also young leaves for salad. It is interesting that they eat with impunity at least several fruits which are poisonous to mammals. They will also join in the termite feasts when alates take flight, but animal prey is most rarely taken. Nests are frail platforms of sticks like those of doves, and their eggs also look like dove eggs. Nests are usually well hidden by the forest species, but in the go'way-birds are often exposed to view. Chicks are fed on regurgitated fruits, and it is interesting that, like mousebirds, turacos will eat the faeces of their chicks. The chicks appear to offer their posteriors when defecating. From an early age they spend much time out of the nest 'branching', and have a thick protective coat of down.

We probably have only four species of turacos in southern Africa, but the classification is still controversial. The problem is mainly our Knysna Turaco (Lourie) and closely related species. They form a species complex found from the Cape to West Africa and the Sudan, with numerous minor differences. These are mainly the length and shape of the crest, minor markings around the eyes, and differences in the extent and shading of the body gloss. It seems ridiculous that such minor points

*The Knysna Turaco* (Tauraco corythaix), *a beautiful bird in which tiny geographical differences are unsatisfactorily 'blown up' to create imagined 'species'.* (Photo: Geoff McIlleron)

can generate such controversy, but that is the position. Moreau (1958), who knew the *Tauraco corythaix* group well, considered treatment as a superspecies. Five species had been split into 17 subspecies by Peters in 1940: *T. persa* in the west, then *T. schuetti*, *T. fischeri*, *T. livingstonii* and *T. corythaix* (the Knysna Turaco) in the south. Moreau (1958) finally concluded that these should be considered as forming one polytypic species. On the one hand, he acknowledged the almost complete absence of transitional forms; on the other, he strongly emphasized 'the fact that the distinguishing characters are almost limited to details of head-feathering and gloss'. Supporting him, Rowan (1983) emphasized that nothing is known of the biology of the birds that militates against accepting them as a single species, and there is no other cause to give separate accounts of them. Clancey (1952) proposed five *T. corythaix* subspecies: *corythaix* (southern Cape to KwaZulu-Natal, shortest crest), *reichenowi* (dune forests in coastal Zululand, longer crest, bluish dorsally), *phoebus* (mountain forests from Barberton to Woodbush, shorter crest, more bluish dorsally), *livingstonii* (eastern Zimbabwe and adjoining Mozambique, crest like *reichenowi* but greener gloss), and *schalowi* (western Zimbabwe, Caprivi, northern Botswana, etc., longest crest, greenish wings and mantle, violet to violet-blue tail). Fry *et al*. (1988) support Moreau (1958) in lumping *reichenowi* with *livingstonii*, but under the latter name as a separate species. Rowan (1983) pointed out that *reichenowi* formed a distinct geographical and ecological entity. Fry *et al*. (1988) also then lumped *corythaix* and *phoebus* with *persa* from central Angola to West Africa, again basically supporting Moreau (1958).

In all this ado about very little, one factor shines out like a ray of hope to provide an acceptable factual solution. This is the most accurate map ever of the distribution of the complex in southern Africa. When the approximate distribution maps like Rowan (1983) and various others are compared with this accurate atlas map (Harrison *et al*. 1997), it is remarkable how the disjunct distributions of the foregoing basically allopatric subspecies stand out clearly. This is obviously why the atlas still supports Clancey's subspecies as a viable classification. Comparing this map with the distribution map of Parker (1999), labelled *livingstonii*, supplies essential insight. It can be seen that this latter map is actually a junction of three disjunct but not intergrading subspecies: the commencement of *phoebus* on the left, the top end of *reichenowi* at the bottom, and *livingstonii* extending into Mozambique. The clinal variation in crest length almost alone does not justify distinct species without substantial evidence certainly not yet forthcoming.

Consequently, if *livingstonii* is classified as a subspecies of the Knysna Turaco as the best solution, and leaving the extralimital taxa in abeyance for the present, we have three remaining turaco species. The first is our Purple-crested Turaco, which is currently classified in three different genera: *Tauraco* (e.g. Parker 1999), *Musophaga* (e.g. Sinclair, Hockey & Tarboton 2002) and *Gallirex* (e.g. Sinclair & Ryan 2003). However, it is a well-known species widely distributed in the moist eastern portion of southern Africa. The second is our even better-known Grey Go'way-bird, even more widely distributed in the northern half of southern Africa and which has colonized Johannesburg in recent years. The third turaco is a relatively recent addition to southern Africa, the spectacular purple Ross's Turaco, which has crossed over our northern boundary limit.

Finally, the brilliant scarlet wings of three of our four turacos are well known. Less well known is that the colour is from a remarkable pigment called uroporphyrin III, apparently unique in the entire animal kingdom. This pigment may yield 8 mg of copper per bird. For more than a century, a charming fable was everywhere accepted that this red colour was washed out from the feathers by rain, and had to be regularly replaced. A feather immersed in a glass of water does turn the water pink, but the basic colour remains. Chapin wore a red turaco feather in his hat for 18 months in the Congo to test the durability of the red pigment, but the only colour change was a slight darkening due to oxydization of the copper.

**Top:** *The Purple-crested Turaco* (Tauraco porphyreolophus) *is an undoubtedly beautiful bird.* (Photo: Fanie Hendriks)
**Bottom:** *The Grey Go'way-bird* (Corythaixoides concolor) *has of recent years colonized our urban areas due to the trees and fruit cultivated there.* (Photo: Clem Haagner)

ORDER STRIGIFORMES

# Barn Owls and Bay Owls

## Family Tytonidae

Owls were long classified with the diurnal or day-active raptors before it was realized that they had developed in parallel directions, but from different origins. Within the owl group, it was also realized that the well-known Barn Owl and its 9–11 close relatives should be separated from the other owls. They justify their own family, with differences like their heart-shaped faces due to facial discs, short rounded wings, long legs feathered to the toes, short-feathered thighs, and a middle toe with serrated claw. Other owls moult their tails from the outer tail-feathers inwards, but this family moults from the inner tail-feathers outwards. In addition to the 8–10 species of the genus *Tyto*, with tails shorter than their wing-tips, two owls from the genus *Phodilus* are classified here, with tails longer than their wing-tips.

The Barn Owl has a world-wide cosmopolitan distribution, but apparently never reached New Zealand. It is probably the world's best rat-catcher, particularly during rodent cyclic outbreaks or 'plagues'. One Barn Owl fed its mate on the nest four prey items in 20 minutes. During such gluts, many carcasses are wasted, even at nests with several chicks. As would be expected in such a widely distributed species, considerable variations in prey selection are found. In the Namib Desert for example, 49% of its prey are lizards. On the coast of Guinea-Bissau, mostly birds are eaten. In Mali some pairs specialize in frogs and toads, which can only be estimated because they are not detected in regurgitated pellets. As in the majority of predators, the most easily available prey is taken. Introduced to combat rodents in the Seychelles, they readily and regrettably switched in particular to the obvious white Fairy Terns roosting in trees at night.

Like all owls, the Barn Owl has outstanding night vision at low light intensities, but its ears are even better. By scientific experiments in total darkness, it was established that this owl could listen to the footsteps of a mouse, and successfully dive onto it when it paused for a moment. The Barn Owl often hunts from a perch, but most close relatives hunt while flying. They do not reach us in southern Africa – with one exception. Our second owl in this family, the African Grass Owl, can be easily confused with the Barn Owl, but has decidedly darker upperparts and clear dark markings on the pale underparts. Unlike the Barn Owl, it is recorded as hunting in the early mornings and late afternoons. However, this activity is rare, much less than in the competing Marsh Owl (Strigidae). Again unlike the Barn Owl, which nests in a variety of sites like caves, hollow trees, human habitations

**Top:** *The Grass Owl* (Tyto capensis) *is similar to the Barn Owl but differs strikingly in the dark upper parts. The prey in the photograph is a mouse.* (Photo: Clem Haagner)

**Left:** *Generally acknowledged to be the world's best rat-catcher, the cosmopolitan Barn Owl* (T. alba) *is an absolute specialist in night-hunting.* (Photo: Fanie Hendriks)

and hamerkop nests, the Grass Owl nests simply on the ground in the tall grass of a vlei. Moister vleis than those used by the Marsh Owl seem to be selected.

Both Grass and Barn Owls commence incubation with the first egg (latter laying up to 19, according to Tarboton & Erasmus 1998), and stagger their egg-laying dates by up to several days on occasion. In a poor year, this ensures that the oldest and strongest chicks will survive, but that all will be raised in a good year. Surplus rodents, usually headless, are stored with the eggs and small chicks. Studies show that the youngest chicks of large broods fledge in the shortest period of 50 days, while unstimulated single chicks may stay in the nest for up to 72 days. In particularly good seasons, even overlapping clutches may be laid by the same pair. In this family two distinctive successive down-coats are produced by the developing chicks.

The Oriental Bay Owl *Phodilus badius* is a similar but smaller species than the *Tyto* owls, and the facial disc is incomplete above the eyes. It is a shy species which lives deep in forests and is relatively unknown. However, the last species in this family can be justifiably described as the rarest bird species in the world. To the surprise of ornithologists, a strange owl species was unexpectedly discovered in 1951 in forest at Muusi, north-west of Lake Tanganyika. The surprise was mainly because it was clearly so closely related to the Oriental Bay Owl of tropical Asia, despite the remarkably considerable distance separating it from this sibling species. This new discovery had differences in plumage and also bill and foot morphology, clearly a different species. It was named the Congo Bay Owl *P. prigoginei* after the discoverer Dr Alexandre Prigogine, who showed it to me in the Royal Museum for Central Africa at Tervuren in Belgium. He explained that although the entire area was scoured in a search for other specimens of this species, it was never collected again. It was an eerie feeling for me to hold this soft unique specimen of which literally nothing is known. One possible sighting was made at a tea estate in Burundi in the mid-1970s, but the mystery persists despite another recent reported sighting.

Owls are well known for their strange nocturnal calls, some of them bloodcurdling, which frighten superstitious people all over the world. The Barn Owl, with its wide distribution, white appearance with a large square head, fondness for isolated church buildings and cemeteries, soundless flight, and surprising variety of frightening calls, is certainly responsible for more ghost stories than any other animal in the world. Previously in South Africa it was known as the 'Doodsvogel' or Death-bird, with the superstition that if it alighted on the roof and called, someone in that house would die.

# True Owls
## Family Strigidae

This closely related family contains about 120–125 species called typical or true owls, despite containing some strange ones. Unlike the Tytonidae, where bills tend to project downwards, these owls have the bill projecting forward. Long divided into two subfamilies on debatable criteria, a division into three groups based on different moult patterns is probably preferable. The family's origin is apparently the Palaearctic, with about 50 fossils known. Their general adaptation to darkness enables them to replace the distantly related falconiform raptors as nocturnal predators, but some owls hunt significantly during the day, although less well adapted.

The eyes and ears of owls are particularly well adapted. The eyeball of the 66 cm Snowy Owl is approximately as large as the human eyeball. Owls have the third eyelid well developed to protect the eye. Their exceptional ears are asymmetrical to be more efficient. Soft feathers for soundless flight are found generally, and made more efficient by filaments on the tips. Their binocular vision is assisted by the fact that owls can turn their heads 270° and more.

Owls are found world-wide except for isolated islands and Antarctica, which is rodentless. They all lay rounded white eggs in nests taken over from other birds like raptors,

**1:** *White-faced Owls* (Ptilopsis granti) *at their nest in a tree hollow, baby visible.* (Photo: Cyril Laubscher)

**2:** *Cape Eagle-Owls* (Bubo capensis) *are among the most powerful in the world, taking prey like* Lepus *hares and Red Rock-rabbits.* (Photo: Geoff McIlleron)

**3:** *The Wood Owl* (Strix woodfordii) *has heavily barred underparts and shadowed eyes that look like 'black eyes'. The pair communicates regularly with hoots, the female higher pitched.* (Photo: Peter Williams)

**4:** *Pel's Fishing Owl* (Scotopelia peli) *is a large ginger-coloured owl which dives into water to catch fish at night.* (Photo: Peter Steyn)

**5:** *The Marsh Owl* (Asio capensis) *is considerably more of a daylight hunter than our other larger owls, much more than the competing Grass Owl. Here it looks over its shoulder.* (Photo: Geoff McIlleron)

TRUE OWLS • FAMILY STRIGIDAE • 65

**Left:** *Our smallest owl is the Scops-Owl* (Otus senegalensis), *which has prominent 'ears', raised feather tufts which help its brilliant camouflage.* (Photo: Peter Williams)
**Middle:** *Pearl-spotted Owlets* (Glaucidium perlatum) *are finely spotted except the streaked breast. Amusing are the 'false eyes' on the back of the head, which are supposed to scare off small birds attacking from the back.* (Photo: Peter Williams)
**Right:** *The Barred Owlet* (G. capense) *is 'earless', like the Pearl-spotted Owlet but slightly larger and heavily barred.* (Photo: Peter Ginn)

woodpeckers and hamerkops, in man-made structures, and in natural sites like tree holes or forks, cliff ledges, caves, or even on the ground. Sizes vary from the tiny Elf Owl (14 cm long) from cactus deserts in North America, slightly smaller than our African Scops-Owl, to the *Bubo* eagle-owls, which are the largest owls in the world, with the Eurasian Eagle-Owl up to 75 cm long. Because owls are often dependent on rodents as their main prey, their numbers also often vary cyclically. To best utilize this unpredictable food source, the numbers of eggs laid also vary from two to as many as the 14 exceptionally recorded in the Snowy Owl (though in the Barn Owl of the previous family, even more eggs have been recorded). Owl nests and roosts are characterized by regurgitated pellets of bones, hair, feathers, and chitinous insect remains.

Ten members of this family occur here. Of the genus *Otus* (in America known as screech-owls), distributed over the world except for Australia, we have from the White-faced Owl to the widespread but small African Scops-Owl. Although the former, at nearly twice the size of the rest of the genus, does take up the elongated vertical 'frozen' protective posture like the smaller scops-owls, this is not as regular and not nearly as camouflaged.

Possibly the best solution is to omit the 'scops' from the vernacular name, and classify it as proposed by Sinclair & Ryan (2003) out of *Otus* and into *Ptilopsis*. The proposed northern and southern species split here is another matter in such similar birds, despite the apparent call differences, and more study seems essential.

Of the 12 eagle-owls, we have three species. First is the Cape Eagle-Owl, which is closely related to the Great Horned Owl and the Eurasian Eagle-Owl, and together with them forms a superspecies. This superspecies probably comprises the three most powerful owls in the world. Although our second eagle-owl, the Spotted, on a large prey sample (Fry *et al.* 1988) took over two-thirds invertebrate prey, it also eats birds and mammals. For example, in a Johannesburg nest near Emmarentia Dam I once found 40 red legs of Crowned Plover under Spotted Eagle-Owl chicks (though not matched for left and right), remnants from adults taken roosting on short grass at night (Milstein 1993). Our third and largest eagle-owl, formerly chiefly known as the Giant, now Verreaux's but also Milky, is also capable of large prey. Where hedgehogs occur, it delights in them, neatly peeling off the prickly skin in one piece and leaving that behind. No one has yet come forward with a reasonable explanation for the striking pink eyelids of this owl.

Endemic to Africa, of the three species of *Scotopelia* fishing owls, we have the best-known, Pel's. They have sharp scales on the soles of their feet, like the Osprey, to ensure that they get a firm grip on their slippery fish prey. Often overlooked is the fact that they require tropical climates as a 'must'. They simply cannot dive into cold water at night without a considerable risk that they will not dry out, but become chilled and succumb. Therefore wandering juveniles, for example to the southern Free State, can really only wander in spring and summer: winter would be too cold and risky.

Our African Wood-Owl was formerly considered to be the only African representative of the genus *Ciccaba*, with another four congeneric species found in Central and South America. Now it has been placed back in the genus *Strix*. The clearly distinguishable male and female calls are constantly uttered to keep in touch with each other while they hunt insects like crickets.

Next are our attractive *Glaucidium* owlets. The Pearl-spotted Owlet has become a great favourite due to its attractive whistled calls, its tiny size, as well as its ready use of old woodpecker and barbet nests, and consequently nest-boxes. The clearly-marked 'false eyes' on the back of its head are supposed to scare birds from making a sneak attack. The reason why small birds dislike it is because it sometimes catches them during daylight hunting. Steyn (1984) amusingly describes the largest known prey item, a Laughing Dove or Cape Turtle Dove at a water hole. Certainly the call attracts various birds to mob it. The one-third larger Barred Owl is also a most attractive species, but lacks the interesting 'false eyes'. It is less able to fit into woodpecker or barbet holes. To considerable surprise, the 'lost' Eastern Cape allopatric population of this species was rediscovered in 1980 after 150 years of no sightings. Its call is slightly different, but it is unlikely to be a distinct species. Our tenth owl species is the Marsh Owl, previously mentioned as a daylight hunting competitor of the Grass Owl (Tytonidae), and whose range extends to East and West Africa.

Like the Barn Owl in particular, owls of this family have also given rise to superstitions all over the world. They are associated with ghosts, phantoms, witches and such supernatural manifestations. Another positive but unjustified belief is the considerable wisdom of owls. However, it is a shining example of the benefit of looking wise and saying little. A further example of this is Steyn's (1984) observation of a Pearl-spotted Owlet repeatedly shamming death by lying on its back with its eyes closed, and also of a Verreaux's (Giant) Eagle-owl, similar to a Barn Owl recorded feigning death in Britain.

## ORDER CAPRIMULGIFORMES

# NIGHTJARS

## FAMILY CAPRIMULGIDAE

This is a fascinating order which the latest DNA research shows is distantly related to the owls. The claw of the middle toe has a comb-like outer edge. One exceptional member is classified in its own sub-order, separate from all the rest. This is the Oilbird *Steatornis caripensis*, named because for centuries the fat chicks, double the weight of their parents, have supplied native Venezuelans with their domestic oil supplies. Although fruit-eating, these oilbirds breed in great numbers up to 1,5 km deep in enormous caves. They are the only birds able to navigate in total darkness by an echolocation system like the smaller bats (Microchiroptera), although their clicks can be heard by the human ear.

Two small families similar to nightjars are found in the Far East and one in South America, all nesting on trees, but 75% of the 100 species are found in the Caprimulgidae, which are all ground-nesters. The American 'nighthawks' are classified in a separate subfamily, and lack the distinctive rictal bristles at the bill which assist in prey gathering, but so does one monotypic genus of nightjars. Nightjars have a cosmopolitan distribution except for some deserts, the polar regions, and New Zealand. We have seven of the 25 African species, including the European Nightjar, which is a regular migrant from the northern hemisphere.

The nightjars are probably the best-camouflaged of all birds. The basic colour combination is brown, grey, black and white in cryptic patterns. The large eyes of nightjars would help give them away to potential predators, so they are kept closed except for a tiny slit to see through until the last moment. Then they launch themselves silently and suddenly into the air to escape, from almost under one's feet. They normally lie flat on leaf-strewn ground, or more rarely (in two species) parallel along a horizontal branch, and are exceptionally well concealed. The nest is a slight hollow on the ground, or even on a boulder in the case of the Freckled Nightjar. In this unlined hollow the clutch of two eggs is laid, with a beautiful marbled pattern, usually in pink or grey. It is interesting that neither these eggs nor the downy chicks that hatch from them are cryptically coloured, unlike so many ground-nesting birds. The reason is simply the incredible camouflage of the adults, and their high degree of parental care in brooding both the eggs and downy chicks, so that the eggs or chicks are extremely rarely exposed during the day when concealment might be needed.

Wings are long and pointed, enabling nightjars to capture flying insects with ease. Like the owls, nightjars are soft-feathered, so that their flight is virtually soundless, not betrayed by whistling feathers. The weak bill is remarkably wide, and can open exceptionally. A series of rictal bristles helps to ensure flying insects go into the gaping cavity, but these are an aid, not essential. Up to 500 mosquitoes have been found simultaneously in a single nightjar, and even small birds may rarely be swallowed. Three species of nightjars collected feeding together in Tanzania contained the same species spectrum of insects of several orders. Due to their relatively inadequate legs, nightjars prefer to fly a short distance rather than walk, a logical choice with other masters of flight as well. They begin to hunt for prey as dusk approaches, and unfortunately for them are fond of sitting on roads. They have consequently been killed by vehicles in horrifying numbers, although this is no longer so apparent and seldom causes an outcry. The reason is that there are far fewer nightjars to kill. From the grille of a big sedan at Kariba, Dave Steyn removed the bodies of 13 nightjars: one night's kill for one vehicle. This cumulative slaughter has undoubtedly had a major harmful effect on our nightjar populations, and many areas have been unobtrusively denuded of all nightjars.

Although conservationists here are understandably concerned at the general decline of nightjars as a threatened group, the rarest of our nightjars is undoubtedly the Natal Nightjar. Not only is this isolated nominate subspecies subjected to the foregoing pressures, but worse. In this case, after widespread sugarcane cultivation, even much of its remaining preferred habitat in Natal of tiny patches of coastal forest in seasonally moist grassland is being destroyed by overdevelopment, mainly for housing. Its name has recently been changed to 'Swamp Nightjar'.

**1:** *This is one of the finest nightjar photos ever taken, of a Rufous-cheeked Nightjar* (Caprimulgus rufigena), *showing the bird in perfect focus, the 'nest' habitat and the eggs.*
(Photo: Cyril Laubscher)

**2:** *A male Pennant-winged Nightjar* (Macrodipteryx vexillarius) *at dusk, showing his remarkable pennants.*
(Photo: Alan Weaving)

**3:** *The Swamp Nightjar* (Caprimulgus natalensis), *our rarest nightjar.*
(Photo: Geoff McIlleron)

One can but hope that this is not due to prophetic insight, foretelling its serious decline in Natal to total disappearance. Fortunately, apparently healthy populations of other subspecies occur further north in Africa.

Nightjars have strange calls, and with us the best-known is that of the Fiery-necked Nightjar, also known as the 'litany bird' from its popular English rendering as 'Good Lord, deliver us!' The Afrikaans rendering involves sage advice: 'Jaag weg die wewenaar!', a warning to chase the widower away. Americans apparently enjoy competing to see who can record the greatest number of calls uttered in succession by a single specific nightjar, or 'nighthawk' to them. The record appears to be a remarkable 1088 times. However, we can boast the most spectacular of all nightjars, separated into a tiny genus *Macrodipteryx*: the Pennant-winged Nightjar, and further north the Standard-winged Nightjar. They have incredibly lengthened second primary wing-feathers, up to 777 mm in the Pennant-winged Nightjar, and 535 mm in the Standard-winged. Tony Tree established by ringed birds that these feathers grow individually slightly longer after each adult wing-moult. Although the Standard-winged moults these amazing feathers on arrival in its Sudan wintering grounds, according to Lynes littering the ground, the Pennant-winged carries them as stumps until time for a normal wing-moult. It is alleged, but not yet proved, that the males bite off these redundant plumes after the breeding season.

The Americans have made various fascinating observations on their species. The great early ornithologist Audubon observed a nighthawk moving eggs to another nest-site by carrying them in its mouth. Despite strong disbelief and opposition for a century, Audubon was finally vindicated. In another case, where a nighthawk always flew to its eggs from the same direction, the eggs were gradually moved 18 m in total from the original site. However, the most remarkable observation was made by native Indians in Arizona well over a century before, but only confirmed in 1946. This was the true hibernation of yet another nighthawk species, in rock crevices in cliffs. The body temperature dropped from 38°C to 19°C, the first hibernation recorded in a bird. Ringed birds returned to the same individual crevices to hibernate in succeeding years.

ORDER COLUMBIFORMES

# PIGEONS AND DOVES

## FAMILY COLUMBIDAE

The dove family is one of the best-known bird groups in the world, and has an ancient relationship with man. Many references indicate that they were among the earliest birds to be domesticated. These descendants of the European Rock Dove have exceptional direction-finding powers, utilized by man for at least 5 000 years to carry messages in particular. The ancient Romans regularly used homing pigeons in their campaigning. It is stated that the news of Napoleon's defeat at Waterloo reached Britain by homing pigeons four days before the fastest horses or ships did. Before and during the First World War, homing pigeons regularly made military history. During the Second World War, their value to secret agents on the European continent was so great that the British military authorities were obliged to officially

*Two male Namaqua Doves* (Oena capensis), *our only long-tailed dove species, showing the male's clear black bib. In treeless areas they are prepared to nest on low grass tufts where they lay cream-coloured eggs, not white.* (Photo: Peter Ginn)

**1**: *The Eastern Bronze-naped Pigeon* (Columba delegorguei): *a little recorded and even less photographed forest species. Note the broad white collar.* (Photo: Nico Myburgh)
**2**: *The African Green Pigeon* (Treron calvus) *with its bright coloration is unmistakable if properly seen, but they tend to creep around in the foliage until a close approach causes them to erupt from the tree, usually simultaneously and at a considerable speed.* (Photo: Clem Haagner)
**3**: *The Rameron Pigeon* (Columba arquatrix), *becoming a suburban bird after the fruit grown there.* (Photo: Nico Myburgh)
**4**: *The African Mourning Dove* (Streptopelia decipiens) *is rapidly extending its range in the Lowveld.* (Photo: Mike Jankowitz)

eradicate all Peregrine Falcons on the southern coasts of Britain to eliminate possible interceptions of vital military messages.

As many as 289 species occur in this family, and are divided into various subfamilies. Only in the polar regions and some isolated islands are doves not found. Most pigeon and dove species (a size-based irregular division) are encountered in the Oriental and Australasian zoogeographical regions, and nearly two-thirds of the world's species are found there. They vary in size from the very small Diamond Dove of Australia to the crowned pigeons of New Guinea, which approach a metre in length. We have 14 species of doves here plus the feral pigeon, which can be considered poultry or a wild species. Of these only our smallest, the long-tailed Namaqua Dove, shows strong sexual dimorphism with the male's black front. Three other species, the Tambourine Dove, Eastern Bronze-naped Pigeon, and Cinnamon (Lemon) Dove, show clear but less dimorphism. However, the last-named is usually seen only as a cinnamon flash when it takes off from the forest floor. Doves have thinnish bills which broaden again towards the tip, and a covering cere at the base houses the nostrils. Their feathers are decidedly loose and easily detached, supposedly a predator escape device by leaving a mouthful of feathers behind. Small heads relative to body size are found throughout the family. They, sandgrouse and mousebirds drink by sucking up water without lifting their heads.

In general, doves lay two pure white oval eggs per clutch, but four of our closely related species lay cream to yellowish eggs. Despite the fact that it is our largest dove, larger than our Speckled Pigeon, our Rameron Pigeon lays only one egg. Our African Green Pigeon also often lays only one egg. Dove nests are mostly built of such thin twigs that the eggs are visible from below. The chicks have little down covering, and are regularly brooded. In general, females brood at night and males during the day. Chicks are raised on the well-known 'pigeon milk', which much resembles mammalian milk in feeding value. It is a cheesy curd derived from layers of the crop-lining skin, secreted under hormonal control. Larger chicks are fed partly-digested grain, as doves are almost totally vegetarian. Chicks reach right into the mouths of their parents to obtain regurgitated food, and grow rapidly on the rich diet which cannot be supplied to large broods. The small broods are compensated for by repeated breeding, usually in winter when much fallen seed is available.

One of the most interesting dove species was the highly specialized Passenger Pigeon. It has been described as the most plentiful bird species that the world has seen. However, as a direct result of man's incredible greed in North America during the nineteenth century, this species was completely eradicated. The reliable ornithologist Wilson attempted in 1810 to estimate the size of a single gigantic flock, and reached a figure of more than 2 billion. It laid only one egg, and nested in tremendous concentrations where suitable food like acorns was available in the enormous forests. At one of the last great breeding concentrations in 1878 in Michigan, a single trader earned 60 000 dollars from more than 3 million Passenger Pigeon

**1:** *The Cinnamon (Lemon) Dove* (Aplopelia larvata) *has absolutely nothing to do with lemons but is strikingly cinnamon!* (Photo: Geoff McIlleron)
**2:** *The handsome male Tambourine Dove* (Turtur tympanistria) *with its white breast.* (Photo: Geoff McIlleron)
**3:** *The Blue-spotted Wood-Dove* (Turtur afer) *tends to be a forest species with a restricted range in the Soutpansberg. Note the bi-coloured bill.* (Photo: Cyril Laubscher)

carcasses. Adults and chicks were mercilessly slaughtered every year on such an incredible scale for financial gain that the numbers finally dropped below a sustainable minimum. Thereafter this specialized species simply stopped breeding, lacking the stimulus of sufficiently vast concentrations. The last wild Passenger Pigeon was observed in 1889. Although desperate attempts were made to conserve the species by breeding in captivity, the last Passenger Pigeon died in the Cincinnati Zoo in 1914.

Much could be written on the remarkable doves, like the 37 species of imperial pigeons (Duculinae) of the Far East and Australia, which feed on nutmegs and other large hard nuts and fruits that are often larger than their heads. They manage to swallow these large fruits by having elastic sockets in their jaws like various snakes. However, to conclude, how do our African Green Pigeons manage to find the widely scattered wild fig trees just when the Lowveld fruit is ripe? And where do the Eurasian Turtle-Doves disappear to in Africa? We have only two currently accepted records in South Africa, with another one near Hoedspruit by Dale van Reenen. Yet millions pour annually into Africa from Eurasia: 20 000 a day in migrational peaks passing through a speck like Malta, a minimum of 3 million passing on a 100 km front near Baghdad, etc. Tens of thousands have been reported in West Africa, but where are 'the millions of (Eurasian) Turtle-doves that must occur somewhere in Africa', emphasized by Fry (1975)? Still the Dark Continent.

## ORDER GRUIFORMES

# BUSTARDS AND KORHAANS
## FAMILY OTIDAE

This Old World family has had its greatest development in Africa, although the oldest fossils, more than 50 million years old, are known from the Eocene of Germany. Despite negative indications from egg-white proteins and mallophaga (bird lice), a close relationship to the Gruidae and Heliornithidae is shown by DNA-DNA hybridization techniques, though not to the Rallidae. The family consists of about 23 species, as experts still differ a little in their recognition. In Africa about 20 species occur, 17 of them endemic. The other species are found in southern Europe and Asia, with one species as far afield as Australia. Lacking a preen gland and only three-toed, this family is usually divided into seven or eight genera, sometimes as many as 10, which is probably unjustified and over-split. A more conservative division could be into two basic genera, with other monotypic

*The Black-bellied Bustard* (Lissotis melanogaster) *is much handsomer than the Red-crested Korhaan, longer, with proportionally longer legs and a totally different display. It is regrettable that the more desirable and more accurate alternative name of Long-legged Bustard has been discontinued.* (Photo: Geoff McIlleron)

genera for aberrant species. These two basic groups correspond in southern Africa with the larger members of the family, which we call bustards, and the smaller members of the family, which we call korhaans.

The bustards have sometimes truly remarkable breeding displays, completely outdoing the korhaans, although these are not insignificant, like the graceful communal displays of the Blue Korhaan. One bustard display is described as a male turning itself 'inside-out', and thereby instantly changing from a brownish bird to a white one, and vice versa, simply by erecting its display feathers. As suggested by Kemp & Tarboton (1976), it is certainly time someone gave serious attention to the mating systems of these fine birds: as an example, whether some pair normally, whether leks of ardent males are the norm, or whether loose relationships are skewed in favour of polygamous males. Actual courtship feeding has been recorded in the White-bellied Korhaan and in the Kori Bustard, the latter male presenting the female with an 80 cm snake!

Bustards and korhaans are in general birds of the open plains, and usually occur in pairs or small groups. Our two most arid-adapted korhaans are Rüppell's from Namibia and the closely related Karoo Korhaan, which slightly overlap in range. Our endemic Blue Korhaan is probably the handsomest of this group, and our South African representative of the White-bellied Korhaan is also the brightest coloured, though not meriting species status as Barrow's Korhaan. However, there are singly-occurring exceptions like our Red-crested Korhaan, which is regularly found in woodland. Here instead of an obscured ground display, it has a spectacular aerial display, rising steeply above the trees and suddenly closing its wings to fall to the ground as if shot. The Buff-crested Korhaan of the Sahel is probably conspecific with it, but Savile's probably not. Originally separated off by Austin Roberts as a distinct species, the isolated and distinguishable southern population of our Black Korhaan (also with an aerial display) has again been recognized as a separate species, probably justified though lacking conclusive evidence either way. The Black-bellied Bustard (male only) with its distinctive long legs also often occurs singly in woodland, and has a spectacular circling aerial display. It may be specifically distinct from the similar Hartlaub's Bustard in north-east Africa.

Then comes Ludwig's Bustard, considerably larger and heavier, with a dry western distribution in Namibia and the Karoo although it used to wander to the Natal uplands, and was once recorded near Barberspan. Slightly larger is Denham's Bustard, formerly known here as Stanley's Bustard. It is a more attractive species, easily distinguished by the grey fore-neck and pied head markings where Ludwig's is brown, though both have rufous hind-necks. It is found in the eastern half of southern Africa, but with a connection through to northern Botswana and the Cunene. Finally, in the western half of southern Africa but with a strip down to the Lowveld, we have the majestic Kori Bustard, simply the world's heaviest flying bird. It is fanatically fond of acacia gum, from which the Afrikaans name of 'Gompou', or gum-bustard, is derived. Although there are allegations that the Great Bustard of Eurasia or the

Australian Bustard is heavier, they do not compare and doubters can consult the Guinness Book of Records. Here the mean of Kori Bustard males is given as 17,8 kg, and old males can be considerably heavier. The mean weights of the two challengers are only 10,7 kg and 13,3 kg respectively.

Regrettably, due to the lethal combination of their edibility and size, bustards and korhaans are in serious danger. Although they are supremely suspicious of men on foot, and ultra-cautious about approaching their precious nest-scrapes with one or two rounded cryptically coloured eggs, or the vicinity of their well-camouflaged chicks, they do not seem to realize the danger of men on horseback or concealed in vehicles.

As long as 2 400 years ago, Xenephon wrote about how bustards could be captured by tiring them out. Data on the positive side, like the 1 477 harvester termites I proved were eaten by a single Blue Korhaan, will not despite their economic value be able to balance man's greed. We must ensure culturally that our bustards and korhaans are not eradicated. The last Great Bustard nested in England in 1832; only in 2004 are viable chick translocations under way from Germany to bring them back to ample suitable English habitat. The threat to our remaining bustards and korhaans here is not the inevitable habitat changes normally brought about by development, but thoughtless or mindless illegal hunting.

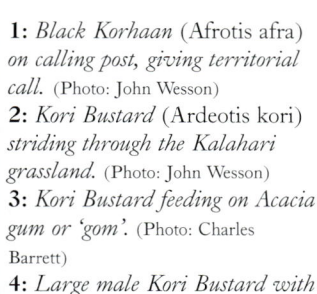

**1:** *Black Korhaan* (Afrotis afra) *on calling post, giving territorial call.* (Photo: John Wesson)
**2:** *Kori Bustard* (Ardeotis kori) *striding through the Kalahari grassland.* (Photo: John Wesson)
**3:** *Kori Bustard feeding on Acacia gum or 'gom'.* (Photo: Charles Barrett)
**4:** *Large male Kori Bustard with neck-ruff partly expanded.* (Photo: Eliot Lyons)

# CRANES
## FAMILY GRUIDAE

There are 15 species in this well-known but threatened family. Despite their spectacular appearance and dancing behaviour, as well as the sentiment which is associated with cranes particularly in the Far East, it would not be exaggerating to state that the continued survival of this specific family, more than any other bird family, hangs in the balance. These large stately birds can be regarded as an ancient group which is struggling to exist, and possibly on the way to extinction. Compared to the 15 living species, double that or 31 fossil species are known. The threatened Whooping Crane of North America enjoys an exceptionally intensive conservation programme from its breeding areas in the Canadian wilderness to its winter quarters in a specially created wetland refuge in Texas. It is even accompanied during its migratory flights by escorting aircraft. Yet there are experts, with whom I disagree, who believe that the remaining population numbers are simply too small to survive. Uncontrolled shooting by occupying forces in the Far East after the Second World War, and again during the Korean War, did probably irreparable damage to various crane species.

The 15 crane species are realistically classified in three genera: 11 in the largest (*Grus*), and two species each in the remaining two genera. Only South America, Malaysia and other islands, and Antarctica are without cranes. We are most fortunate in southern Africa that, with only three crane species present, we have representatives of all three genera. Two additional European crane species migrate to northern Africa, the Common and Demoiselle Cranes.

*A* Wattled Crane (Bugeranus carunculatus) *stands attentively over her egg in its marsh nest.* (Photo: Darrel Plowes)

**Top:** *Pair of Wattled Cranes with tiny chick under female (front crane).* (Photo: Peter Milstein)
**Above left:** *A pair of Blue Cranes* (Anthropoides paradiseus) *at their 'nest', the chick's head visible among the female's tail feathers.* (Photo: Cyril Laubscher)
**Above right:** *Tertial feathers of the Blue Crane, which conceal the absence of moulted flight feathers while they regrow (see text).* (Photo: John Wesson)

As a group the cranes are characterized by long legs and long necks with relatively short tails, but beautiful coverts which are actually the tertials, or innermost flight-feathers. Their bills are relatively short, and their faces relatively bare.

The cranes fly with their necks and legs fully extended. A family characteristic is their well-known bugling calls particularly during flight to keep the group together, but also uttered on the ground. These calls are emitted through a strongly convoluted trachea or windpipe, differently shaped in each species. Only the two relatively silent crowned crane species have a simple windpipe. The hind toe of cranes is placed higher than the other three toes, and does not normally carry any of the crane's weight. The front three toes are joined by a web at their bases. The nostrils are housed in a groove about halfway along the bill. Their short straight bills are used to feed mainly on vegetable matter, but they also prey on available animals like insects, rodents and small birds. Cranes are well known for their attractive dancing displays. It is interesting that this dancing is not confined to the breeding season, but can be seen at any time of the year. Furthermore, cranes apparently pair for life.

Our largest crane species is the Wattled Crane, which is undoubtedly our rarest and most threatened. Its declining numbers place this spectacular species on our Red List of most threatened species, due to the destruction of its essential marsh habitat. Also to short-sighted deliberate disturbance, which even includes the regular illegal removal of chicks. As our representative of the true cranes, it breeds characteristically only in a marsh, and of the two eggs at most only one chick survives. Indicating their marsh origins, crane chicks are not adequately cryptically coloured like most other terrestrial birds. Wattled Cranes relatively seldom flock, but even their biggest concentration on the Kafue Flats in Zambia is threatened by future hydro-electric projects.

The spectacular sibling pair of Grey and Black Crowned Cranes, ours here with a grey neck, and another with a black neck in north-east Africa, which extends in scattered localities to West Africa, have remarkable rounded spiky crests affording instant recognition. They are often regarded as more 'primitive' than other cranes, for apart from their simple windpipes, the two crowned cranes lay unspeckled plain blue eggs, unlike other cranes with their brown-spotted eggs. Although decidedly similar,

*One of two closely related species endemic to Africa, the spectacular Grey Crowned Crane (*Balearica regulorum*) male stands proudly next to his incubating mate.*
(Photo: Warwick Tarboton)

apart from the differently coloured necks, the two cranes have differently coloured cheek patterns, different-sized wattles, and different unison calls. Confirming differences in biochemical electrophoretic analyses indicate species levels have been attained (Ingold, Guttman & Osborne 1987). These two cranes and the Demoiselle Crane are reported to moult their primary and secondary flight-feathers gradually, exceptional for cranes.

The handsome Blue Crane appears on the reverse of our 5c coin, and is endemic to southern Africa. It is supposedly closely related to the Demoiselle Crane and placed in the same genus, but apparently differs dramatically in the mode of its flight-feather moult. Although no longer tied to wetlands and marshes, where other crane species can totally moult their flight-feathers in relative safety every second year, this species largely of our dry plains still remarkably retains the complete simultaneous moult of its remiges every other year. For a terrestrial bird this would appear to be suicidal, but it conceals this handicap so well under the attractive tertial coverts that this mode was only discovered in 1975 by a well-known aviculturalist (Lötter 1975). The flightless moulting Blue Crane simply ensures that it sees approaching danger on the plains in time, and moves well away from it. However, when pressed it takes refuge in water if this is available. The large Blue Crane flocks that once caused damage to grain have been largely eliminated by pesticides and other poisons.

# Finfoots

## Family Heliornithidae

Many South Africans have been puzzled by a strange bird which tends to frequent our quiet stretches of river with well-vegetated banks. Clearly not a duck though duck-sized, it resembles a cormorant, though less uniformly coloured and lacking a hook at the tip of its bill to clamp fish securely. Its neck is considerably shorter and less graceful than that of the darters, although the head is similar, and it also swims low in the water. If surprised, it runs splashing along the water with flapping wings until it has gained sufficient momentum to take off, like a coot or a grebe, and disappear around a

*Male African Finfoot* (Podica senegalensis), *note the flattened tail feathers on the water surface.* (Photo: Johan Boshoff)

convenient bend or deliberately hide in a distant patch of thick cover. The Afrikaans name of 'Watertrapper' or water-trampler is derived from this spectacular escape habit. Otherwise it swims quietly and unobtrusively along the water's edge, delicately removing insects and other prey from aquatic plants and the water surface with its sharply pointed bill. In the Levubu River I watched such a feeding female approach within 1,5 m of a small sleeping crocodile, carefully skirt around it, and then resume normal feeding. Usually shy and suspicious, it can dive soundlessly and reappear some distance away, but is reluctant to do so.

If the first-time observer then succeeds in obtaining a close view, puzzlement is likely to increase rather than decrease. The spread tail of 18 feathers lies flat on the water, unique in South African birds. Should the bird preen while standing on a rock or log, its legs and feet are seen to be a spectacular scarlet in colour, uniquely augmented by brilliant yellow claws. No satisfactory explanation has yet been provided for these bright colours, but it will probably involve breeding display. Should the observer then have the much rarer privilege of detecting its platform-like stick nest built low in dense overhanging vegetation, what seem to be the rounded camouflaged eggs of a korhaan or bustard, in a bizarre situation where their shape and colour are of little survival benefit, may be seen.

Clearly a remarkable bird and found from the Eastern Cape across to West Africa, our African Finfoot is one of only three species in its discontinuously distributed family. The other two are found in the East Indies (Assam to Malaysia and Sumatra) and South America (southern Mexico to Argentina), also with strange lobed toes like a grebe, phalarope or coot. This is a most unusual family, thought by some experts to be most closely related to the crakes. However, DNA-DNA hybridization studies (Urban *et al*. 1986) show close relationship to Gruidae (cranes) and Otididae (bustards), but not Rallidae (crakes). Our finfoot is the largest of the three species, with the male and female sexually dimorphic and the youngsters resembling the female closely, but browner with a dark bill. She is apparently solely responsible for incubating the eggs.

However, on balance the American Finfoot must be awarded top marks due to an almost unbelievable adaptation which was ignored as a fable for almost 140 years after its discovery by a Jesuit missionary in 1833. A Mexican ornithologist was keeping one of these nests under observation during fieldwork (Alvarez del Toro 1971). Despite the remarkably short incubation period (10,5–11 days in this species), he was disappointed when the two chicks disappeared without trace from the nest. However, the male was acting strangely, so using a boat he flushed the male into flight. When it flew back over him, he could clearly see two little heads protruding under the male's wings. Further investigation revealed that a unique pouch was found under each wing in males only, in which the still helpless chicks were carried and even fed.

Although an epoch-making event like the discovery of the American Finfoot male's unique underwing pouches is unlikely to occur again, there are many aspects of our African Finfoot that still require the attention of birders. For example, Mitchell (1977) has pointed out that our finfoot is not confined to well-shaded stretches of rivers, but is prepared to utilize large impoundments with relatively barren shorelines. Observed as close as 3 m, they were feeding here on mayflies (Order Ephemeroptera), from bare rock a few centimetres above water-level: an important short-lived fish prey. I know our finfoot when undisturbed as a quiet bird, yet various calls are recorded, including a bull-like roaring. Few birders seem to know that our adult finfoots have a sharp 4 mm claw on the first digit of their wings, and that immature claws can be up to 18 mm long! They are apparently used to clamber into trees, which is completely logical but not yet proven. Whately (1982) saw an adult finfoot passively anting on a causeway in Hluhluwe Game Reserve, rarely seen in non-passerines. Prey items still need study, and can be as large as a much-bashed 50 cm *Philothamnus* snake or an adult *Rana* frog.

For years I was puzzled that I saw so few adult male finfoots compared to the number of adult females that I encountered, often with the juveniles that resemble them. The ratio was definitely skewed, and not what one should reasonably expect. If one consults our latest field guides, and even 'Roberts', the male is always figured with a dark bluish-grey foreneck, throat and chin, blackish hindneck and crown, and shows a negligible eye-stripe. This is unlike the female's relatively broad eye-stripe, and white foreneck, throat, chin and lores. Then I realized that our adult male finfoot has a strongly white non-breeding plumage, which surprisingly seems almost unknown to birders. Although distinguishable, this closely resembles the plumage of the adult female. It is figured only in Urban *et al.* (1986). Problem solved.

**Above:** *Female African Finfoot leaving nest, note the scarlet legs and yellow claws.*
**Left:** *Nest of an African Finfoot with egg closely resembling that of a bustard.*
(Photos: Peter Ginn)

# CRAKES, RAILS, GALLINULES, FLUFFTAILS AND COOTS

## FAMILY RALLIDAE

Although related to the cranes, this entire family of about 132 species world-wide is small to medium-sized. Plumage is usually dull and cryptic, with some notable exceptions. They seem to have a good sense of smell, unusual in birds. Although they do not seem to be strong flyers, this family has one of the widest distributions in the world. A characteristic is their ability to establish themselves on the most distant islands. Only the frozen wastes or waterless areas are avoided. It appears that another family characteristic is to fly at night, when the rounded wings and long legs are usually invisible. Even species like our apparently tame coot, which seems reluctant to take off by day, fly considerable distances at night. This explains their sudden appearances and disappearances at small isolated bodies of water, which reflect in moonlight and starlight.

Divided with difficulty into a logical framework, the Rallidae form three basic groups. First are the more typical members of the family, unspecialized and found in marshes where their slim bodies ('as thin as a rail') easily negotiate the dense marsh vegetation. Second are those with long toes to spread their weight, walking on floating vegetation with ease. Others with lobed feet are found on open water, like the coots and moorhens. Relatively few are found in grassland, like the Corn Crake and our African Crake. Forms considered most primitive are found in dense vegetation on forest streams. Some movements seem purposeful, others appear by chance, like the more than 20 records of the American Purple Gallinule in the Western Cape. It is a smaller edition of our well-known African Purple Gallinule, with yellow instead of red legs. Usually found exhausted or dying, it seems unlikely to be able to establish itself in the face of strong competition. Our Common Moorhen has the widest distribution of the Rallidae, almost world-wide.

Commencing with the flufftails, a distinctive genus of nine species, we have five of the seven African species (two in Madagascar). They are strongly sexually dimorphic, unusual in Rallidae. Of *Crex*, we have both species, the African Crake endemic and the Corn Crake a migrant, but with the bulk of its world population apparently wintering in Africa. Of *Rallus*, we have one endemic, the African Rail, of the world's nine species. Of the large genus *Porzana*, still disputed, we have two of the three African species, the Spotted and Baillon's, with the third likely, the Little (as far down as Zambia). Our Striped Crake is very closely related to this genus. Of the six *Amaurornis* crakes, we have the Black Crake, endemic to Africa. Of the five *Porphyrio* gallinules, we have the African Purple Gallinule, Allen's (Lesser) Gallinule, and the vagrant American Purple Gallinule. The flightless Takahe *P. mantelli* is also included here. Of the eight

*African Crake* (Crex egregia), *more a grassland species than water associated.* (Photo: Peter Ginn)

*Black Crake* (Amaurornis flavirostris) *incubating its eggs.* (Photo: Will Nichol)

*Common Moorhen* (Gallinula chloropus), *the most widespread of the rail family.* (Photo: Charles Barrett)

*African Purple Gallinule* (Porphyrio madagascariensis) *standing in shallow water.* (Photo: Louwtjie Viljoen)

*The Buff-spotted Flufftail* (Sarothrura elegans): *the strange booming call, usually given during the nocturnal hours, is so odd that many tribesmen refuse to believe that it is uttered by a bird. Here the male approaches his nest.* (Photo: Peter Ginn)

*Gallinula* species, we have the Common Moorhen as well as the Lesser Moorhen, which is endemic to Africa. One member of this genus has lobed feet, providing a link to *Fulica*, the coots. Finally, of the world's nine species of coots, we have here our Red-knobbed Coot, and in the north the Eurasian Coot, which is both resident and a migrant to North Africa. Large numbers of Red-knobbed Coots have been ringed at Barberspan, with 70% of recoveries within 300 km, but one near Cape Town (1 072 km). Here the large population numbers (over 25 000) are carried on floating sago pondweed (*Potamogeton*). No flightless rallids are found in Africa, probably due to the high predator pressure, but some have flightless moults.

The tendency to colonize distant localities, which are often small islands, has resulted in various rallid species which have become flightless. The problematic combination of flightlessness combined with these small areas has resulted in no fewer than 15 species of the Rallidae becoming extinct during the past century. Because of their secretive habits in dense marsh vegetation, from which they give strange loud calls requiring expert knowledge for identification, conservationists cling to the hope that somewhere populations of apparently extinct species have survived. A good example of this is the Takahe of New Zealand, a large clumsy flightless type of purple gallinule undoubtedly related to our smaller African Purple Gallinule. It was described from bones discovered among moa remains on New Zealand's North Island, not from a feathered specimen. By the end of the nineteenth century the Takahe had been seen only four times, first in 1846 when one was run down and captured by seal hunters, then in 1851, 1879 and 1898. With none then seen for 50 years, it was assumed that these sightings were the very last members of a vanished species. Fortunately in 1948 G.B. Orwell rediscovered the species in the remote Lake District of South Island, and estimated seven pairs. These turned out to be far more, but fewer than 500 birds in a few isolated valleys, where strict conservation will probably be able to save the species.

In South Africa and Ethiopia tiny separate populations of the White-winged Flufftail were known. According to a monograph (Keith *et al*. 1970), these numbered 21 adults and one immature from Ethiopia, and only three females from South Africa. No records were accepted by these experts since 1901 in South Africa. Then incongruously the species was rediscovered in South Africa (Wolff & Milstein 1976): a female was picked up dead under a powerline in the Suikerbosrand Nature Reserve. We published this including a photograph of the mounted specimen with one obvious white wing open, to bring it to the attention of South African birders. Mendelsohn *et al*. (1983) then excitingly found the first live population of a dozen in the Franklin Vlei (KwaZulu-Natal), and further findings followed. I made an innocuous allusion referring to this as an example of birder awareness (Milstein 1999), and to my surprise was scathingly criticized by Coetzee (1999). Fortunately I was able to reply (Milstein 2000a), and further increased birder awareness has resulted in more observations at more localities ever since. As an example, at the BirdLife South Africa wetland centre of Wakkerstroom, the first record of White-winged Flufftail was made by André Botha and Rick Nuttall in February 2000 (Anonymous 2000) followed by André Marx (November 2002), Richard Webb (October 2003), and the Warden, Nigel Anderson, flushing twice on 31 December 2003 with Steven Evans and Lucky Ngwenya (pers. comm.). Various subsequent observations continue to follow. Like Rudd's Lark, our White-winged Flufftails clearly had no links to the Ethiopian population. They were surprisingly overlooked breeding residents after all, and can undoubtedly be conserved here for the future if only sufficient suitable wetland habitat can be conserved, e.g. Zaloumis & Milstein (1975).

## ORDER CHARADRIIFORMES

# SANDGROUSE

## FAMILY PTEROCLIDAE

The sandgrouse family has been long considered intermediate between the doves (Order Columbiformes) and waders, etc. (Order Charadriiformes), e.g. Urban *et al*. (1986). However, in the modern classification followed here, they have now been classified as the first family of the Charadriiformes, with the Gruiformes (cranes, etc.) interspersed between the Columbiformes and the Charadriiformes. Sandgrouse comprise 16 species classified into two genera: 14 into the uniform *Pterocles*, and two into *Syrrhaptes*, found in cold Asiatic deserts. This latter small genus does not concern us except to note that it lacks the hind-toe altogether, that the legs and feet are completely feathered (which is supposed to assist in sand, but is clearly rather a temperature-related

*The Burchell's Sandgrouse* (Pterocles burchelli) *male wetting its highly specialized belly-feathers to transport water to its chicks (see text).* (Photo: John Wesson)

adaptation), and that in at least one species (*S. tibetanus*) the male's water-absorbent belly-feathers are lacking. Of the typical sandgrouse (*Pterocles*), six species are endemic to Africa, and six shared between Saharan Africa and adjacent Asia. There is one endemic sandgrouse in India, with another in Madagascar. In southern Africa we have four sandgrouse species.

In general appearance our sandgrouse resemble doves, despite a reduced hind-toe, and are approximately dove-sized. They resemble nightjars in their cryptic coloration: earthy colours like brown and yellow, but also have black and white markings which aid the general camouflage effect. Unlike most doves they are sexually dimorphic in plumage with breast-bands in most species, particularly the males. Instead of a cere as in doves, the nostrils are covered by bristly feathers. There is a dense undercoat of the down, even covering areas of skin on which no feathers grow. Their crops are large, enabling sandgrouse to drink large quantities of water at speed. However, more importantly it enables them to eat large quantities of the small seeds that they subsist on. Only the seed-snipes (Thinocoridae) of South America and the sandgrouse subsist on large quantities of tiny seeds.

Dependent on the size of the seed, Lloyd (1997) indicates that our Namaqua Sandgrouse will each consume between 5 000 and 80 000 seeds per day, and that their selection is so efficient that a full crop of more than 40 000 seeds may contain as few as 10 seed-size sand-grains. He emphasizes that some seeds are so small that 5 000 seeds may weigh only 1 g. Ephemeral seed-production by mainly legumes after unpredictable rains necessitates a nomadic life for sandgrouse. This and widely spaced watering-points demand adequate powers of flight from sandgrouse, and their long pointed wings undertake the task with ease. For their daily drink to balance the ultra-dry seed, a round trip of 150 km at a cruising speed of 80 kph is covered effortlessly (Lloyd 1997). Sandgrouse drink in large numbers at speed as an anti-predator strategy. In less than 60 minutes, 15 000 Namaqua and Burchell's Sandgrouse have slaked their thirst (Anderson 2000b). Attacking falcons are confused by the milling mass of drinking sandgrouse, resulting in a low rate of successful kills at waterholes (Lloyd 1997). Sandgrouse gulp water down without raising their heads until they need to swallow.

The greatest danger to sandgrouse survival appears to be mongoose predation on eggs and chicks, with survival sometimes less than 10% (Lloyd 1997). It has been postulated that this is a direct result of sheep-farmers over-culling mongoose enemies like large raptors and jackals. The mongooses have possibly either increased numerically or can forage with impunity. Lloyd (1997) emphasizes how sandgrouse parents immediately remove hatched egg-shells to 20–30 m away from the nest-scrape to outwit scent-hunting predators.

**Top:** *Namaqua Sandgrouse* (Pterocles namaqua) *male collecting water as indicated for the Burchell's Sandgrouse male.*
(Photo: Tony Heald)
**Bottom:** *A male Double-banded Sandgrouse* (P. bicinctus) *prepares to settle on his unusually exposed eggs.* (Photo: Darrel Plowes)

Of our sandgrouse, the Namaqua (with elongated central tail-feathers in both sexes) is found on stony and gravel desert, while the Burchell's Sandgrouse selects Kalahari sand. Both are typical desert inhabitants, often drinking in the mornings at the same waterholes. The largest of our sandgrouse is the Yellow-throated, which prefers moister soils than our other sandgrouse, often on alluvial plains near rivers and marshes. While the Namaqua is the earliest morning drinker, the Yellow-throated is the latest. The Double-banded Sandgrouse selects more woody habitat, and with us is consequently found further east than the other species. Although it does occasionally drink in the morning, it definitely prefers to drink later, and often waits until dusk. It is clearly less mobile than our other sandgrouse, flying shorter distances. As utilizable gamebirds, sandgrouse require careful management, and Crowe (2000) was justifiably criticized by Anderson (2000a) for making misleading and incorrect comments on sandgrouse hunting seasons.

Finally, the most remarkable aspect of sandgrouse biology is the now well-established carrying of water in specially evolved male belly-feathers to the totally dependent chicks. Gordon Maclean and Tom Cade in particular were severely criticized by opposing authorities like Richard Meinertzhagen (a noted desert authority) for their accurate description (e.g. Cade & Maclean 1967) of this unique phenomenon. Meinertzhagen (e.g. 1964) stated flatly 'that is not so', and claimed to have seen males giving chicks water bill-to-bill in captivity. The first observation of what became this controversy was by an amateur aviculturalist, who observed his male sandgrouse soak its belly-feathers in water, and then fly to the back of his aviary where the chicks sucked the water from his feathers. It was further proven when incubator-hatched sandgrouse chicks survived only when water-soaked cottonwool was hung up within reach for them to drink from.

Lloyd (1997) has ably summed-up this fascinating adaptation, achieved by modified feathers with thousands of tiny feather filaments which are tightly spiralled around one another. These uncoil when immersed, and by capillary action trap water in the tiny spaces between them. Like blotting paper, they can absorb up to 20 ml of water. The chicks scurry to the arriving male, and commence stripping the water from his belly-feathers, likened by Lloyd (1997) to a litter of puppies. To avoid hot desert sun, the male will turn so that his belly with the precious water is preferably in the shade. This continues daily for two months, until the chicks fly to waterholes. When the chicks have finished drinking from his feathers, the male deliberately dries his belly in the dust by rubbing it. This is to eliminate the strong 'birdy' scent of wet feathers to predators. Sandgrouse are truly remarkable birds, but the high nest mortality appears excessive and cause for concern. Even the lumbering Aardvark will eat discovered sandgrouse eggs.

# WADERS

## FAMILY SCOLOPACIDAE

This family consists of over 80 species, with over 40 recorded in Africa, and 32 species recorded with us in southern Africa. They are small to medium-sized wading birds up to the size of curlews. Easily distinguished from the short-billed plover family (Charadriidae) with their more tropical distribution, wader bills are thin and generally straight or down-curved, at least as long as the head, and sometimes considerably longer. The outstanding characteristic of this family is that they are all long-distance migrants, breeding at high latitudes in the Palaearctic Region, with the sole exception of the African Snipe. Some North American vagrant waders also reach us in small numbers. Waders therefore winter with us in drab non-breeding plumage of mainly grey, brownish and white, but some arrive with traces of much brighter plumage, and a few assume almost full breeding plumage before leaving us to breed in the north.

First the snipes: the Great Snipe, which is a shorter-billed non-breeding migrant that winters entirely in Africa, and our African Snipe, an endemic resident.

**Above:** *The Great Snipe* (Gallinago media) *visits South Africa as a non-breeding migrant, and its occurrence is probably consistently overlooked.*
(Photo: Clem Haagner)

**Left:** *The African Snipe* (G. nigripennis) *is one of the few waders to breed in the southern hemisphere. It is extremely well camouflaged and blends into the background.*
(Photo: Garth Batchelor)

The latter is possibly the only wader to breed away from the Holarctic Region. The true snipes are a reasonably similar group world-wide, with shortish legs. They are characterized by a relatively long bill, which is pushed deep into soft mud to find worms, molluscs and other mud-dwelling animals. Due to their elusive jinking flight when put up, they have been considered gamebirds for centuries, a delicacy. However, apart from their remarkably evasive flight after rising with a sudden sucking noise unexpectedly from their marsh, snipes have another even more remarkable flight. This continues to the end of incubation of their eggs in a grass-tuft nest. Snipes patrol low over their breeding territories by day and by night, with a ghostly 'whu-whu-whu-whu' sound usually described as 'drumming'. One of the great British ornithologists, Lord William Percy, gave a famous demonstration of how this sound was produced. He took the outer tail-feathers of a snipe, inserted them into a bottle-cork, and whirled the cork around his head on a piece of string. The vibration of the snipe's outer tail-feathers clearly produced the 'drumming' sound as long as he whirled the cork and tail-feathers. However, when circling snipe are hardly visible drumming in the dusk or darkness, such a simple explanation of the ghostly phenomenon seems far-fetched to many hearers.

Next come two large Palaearctic waders and one Nearctic vagrant, classified in *Limosa* and named godwits. The Bar-tailed Godwit has recently achieved fame as the fastest migrant between its Palaearctic breeding grounds and its winter quarters in New Zealand, but this is unlikely to be the final chapter in the competitive world of speed. Then come two waders with strongly decurved bills: the Eurasian Curlew, which is our largest wader, and a similar smaller species called Whimbrel in the Palaearctic, but Hudsonian Curlew in the Americas. Next are 25 relatively undistinguished wader species when in their winter plumage, including several Nearctic vagrants which end up here after becoming lost on their normal southward migrations. At least the Terek Sandpiper is distinguished by an upturned bill, and the Sanderling by the fact that it is our only wader with only three toes. The Ruddy Turnstone distinguishes itself by its peculiar stone-rolling behaviour. The smallest waders are hardly larger than a sparrow.

Then comes the most spectacular of all waders, the Ruff. The much smaller female is called 'Reeve', but this is best disregarded as it is merely one of the surviving venery terms, the naming of quarry species which was one of the very few forms of education endured by gentlemen in the Middle Ages. The Ruff develops a spectacular breeding plumage in the Palaearctic, with the males gaily coloured in different combinations of red-brown, black and white, but amazingly with no two males identical. The most spectacular component is a large ruff of erectile feathers around the neck. The males take up dancing positions in a display area called a 'lek', and display assiduously and remarkably to attract the attention of females which wander among them. The impressed

*This rare wader, the Asiatic Dowitcher* (Limnodromus semipalmatus), *which recently caused a stir near Benoni, is not only the first record in southern Africa, but the first for Africa.* (Photo: Clive Kaplan)

**Top:** *The female Ruff* (Philomachus pugnax), *archaically called a reeve, is considerably smaller than the male. Females, as in the Middle Ages, never achieve the spectacular plumage of the jousting males.* (Photo: Geoff McIlleron) **Bottom:** *In non-breeding plumage, a rather unusual male Ruff, which is almost pure white but not albino or leucistic, merely an example of the fascinating colour schemes produced for the Ruff jousting where they strive, as did the knights of old, to win the ladies' hearts!* (Photo: Charles Barrett)

female makes her choice, mates then and there with the chosen male, and goes off by herself to raise a family. The spectacular display grounds remind one of the tournaments of the ancient knights in armour, with the same objective of winning the adulation of the most attractive females.

Last are the three swimming 'waders', two species from the Palaearctic and another vagrant from America. Called phalaropes, they have lobed feet like finfoots, coots and grebes. They swim around in a circular or spiral direction, kicking with a spinning motion to stir up micro-organisms which they feed on. Like our other waders, they are hardly recognizable in their breeding finery, of which we so regrettably see only the remnants or the commencement. Occasionally some waders like the Curlew Sandpiper let us see their beautiful breeding plumage, so strikingly different from their drab non-breeding plumage, before departure.

# PAINTED-SNIPES

## FAMILY ROSTRATULIDAE

There are only two species in this family, closely related to each other and also to the Jacanidae (Tarboton 2001), shown by similar downy chick patterns and only 10 primary flight-feathers present. The sternum has two notches on the posterior border, like the Jacanidae and Gruidae. Basically the two species have more or less the same appearance and habits. However, each is classified in its own monotypic genus, probably an indication of long separation despite the retention of aberrant habits. Our species, now termed the Greater Painted-snipe, has an extensive and continuous

**Above:** *The painted-snipes are another example of sexual reversal; here the Greater male* (Rostratula benghalensis) *is incubating his eggs. The female is considerable more attractive, does the courting and then leaves the male in sole charge.* (Photo: Will Nichol)
**Left:** *The female Greater Painted-snipe is clearly seen to be more beautiful than the male.* (Photo: Tony Heald)

distribution in Africa, Madagascar, the Middle East, Asia to China and Japan, the Philippines and Australia. The Lesser or American Painted-snipe in contrast occurs only in a limited area of southern South America.

The general appearance, with long bill, short legs, short tail and white underparts, superficially resembles that of a true snipe. However, the mode of flight differs clearly. True snipes utter a soft squelching call on taking off, while the painted-snipes rise silently. True snipes fly jinking rapidly with their legs tucked in, while painted-snipes fly strongly but relatively poorly, trailing their legs initially like crakes. After landing, painted-snipes hold their wings momentarily open and bob their tails like a sandpiper. The bill of our painted-snipe has no pitting, unlike a true snipe, while the Lesser Painted-snipe has it at the distal end. Painted-snipe bills are hard and rigid, with a long groove culminating in the nostrils.

The clear white 'spectacles' or eye-rings of our Greater Painted-snipe, which extend backwards in extension stripes, are an excellent diagnostic criterion. Here the Lesser Painted-snipe has only a long supra-orbital stripe above the eye. Our painted-snipe has no web between its toes, but the Lesser has a slight web between the middle and outer toes. The wind-pipe or trachea of our female painted-snipe has four convolutions before reaching the lungs, enabling her to give a deep echoing call compared to the peep of the male with his straight wind-pipe. In both species, the females are also larger and more beautiful than the males.

As in the polyandrous button-quails, all three of these typical characteristics together indicate a reversal of sexual dominance in favour of the Greater Painted-snipe female at least. She does the courting, lays a clutch of usually four eggs for each of several successive males in nests that they have built, and leaves them to raise the family alone. However, in the Lesser Painted-snipe, the similarly larger, more beautiful and noisier female is alleged (Pitman 1964) to incubate the normal clutch of two eggs herself. This is an unlikely contradiction, and it appears far more likely that she also selects and courts the male, and completes the reversed sexual role as is the case with the polyandrous Greater Painted-snipe female. Tree (1989a) points out that here the principal display with spread tail and fanned wings partially turned, and showing the beautiful golden spots, is used both as a mating display and as a threat to other females. He describes specific vocalizations given by the usually silent Greater female at these times, including during territorial defence. The female has an oesophageal crop unique in the entire order, which is used as a resonance chamber.

Both Tree (1989a) and Tarboton (2001) emphasize the strongly nomadic behaviour of the Greater Painted-snipe, which appears to be rarer than it actually is, due to its skulking crepuscular habits and use of vegetative cover. It clearly prefers seasonal or ephemeral wetlands when the water-level is receding but still enables sufficient time for breeding. However, the Greater Painted-snipe is prepared to compromise and utilize less ideal sites rather than not breed at all. Ideally short vegetation of grasses and sedges is selected, where a canopy of live vegetation can be drawn over the nest-pad of plant stems to hide it, but compromises extend to more exposed nests and finally to the exposed plover-type nests described by Tarboton (2001) away from vegetation on islands in the Zambezi. Possibly reflecting to a degree the reversed polyandrous sexual roles, nests tend to be clumped, and Tarboton (2001) records up to 20 nests in the vicinity of each other under ideal conditions. With low breeding density, Tree (1989a) has interestingly recorded occasional reversion to a monogamous mating system, where the female remains with the family.

# Jacanas

## Family Jacanidae

This is a remarkable family found in the world's tropical and subtropical regions, consisting of eight relatively small species. In Africa we have two endemic species, with another closely related in Madagascar, two in Asia, one in Australia, and one each in Central and South America. The most remarkable feature is the foot, with excessively elongated toes and long straight claws. In particular, the claw of the hind-toe is much longer than the toe itself, and tapers to a fine point. Tails are short with the exception of the aberrant Pheasant-tailed Jacana of Asia, the largest species, with a long flowing tail, the only seasonal breeding plumage encountered, and unscrolled eggs. Most species have a bright frontal shield (red, yellow or blue), rudimentary in the juveniles. Bills are moderately long and straight, decurved slightly at the tip. For combat the carpal joint carries a blunt knob or small spur, up to 23 mm long. Sexes are alike, but the female is usually larger.

The name 'jacana' originates with the Hopi Indians of the Amazon Basin, but the original Spanish-Portuguese pronunciation of 'jaçaná' has been widely anglicized.

Our Lesser Jacana (front cover photo) is the world's smallest jacana species, and is considerably rarer than the more familiar and widespread African Jacana. Its stronghold in southern Africa is the Okavango Delta, where Tarboton (2001) indicates it breeds regularly, but more sporadically elsewhere. Tree (1989b) points out how the Lesser Jacana moves in from the north to breed on suitable Kalahari pans in Botswana after good rains. The Lesser Jacana resembles the juvenile African Jacana, but is much smaller, and can be clearly distinguished. The best criteria include the colour of the crown and eye-stripe: warm rufous-brown, compared with the dark brown of the African Jacana. Furthermore, the white superciliary eye-stripe extends far further back in the African Jacana.

Most important is the white trailing-edge of the Lesser's wing with a pale brown crescent from wrist to tertials, while the African Jacana's wings are blackish-brown.

The nest and eggs of the Lesser Jacana are much smaller than those of the African Jacana, but otherwise remarkably similar. However, the greatest difference between the two species is that the Lesser Jacana is monogamous, and shares short sessions of incubation duties with high nest attendance (82%). In contrast the African Jacana has a highly evolved, polyandrous mating system, and only the male incubates, with low nest attendance. It utilizes solar radiation to help hatch the eggs, shading or incubating only when necessary. Tarboton (1996) indicates that this polygamy is the most extreme form of simultaneous polyandry yet recorded in birds. ('Simultaneous' polyandry is where a female is mated to more than one male at the same time, and 'successive' polyandry is where the female mates sequentially with successive males.)

The remarkably long toes serve to distribute the weight of the jacana more widely, so that it is able to walk on relatively flimsy floating vegetation, and feed on the aquatic insects, molluscs and tiny crustaceans found there. The larger and heavier African Jacana female sometimes sinks a little through the floating vegetation, because as Tarboton (1996) shows, her weight is nearly double that of males, but her toe-spread only 5% larger, and so she cannot reach some feeding areas available to males. He also indicates that she spends more time feeding (75%) than do males (69%). With the high nest mortality in this species, Tarboton (1996) considers that the most plausible reason for reversed sexual size dimorphism here is the enablement of larger females to lay more eggs more quickly. However, this may be a chicken-and-egg situation, and as with other reversed sexual dimorphisms the usual advantage of female dominance over the male may be holistically the primary reason. The correlated larger size and increased egg production may be secondary.

Jacana eggs are among the most beautiful of all bird eggs. With our two species they are pointed, rich brown in colour, and heavily overlain

*An African Jacana* (Actophilornis africanus) *and hatching brood. Note the blue frontal shield.*
(Photo: Tony Heald)

with thick scrolled black lines. They are decidedly glossy due to a unique pore structure, which reduces the wetability of the eggs, definitely advantageous with a damp nest. The nests are small platforms of water weeds, continually added to during the incubation period. When water-levels rise, incubated eggs (which float) have been moved from a sinking nest to a safe position nearby, but this appears to be rare.

Dominated males also take up territories, advertise for polyandrous females, but only dare to approach them when the females take up a submissive posture. After copulation, the female lays eggs daily till clutch completion. On a 12-day cycle, the female may repeat the process with another male, but if the previous clutch has been lost at this stage, she may replace it. Tarboton (1996) suspected that if each clutch survived, a female could mate with as many partners as the number of clutches she could lay per season. One large female laid 10 clutches for at least six (probably seven) males, and several others laid clutches for four or five males during the same period. Such males did not remain loyal to individual females, but courted and mated females where they could, moving to new territories if their female was not ready when they were ready for a clutch. One male received clutches from three different females in a season, and several others from two different females. The female polyandry was nearly matched by the male polygyny. Tarboton (1989b) emphasized that females paid a high price for their system, continually pressurized by other females, with fighting that led to injuries and near-drownings. In time even the most dominant and successful females were ousted by newcomers wishing to breed. Nests are seldom less than 50 m apart.

Jacana chicks are decidedly precocial, following the male soon after hatching, and feeding themselves. Tarboton (1989b) emphasizes that the chicks are adept swimmers from hatching, and dive underwater to escape danger. They may cling to an underwater stem, showing only their bills and faces. Hancock (2001) noted that the submerged chick's eyes are unblinking, whether above or below the surface. All jacana species brood their chicks under their wings for warmth, and place their wings under the eggs when incubating on the damp nest-platforms. However, in at least three species, the chicks are actually gathered up and carried away under the male's wings to take them from potential danger, up to 70 m recorded. This continues up to 18 days of age. Males give impressive distraction displays to lure potential predators from the vicinity of their chicks (Urban *et al.* 1986).

A final remarkable adaptation is that in the 'carrier' species the radius bone in the wing is bow-shaped and flattened (Tarboton 1996). Three species are known not to carry their chicks in this unusual way, and do not have the modification. Neither does the Lesser Jacana, though this has been reported to carry its chicks 'sometimes' (Urban *et al.* 1986). However, Hancock (2001) proved conclusively (including colour photographs) that the Lesser Jacana certainly carries its chicks, so the modified radius bone cannot be essential.

# SHEATHBILLS
## FAMILY CHIONIDAE

Sheathbills are two species of strange little pure-white birds which are usually likened to pigeons or bantams, quite incongruous in the Antarctic. Stokes (1968) emphasizes that, when courting or 'barnyarding' around human habitations, they behave astonishingly like the pigeons they resemble. He describes them as strutting and mincing around in circles, bobbing and bowing and cooing as if they were in Trafalgar Square, on the steps of St Paul's, or the Piazza San Marco. They are distinguished as the only bird species without webbed feet to reach the shores of Antarctica, although rudimentary web remnants can be seen between the three front toes. The hind-toe is well developed, and the legs are sturdy. The name is clearly derived from the peculiar sheath, rough and horny in texture, which covers the base of the short stout bill and partially covers the round nostrils. In the Greater Sheathbill, which is increasingly reaching South Africa by ship assistance,

*The Greater Sheathbill* (Chionis albus) *(left), which is found in the Antarctic proper, has a distinct yellow or flesh-fronted shield. Apart from the coloration of the shields and a more northerly distribution on the sub-Antarctic islands, the Lesser Sheathbill* (Chionis minor) *(right) with its black shield is remarkably similar to the Greater. They are the only birds in the Antarctic not to have webbed feet.* (Photos: Allan Batchelor)

the bill is yellow or flesh-coloured. In the more sedentary and slightly smaller Lesser Sheathbill, the bill is entirely black. Juveniles moult from their grey down directly into white adult plumage, and can then only be distinguished by the less-developed sheaths and fleshy wattles, called caruncles, on their faces.

Sheathbill flight is also described as pigeon-like, though the resemblance to pigeons is only superficial, like the sandgrouse (Pteroclidae), and they are also clearly charidriiforms, albeit aberrant. During short flights the legs are often dangled, but over the ocean they fly more strongly with retracted legs. Harrison (1983) indicates that the ranges of the two species are not known to overlap, with the Greater Sheathbill found on the Antarctic Peninsula and Scotia Arc, while the Lesser Sheathbill is apparently confined to the sub-Antarctic islands of the Indian Ocean. The sedentary nature of the Lessers is emphasized by the proposal of four subspecies, which differ mainly in sheath shape and the colour of the facial wattles, legs and feet. Adult Greaters apparently undertake only limited dispersal during the winter, but their juveniles fly north over the Scotia Sea and Atlantic Ocean to the Falklands, Tierra del Fuego and Patagonia, occasionally reaching Uruguay. They readily pitch onto the decks of ships, and with the increased marine traffic during the Falklands War, actually reached Britain by ship assistance. Sheathbills have been seen in flight and on ice floes several hundred kilometres from the nearest land, and are accepted as seabirds.

Inquisitive and fearless of men, sheathbills rely on their running and dodging ability, and are reluctant to fly even when pursued. Between breeding seasons, they tend to live communally in small flocks, often quarrelling among themselves. They use their short carpal wing-spurs in fighting. The secret of their success is their remarkable scavenging ability as opportunistic feeders. Sheathbills let nothing go to waste. Stonehouse (1964a) indicates that they feed on shore animals of the intertidal zone. Here they consume large quantities of *Ulva* and other algae (presumably for the animals which live amongst these), stranded plankton, seal and penguin faeces, carcasses, eggs, unhealthy chicks, spilled food, and induced dropped food from penguins trying to feed their chicks. Any edible human waste at rubbish tips is much utilized in the winter, but one of the peak food sources is when the seals give birth. Placental blood, the placentas themselves, or any waste matter is consumed. Stokes (1968) records how they have even been observed plucking at the umbilical cords of newborn seals before separation from their mothers has occurred.

Their nests are built in crevices and under boulders, often for convenience on a rocky ridge overlooking a penguin colony (Stonehouse 1964a). Although they continue to feed communally and gregariously, sheathbills separate into their own nest sites per pair. Probably they do not trust each other. Nests are well hidden and approached by deliberately indirect routes. Materials used include grass, moss, feathers and any suitable rubbish they can find. Mostly two largish eggs, but occasionally three, are laid. Usually pale brown in ground colour, they are blotched with darker brown, and finely speckled with black or brown. Stokes (1968) states that they are laid at intervals of more than a week, which seems unusual, but that incubation commences with the first egg. Apparently this results in only one chick being fledged per brood.

A final point is that despite their habitual scavenging and often repulsive diet, Stokes also recorded that the Norwegian whalers called the sheathbills 'ptarmigans', and considered both them and their eggs delicious to eat. It is indeed strange to have such birds as the adaptable sheathbills in the Antarctic. Perhaps there is a correlation with Austin (1962) emphasizing that the sheathbills are structurally a connecting link between the waders and the gulls, and also perhaps fairly direct descendants of the ancient common ancestor from which both groups diverged.

# DIKKOPS (THICK-KNEES)
## FAMILY BURHINIDAE

The dikkops are a small family of nine mostly dryland nocturnal waders, in size approximately equivalent to medium-sized or large plovers. They are also known as stone-curlews or stone-plovers from their preference for bare stony habitat; Norfolk plover as a limited geographical name; goggle-eye from their appearance; willaroo as an aboriginal name in Australia; and thick-knee from their swollen tibio-tarsal joints, which is the most commonly used name clearly and the greatest misnomer. The tibio-tarsal joint is a bird's ankle, most definitely not its knee, as anyone who has eaten a roast chicken will know. Consequently the South African name of dikkop, derived from its decidedly large squarish head, is used here without apology as the best of a dismal list. The typical dikkop species are seven in number, classified in the genus *Burhinus*, with two more aberrant species classified in *Esacus*. With the exception of North America and Antarctica, the dikkop family consequently has a world-wide distribution from Central and South America to Australia. Of the four African species, only the Senegal and Water Dikkops are endemic to Africa, as the Spotted (Cape) Dikkop extends into southern Arabia, and the Eurasian Dikkop is widespread. This latter species is also the only true migrant in the family, with a gathering of as many as 300 of this species observed in Europe (Urban *et al*. 1986).

*The Spotted Dikkop* (Burhinus capensis) *is typical of its genus, camouflaged and easily recognized as a nocturnal species by the large eyes*. (Photo: Tony Heald)

The basic plumage of the dikkop family is a tawny or buff colour, cryptically patterned with bars, streaks, speckles and shaft streaks of blackish, dark brown and greyish. The underparts tend to be paler, but the general effect is an excellent cryptic blending with their chosen arid environment. Legs tend to be yellowish, and bills yellowish at the base, becoming blackish towards the tip. The wings of each species have basically a striking black and white pattern, but which varies from species to species. This contrasting pattern is suddenly flashed when wings and tail are opened in threat displays, and clearly has an impressive effect. However, the surprise may also help dikkops to escape from dangerous situations. I have seen a Spotted Dikkop bravely standing its ground to protect its nest from a thirsty herd of cattle. These were on their way to drink, and the dikkop actually succeeded in splitting the herd, which passed on both sides of the impressive outstretched wings. Even elephants have been diverted by this dikkop's spread-wing threat, although presumably a really large herd would overrun it. However, the most striking feature of all the dikkops is their large yellow eyes, normally augmented with white embellishments nearby. These clearly identify the family as nocturnal feeders, preying on various insects and other small animals. The irises can dilate remarkably.

During the day, dikkops lie prone on the ground, sometimes with legs outstretched behind them, or squatting on their tarsi. They are normally well camouflaged, rising to their feet only when forced to do so by a close approach. Dikkops then run off reluctantly, hunched and tending to look at you over their shoulder, for a short distance before pausing, only running further if pressed. Several dikkops may share the same cover during the day if this is in short supply. However, when night falls, it is a different matter altogether. They immediately exert their territorial rights and noisily defend their territories against all-comers, emitting weird calls which many people do not recognize in suburbia as emanating from such a relatively large bird. It is said that one of the Australian dikkop species lies so still that it can be picked up from the ground and replaced without moving. However, this seems more than a little far-fetched, and is probably a charming fable.

**Right:** *Spotted Dikkop threat display near its nest (see text).* (Photo: Cyril Laubscher)
**Below:** *Water Dikkops* (Burhinus vermiculatus) *are easily distinguished from the Spotted Dikkop by a clear horizontal wing-bar.* (Photo: Geoff McIlleron)

The two eggs appear to be laid on the ground without any attempt to make a nest-scrape, but the site is probably chosen at least for visibility of potential danger. Both sexes incubate, with two brood patches positioned laterally rather than centrally. The eggs are considered large for the size of the bird, and are cryptically coloured with a cream or pale brown ground-colour, boldly blotched with dark brown and blackish over underlying grey speckles. Tarboton (2001) indicates that it is possible to distinguish the slightly smaller eggs of the Water Dikkop from those of the Spotted Dikkop on coloration. Erythristic eggs have been recorded in the Senegal Dikkop, described as a beautiful salmon pink, but not apparently in other species of dikkop. They would probably be fairly strongly selected against. The Senegal Dikkop is also recorded as nesting on flat house roofs in Egypt. Water Dikkop eggs have been recorded as laid on dry elephant, hippo or buffalo dung, and a close association between nests of this species and crocodile haul-out places has been alleged. Dikkop chicks are well camouflaged by cryptically patterned down-coats, and lie prone with large eyes closed or showing only tiny slits when endangered.

# Oystercatchers
## Family Haematopodidae

The oystercatchers are a small family of largish three-toed specialized waders, all similar and classified in the same genus. They have practically a world-wide coastal distribution, except for polar regions and oceanic islands, also tropical Africa and southern Asia. Powered by strong neck-muscles, the outstanding characteristic of oystercatchers is a long vertically-flattened bill, which has been likened to a double-edged oysterman's knife. This is used for the same expert purpose, to slip suddenly between the slightly opened half-shells of oysters, mussels and clams, usually when they are feeding by filtering seawater, to sever the strong muscle which holds the two half-shells together. This leaves the shellfish unable to close its shell again, and allows it to be eaten at leisure.

The specialized bill is also used to chisel limpets off rocks, dislodging them by a sharp blow to the edge of the shell, usually the edge away from the head. It is also used for more general purposes, like probing deep into mud for worms, and killing small crabs. Due to this specialized diet, found adequately only in the narrow inter-tidal zone, it has been said that oystercatchers are nowhere abundant. A further indication given by Hockey (1997), is that while plover chicks for example commence feeding themselves on the day they hatch, oystercatcher chicks have to be fed by their parents, one food item at a time, until well after fledging. This is because the chicks at this stage have neither strong enough bills nor the physical strength to tackle shellfish on the shore. Parents bring the shellfish singly to the vicinity of the chicks, and if necessary open them up for them, the jettisoned shells accumulating to form chick middens.

Oystercatchers have only two basic plumage patterns world-wide, which together with their being of approximately the same size, with similar shrill whistled calls, has led to considerable differences of opinion with regard to their classification. Earlier some authorities held that there were only four species with several subspecies of the two plumage types, but today it is accepted that there are at least six or seven species, and up to 11 species may be valid. Both plumage patterns are conspicuous, either melanistic – sooty black with sometimes extremely limited white areas, or pied – with black or dark brown upperparts and white underparts.

*The handsome African Black Oystercatcher* (Haematopus moquini), *one of the rarest oystercatchers in the world.*
(Photo: Nico Myburgh)

*Unlike the African Black Oystercatcher, the pied Eurasian Oystercatcher* (Haematopus ostralegus) *shows considerable white markings.* (Photo: Jarle Vines)

In southern Africa we have two oystercatcher species, one of each type. Our African Black Oystercatcher is sooty black with an orange eye-ring, a red bill with an orange tip, and pinkish to reddish legs. It is an endemic coastal breeding species found from the Hoanib River in Namibia to the Bashee River in Transkei, but not breeding over the total area. Then we have the Palaearctic migratory Eurasian Oystercatcher, pied in colour, with an orange bill and pink legs, no orange eye-ring, and a white throat crescent in juveniles and most non-breeding adults as well. It also has a conspicuous white wing-bar, a white rump and white base to the black-tipped tail. Occurring less frequently on rocky shores, it prefers sandy coasts, coastal lagoons and estuaries. However, when high tides preclude feeding in the inter-tidal zone, both species may roost together. Further north in Africa, some large concentrations of Eurasian Oystercatchers are known, possibly subsisting on *Donax* mussels from the sand. Examples are Morocco with up to 2 500, and Mauritania with a midwinter peak of 10 000–11 000 birds (Urban *et al.* 1986). However, only small numbers of this species reach as far south as the coasts of southern Africa.

In contrast, the African Black Oystercatcher is the world's third rarest oystercatcher, with a total population of only 4 800 birds estimated in the early 1980s (Hockey 1997). Not only is this population dangerously small, but its limited mainland breeding habitat is subject to increasing human pressure. Many nests are destroyed by the proliferation and recklessly thoughtless use of off-road motor vehicles and motorcycles. Heavy exploitation by man takes place in the limited inter-tidal zone for food and for bait, apart from the general tourist disturbance to these mainland breeding areas. Fortunately high breeding concentrations on offshore islands still compensate for the low mainland production of chicks, though even here a thoughtlessly built causeway has enabled island access by dangerous mammalian predators.

Mainland beach espacement of breeding pairs has been indicated by Tarboton (2001) as 100–600 m, but on offshore islands 20 m, or even 6 m. Maximal density on prime islands has been stated by Hockey (1997) to be only 1,5 m between nests. Mainland nests are unlined sand-scrapes, about 210 mm in diameter and 40 mm deep, but Tarboton (2001) indicates that in contrast island nests are typically well lined with shell fragments, apparently to conceal them from predatory Kelp Gulls. With their longevity and permanent pair-bonds, pairs may return annually to breed in the same territory. Favoured nest-sites include rises offering a wide view, among beached kelp, or among stones or low scrubby vegetation which provides some concealment for eggs and parent. Single seasonal clutches of sand-coloured finely speckled eggs are laid: usually 2 (1–3), rarely 4, laid at two-day intervals. Occasional clutches are laid on bare rock, or ledges of rock stacks. Incubation commences intermittently from the first egg, and incubating birds sneak off from the nests, warned by their mates of the approach of potential predators. Fortunately this oystercatcher is prepared to lay up to three replacement clutches (Tarboton 2001). Hockey (1997) ably explains the fascinating and intricate ecosystem by which the small islands around Saldanha Bay support possibly the highest breeding densities of any oystercatcher anywhere in the world. However, high mortalities can be caused by diseases like paralytic shellfish poisoning and avian cholera, great potential dangers.

# Avocets and Stilts
## Family Recurvirostridae

This is a small world-wide family of medium-sized attractive and particularly elegant wading birds. Formerly considered to comprise seven species, there are still differences of opinion concerning their classification. The aberrant Ibisbill *Ibidorhynchus struthersii* of Central Asia was formerly included in this family, despite its downcurved scarlet bill, relatively short legs and slightly lobed toes. As a family they are remarkable for the relative length of their legs, and only the flamingoes are considered to have proportionately longer legs. Most have the characteristic coloration of black and white plumage, some with a suffusion of cinnamon to reddish brown.

Four species in *Recurvirostra* have the characteristic upturned (recurved) bill, and are represented here by the Pied Avocet. One species with a slender straight bill and several subspecies world-wide is classified in *Himantopus*, our Black-winged Stilt; but another slightly aberrant stilt, the Banded Stilt, is found in Australia together with the Australian subspecies *H. h. leucocephalus* of the Black-winged Stilt. Endemic to Australia, it is found near salt lakes in the interior. Classified as *Cladorhynchus leucocephalus*, it has a bright chestnut breast-band with yellow legs, and has long been isolated. Olsen & Feduccia (1980) have proposed that flamingoes are descended from this family and not ciconiiform waders, and regard the Banded Stilt as intermediate between the Recurvirostridae and the Phoenicopteridae, based on a number of unique traits which it shares with flamingoes. The hind-toe is missing or rudimentary in both avocets and stilts, but there are also clear differences with regard to their toes. The avocets swim well, and have webs between their toes, while the stilts have only partial webbing.

Our Pied Avocet is one of four closely related species in the genus, and extends from South Africa to Europe and Asia. The American Avocet occurs from southern Canada southward, and winters in Central America. It has a suffusion of cinnamon colour on the head and neck in the breeding season. The Red-necked Avocet with

*The Pied Avocet* (Recurvirostra avosetta), *our local variety, where it can be seen that the optimal clutch is four eggs, grouped with their points together.* (Photo: Nico Myburgh)

*The Black-winged Stilt* (Himantopus himantopus): *only the flamingoes can boast longer legs in relation to body size.* (Photo: Eliot Lyons)

head and neck reddish-brown is endemic to Australia, although occasionally recorded in New Zealand. The Chilean Avocet, which is darker above than its congeners, is found on saline lagoons in the Andes.

The avocet's recurved bill is often used to sweep up plankton from the water surface (or deeper) with graceful sideways sweeps, a beautiful sight. Avocets also up-end like ducks in deeper water: tail in the air, blue-grey legs waving, and head under water. The plover-like eggs are laid in a bare unlined hollow on sandy soil or indentation in dried mud, but in muddy soil the hollow is properly lined, and lining is regularly added. From one to even 1 000 nests can be found, but Tarboton (2001) emphasizes that, because conspicuous breeding adults leave the nest at the first sign of danger, their nests can be easily overlooked.

Stilts with their long red legs are less tolerant of bare nest-sites than avocets, and prefer marshy vegetation in shallow water. Tarboton (2001) points out that they habitually raise their nests with additional material should water levels rise, but that conversely nests can be left high and dry with receding waters. Stilts are also more conspicuous than avocets when breeding, as they call a great deal, and fly to mob intruders approaching the nests. Although rarely hundreds of nests can be found together in ideal conditions, stilts are less inclined to the large concentrations sometimes found with avocets. They are conversely more inclined than avocets to pick up tiny prey items from the water and mud. Both stilts and avocets apparently prefer to nest in small colonies of fewer than 10 pairs (Tarboton 2001).

It is interesting that, unlike the preceding family of oystercatchers with their greater parental care, clutches of four eggs are the normal size here, and not exceptional in both avocets and stilts. The pointed cryptically coloured eggs fit together optimally in the nest, and the precocial chicks readily feed themselves. Stilts breed in a greater variety of wetlands than do avocets, but sporadic breeding seldom occurs regularly at the same individual sites. Stilts obviously take greater care to site their nests in shallow water with emergent vegetation than do avocets. They have also been recorded as nesting in every month of the year, whereas avocets are more inclined to a spring peak (August–November). Tarboton (2001) indicates that the stilt breeding peak occurs later in Namibia than elsewhere: February–April rather than mainly August–November.

When suspicious or excited, avocets bob their heads up and down without moving their bodies. Should they capture a fish, they walk to the shore, repeatedly beat it on the ground for several minutes, swallow it, and return for another. Finally, the close relationship between the genera *Himantopus* and *Recurvirostra* has been confirmed by behavioural studies and study of a captive hybrid between the American Avocet and a Black-winged Stilt.

# PLOVERS

## FAMILY CHARADRIIDAE

The plovers are a large well-known family of about 63 species, world-wide in their distribution except for frozen areas and dense vegetation. In many ways they resemble the waders (Scolopacidae), except for a reluctance to wade, preferring to run in as the waves recede, feeding on stranded organisms. However, they are easily distinguishable by their relatively short bills, sometimes described as pigeon-like, which are never longer than their heads, and are slightly swollen near the tip, although there are no nerve-endings there. This confirms that plovers do not 'feel' for prey, but rely on locating it visually. Their heads are proportionately large and rounded, with large eyes, and joined by a short thick neck to a plump or 'chunky' body. Their tarsi are fairly long with reticulated scales, although a few have transverse scutellae. Plovers in general have only three toes, although there are a few vestigial indications. Our Grey Plover, known in America as Black-bellied Plover despite less of a black belly than the golden plovers, has a rudimentary hind-toe still present. Plumage colours are basically brown, black, white and olive-grey, but often attractively patterned in striking combinations. Yet

**Above:** *The Long-toed Plover* (Vanellus crassirostris) *shows clear adaptation to the marshy meadows it favours. The toes and claws have grown out long, enabling the plover to spread its weight over a larger area, as the jacanas do, and reach feeding areas and food where a short-toed equivalent cannot.* (Photo: Clem Haagner)

**Right:** *The White-crowned Plover* (V. albiceps) *has a strident call, and there are crocodile hunters that swear that this call warns crocodiles to take to the water. One of the 'spurred' plovers, the White-crowned has a spur on each wing which it uses in fighting.* (Photo: Clem Haagner)

they provide concealment by what are called disruptive effects – like zebras, with their alternate black and white stripes, which should in theory be totally obvious, but most certainly are not, particularly in shade.

Causing increasing controversy, there is now a most regrettable taxonomic tendency to force plover classification willy-nilly into one of two subfamilies: the Charadriinae or smaller 'ringed' plovers, and the slightly larger Vanellinae, or so-called 'lapwings'. Regrettably this does not fit all the facts. In his classic review of the plovers, Bock (1958) corrected much of the over-splitting, for example recognizing 24 species of lapwings in a single genus, *Vanellus*, where Peters had classified 26 species of plovers into 19 genera. However, Bock (1958) realistically saw no benefit in a subfamily Vanellinae, and classified 26 species into five genera. Apart from the major disruption caused to long-standing vernacular names in Africa and elsewhere, this is not merely an abstruse academic issue to us, as in Africa we have most of the 'lapwings' (though always known as plovers and none with proper 'lapwings'), and Africa appears to be the centre of their distribution with over 20 species present. Already *Hoploxypterus* merits reclassification on differing jaw musculature, and classificatory doubts are reasonably expressed on distinct species like the Long-toed Plover with no close relatives and major adaptations like its exceptionally long toes, so that the monotypic genus *Hemiparra* is likely to be generally recognized again. The only South African record of this plover is by well-known ranger Gus Adendorff, who clearly observed a Long-toed Plover floating down the Pafuri River on flood debris.

With a variety of divergent characteristics, like differing facial wattles, carpo-metacarpus knobs or spurs, bare skin around eyes, crests, etc. present, the debatable Vanellinae as a 'hold-all' is unlikely to stand the test of time and careful studies. Consequently, for the present it seems preferable to retain 'plover' rather than force introduction of the suddenly fashionable 'lapwing', a somewhat frivolous name of irrelevant origin. The proper Lapwing, *Vanellus vanellus*, is much more famous for its highly regarded 'plover eggs' than for its unusual irregular wing-beat, absent in every one of our plovers. These eggs are still collected for gourmets on a large scale in Belgium and the Netherlands, with a cut-off collection date after which replacement clutches will not be laid. However, this exploitation is minor compared with the 'countless thousands' previously collected from this plover in Europe.

Plovers share incubation and chick-raising duties between the sexes, although chicks feed themselves from the day of hatching. Migratory plovers nearly outnumber our breeding species, which are all endemic to the Afrotropical Region (Tarboton 2001). Several plover migrants are strongly nomadic, seeking out areas of short or burnt grass in their winter quarters. More conventional migrants include three *Pluvialis* species, of which the two species of golden plover (*P. dominica* and *P. fulva*) were only relatively recently realized to be full species, and the closely related Grey Plover is much commoner with us. The Little Ringed Plover has only recently been photographed in Zimbabwe, to join the Common Ringed Plover, Kentish Plover, Lesser Sand (Mongolian) Plover, Greater Sand Plover and Caspian Plover as Palaearctic migrants here. The vagrant Spur-winged Plover has probably recently expanded its range to us. The Crowned Plover, Blacksmith Plover and Wattled Plover are common well-known breeding plovers here, adept at distraction displays and mobbing, with the noisy White-crowned Plover much rarer, usually along Lowveld rivers. Similar in appearance, Black-winged and Lesser Black-winged Plovers are also less common breeders, selecting heavily grazed or burnt habitat.

Although the little Three-banded and Chestnut-banded Plovers do not cover up their eggs to outwit predators, the Kittlitz's Plover fascinatingly does this habitually and completely when disturbed, causing the dust to fly as it does a little rotating 'war-dance', and uncovering the eggs on its return. With regular incubation relief between parents, often with water-immersed bellies in hot weather to cool eggs, in general no protective covering of the eggs takes place. Carl Vernon showed me a Kittlitz nest at Barberspan where the tiny covering pebbles had clearly been carried

*The Kittlitz's Plover* (Charadrius pecuarius) *busy doing a little war-dance, either to kick the sand covering off her eggs or to cover them completely when danger approaches.* (Photo: Cyril Laubscher)

*A sequence of photographs showing the progressive covering of the Kittlitz's Plover eggs from exposed to covered and vice versa. The stratagem even requires fetching tiny sticks, stones, seeds, etc. from several metres away if there are insufficient debris at the chosen nest-site, simply to have a sufficient stockpile to conceal her treasures in emergencies. Just a few seconds are required, the dust flies in her war-dance, and to the casual observer the eggs have vanished.* (Photos: Peter Milstein)

*Our Crowned Plover* (Vanellus coronatus) *(top), Wattled Plover* (V. senegallus) *(left) and Blacksmith Plover* (V. armatus) *(right) are common breeding plovers well known to many South Africans.* (Photos: Eliot Lyons)

**Above:** *The Lesser Black-winged Plover* (Vanellus lugubris) *which prefers to nest on recently burned veld or heavily overgrazed veld.*
(Photo: Martin Goetz)
**Left:** *The Little Ringed Plover* (Charadrius dubius*), here recently photographed in southern Africa for the first time.*
(Photo: Graeme Stewart)

from considerable distances to accumulate around the nest. Finally, the White-fronted Plover may also be developing egg-covering by sand, but this appears to be still haphazard, and the kicked-in sand is apparently not regularly removed as by the little Kittlitz champions of concealment.

In contrast, I well remember a Crowned Plover nest with eggs in a hollow precisely on a whitewashed rugby field touch-line, an incomprehensible siting decision totally negating the cryptic coloration of the eggs, which nonetheless survived. Van Reenen (2004) narrates another two remarkable Crowned Plover cases. One was a nest with three eggs in the middle of the main rugby field at a Welkom school, laid during the holidays. His father solved this problem by appointing a scholar 'guardian', whose duty it was to remove the plover eggs to a cottonwool-lined box before every match and practice, and replace them afterwards, all hatching successfully. The other was an exceptionally brave plover in a White River school parking ground, which adamantly refused to leave its eggs for a photograph, even when his son placed his finger into its open bill. These trusting plovers were decidedly fortunate, as another example shows. I once found Spotted Eagle-Owl chicks sitting in a willow nest-cavity on 40 red Crowned Plover legs, obviously from adults taken at night roosting on short grass.

# CRAB PLOVER
## FAMILY DROMADIDAE

The Crab Plover is indeed a remarkable bird, and Tree (1989c) has stated: 'It looks, and often acts, like a cross between a plover, a dikkop and an egret'. The only member of its monotypical family, it has a number of strange characteristics for a wader. However, these add up to much more than merely an aberrant wader, and the Crab Plover has no close relative, although the dikkops (Burhinidae) were proposed. Austin (1962) has pointed out that its internal anatomy is plover-like, and that its long legs with partly webbed front-toes resemble those of avocets. The grey unpatterned natal down has caused an affinity to the gulls (Laridae) to be suggested, and its burrow-nesting to the auks (Alcidae), according to Urban *et al.* (1986). However, Hockey & Aspinall (1996) indicate that from DNA genetic evidence, its closest relatives are probably the pratincoles and coursers of the Glareolidae. They point out that its lineage probably diverged from them

**Above:** *Part of a flock of Crab Plovers* (Dromas ardeola) *in flight along the shore.*
**Left:** *A small group of Crab Plovers resting on the shore.*
(Photos: Alan Weaving)

in the Oligocene, and its unique attributes may have developed over the past 35 million years.

Occurring on desert Indian Ocean coasts, but occasionally wandering as far as the Cape in the west (including Madagascar) to Malaysia in the east, it is a medium-sized mainly white wader with black markings, and long grey legs with a sturdy hind-toe. The powerful black bill, resembling that of a tern in shape, is one of the major clues to what makes it different. This strong bill, usually likened to a dagger, is used to dismember the large crabs which form its staple diet. Other crustaceans are also included, as are molluscs, for shellfish shells are 'easily pounded to pieces with the heavy bills'. Crab Plovers are decidedly sociable, and a single flock of 3 000 birds has been recorded (Tree 1989c). Hockey & Aspinall (1996) have given an excellent preliminary account of its distribution, but emphasize that other breeding colonies remain to be discovered in the little-known arid islands of the sparsely populated coasts that they frequent. They indicate clearly and reasonably that the 1994 world census of 43 000 undertaken by the International Waterfowl and Wetlands Research Bureau is an underestimation, with major breeding areas yet to be discovered, and the Bajun Islands off Somalia strongly suspected as major breeding sites. Thus far all breeding colonies have been sited on islands. Waders do not normally nest colonially, and the only other ones to do so are pratincoles, avocets and stilts.

Crab Plovers are essentially a coastal species, and are not found inland. Perching on hippo backs in seawater has been recorded, but appears unusual. They are found on coral reefs, sandy beaches and coastal mud-flats, and seem to favour estuaries and tidal lagoons. Often associated with mangroves, here they specialize in crabs as indicated, but feed on other prey in the inter-tidal zone as well. On reaching a tidal pool and sighting a prey item, Crab Plovers stretch their necks forward slowly, and then strike suddenly (Tree 1989c). Usually they run after receding waves to seize crabs and other stranded prey organisms. They fly well and utilize regular roost sites, with birds congregating from up to about 20 km away. Tree (1989c) details how Crab Plovers vary their take-off according to wind conditions: 'When there is little wind, it runs, crouched, before becoming air-borne, rather in the manner of a dikkop but with more even wing beats. In windy weather it is more inclined to spring straight into the air when flying off.'

Post-breeding movements of the adults accompanied by their chicks involves the majority moving south, about 20% remaining in the breeding areas, and about 10% moving south-east (Hockey & Aspinall 1996). Prolonged parental care continues on the wintering grounds, and such feeding of soliciting chicks has been misconstrued as southerly breeding. In the southern parts of the species range, there is no doubt that Crab Plovers are non-breeders which return to their breeding colonies in the north. They are not shy, and are noisy birds. Austin (1962) describes them uttering their 'loud, chattering, hoarse, crow-like calls both when flying and when running about on the shore'. Unless alerted, when the whole flock stretch up their necks, the Crab Plover has a stance resembling that of a dikkop, with the head and neck pulled down onto the shoulders.

Apart from the colonial breeding, other really remarkable breeding aspects occur with Crab Plovers. The first is their being the only waders to nest in burrows. The burrows are excavated in sand banks using their powerful bills, either horizontally into vertical walls or downward into flattened sand-dunes, precisely as carmine bee-eaters nest. However, remarkably the burrows incline downwards soon after the entrance, then rise up again to an unlined terminal chamber. In such an arid habitat, this peculiarity presumably cannot be intended as a necessary rainfall protection device unless dating back to some long-forgotten pluvial period in the history of the species. Burrows are indicated by Urban *et al*. (1986) as 120–188 cm in length, but some exceeding 2 m are also recorded. Situated in raised dune areas near the sea, the entire area of nest colonies may be honeycombed with burrows. There appears to be only one acceptable reason for the development of burrows: the advantage gained with considerably decreased approximately constant temperatures in extreme habitat where noon surface temperatures are well over 40°C, nearly 50°C, and drop to 30°C at night. Crab Plover eggs are laid well into May, with the first fledglings emerging towards the end of July/beginning of August (Hockey & Aspinall 1996). Young Crab Plovers only seem to emerge from the burrows when well grown, in the early mornings and late afternoons. Austin (1962) states that they are able to run soon after hatching, so this incarceration is presumably beneficial.

Another remarkable aspect is that the Crab Plover is the only wader in the world to lay pure white eggs. Presumably the 'advantage' of cryptically coloured eggs has never been an issue in the dark burrows. Furthermore, the proportionately large egg is always single, which in itself raises several interesting questions. Arguments of low predator risk, possible food shortages, difficulty in supplying the chick with single food items, a round trip of 12 km or more to feed the chick, etc., are unconvincing. The large egg gives the chick a good start in life, and enables it to fledge early, adequate advantage which does not need to be queried. Human predation of eggs and chicks has occurred at some nest colonies, but conversely conservation efforts have also been instituted (Hockey & Aspinall 1996). Although potentially endangered, and at high theoretical risk, it does not appear that the Crab Plover is actually endangered. More data should, however, be obtained.

# Coursers and Pratincoles
## Family Glareolidae

This is a small interesting Old World family, clearly divided into two subfamilies, the coursers (Cursorinae) and pratincoles (Glareolinae) with two extralimital aberrant species. The coursers are three-toed ground-feeders, proportionately longer-legged than the plovers, and usually in dry habitats. The water-associated pratincoles are long-winged aerial-feeders with four-toed shortish legs, but can run fast. The first aberrant species is the misnamed Egyptian 'Plover' *Pluvianus aegypticus*, which is probably a courser, but may be nearer to the pratincoles. It lacks the transverse leg scutellation found in all other members of the family, and also lacks the comb on the middle toe. The second aberrant species is the Australian Pratincole *Stiltia isabella*, long-legged and also lacking the middle-toe comb, but clearly long-winged as well. Urban *et al*. (1986) are unrealistic in placing all our other African coursers into *Cursorius*. Certainly this is valid for Burchell's Courser, clearly closely related to the Cream-coloured Courser which extends from North Africa into the Middle East and Asia, and for Temminck's Courser. The latter is believed to mark veld-fires by the smoke, arrive within hours, and commence breeding forthwith (Tree 1989c).

However, our larger coursers show clear divergences, with aspects like neonatal down patterns (Maclean 1970, Kemp & Maclean 1973a), and the placing of the distinct Double-banded Courser into *Smutsornis*, as done by Maclean (1993) and Tarboton (2001), makes much better sense, with the nocturnal Three-banded and Bronze-winged Coursers placed tentatively in *Rhinoptilus*, though probably not congeneric. Our handsomest, the unusual Three-banded Courser, prefers acacia- and mopani-covered alluvial soil along Lowveld rivers for nesting (Tree 1989c). They sit tight, but most remarkably allow their eggs to become embedded in soil particles, only one-third exposed, and apparently not able to be turned. If the eggs are artificially loosened, the parent uses its bill to side-throw soil particles to refill the nest cavity around them, not kicking soil in (Kemp & Maclean 1973b). Our Bronze-winged Courser is the least known, described by Tree (1989c) as 'mysterious' for good reason.

**1:** *Burchell's Courser* (Cursorius rufus) *has a blue patch at the back of its head.* (Photo: John Wesson)
**2:** *Temminck's Courser* (C. temminckii) *has a plain red crown.* (Photo: Terry Carew)
**3:** *The Bronze-winged Courser* (Rhinoptilus chalcopterus) *is most attractive with metallic spots on the feathers. It has sporadic movements in the Lowveld, which we do not yet understand.* (Photo: Nigel Helm)
**4:** *The Three-banded Courser* (R. cinctus) *is one of the rarest coursers.* (Photo: Peter Steyn)

A number of the valuable findings of Maclean (1967) on the Double-banded Courser are applicable to other coursers. Examples are substrate colour-matching and good visibility being essential features of the unmodified nest-site, selection of disruptive factors like mammal droppings (60%) and small greyish-white calcrete stones, incubating with back held to the sun all day, and recognition of eggs by shape alone. He noted that the egg may be left unattended between 20° and 30°C, but are constantly attended with higher or lower temperatures. Between 30° and 36°C, the egg is frequently shaded and not incubated. Above 36°C, the egg is always incubated, possibly to shade it from the effects of radiation. In two cases where the parent was kept from the nest for over 15 minutes, the sun killed the embryos. When one courser is engaged on its two-hour incubation shift, its mate usually stands nearby in the shade of a shrub.

With approaching terrestrial predators, incubating coursers leave the nest early, but with aerial predators like a chanting goshawk, the mate gives a high-intensity contact call, and the incubating bird flattens itself on the nest. Small non-predators like larks are only chased when nearer than 0,6 m, but large non-predators like antelope are subjected to the full threat-display of the courser rushing head-down at the intruder, with wings and tail fully spread like a dikkop. Chicks take up to three days to hatch, probably due to the thickish shell and relative weakness of the chick, which leaves the nest within 24 hours, but stays a few metres away for 3–4 days. From the first day after hatching, white crystalline salt deposits from salt glands can be seen around the chick's nostrils. Successive Double-banded Courser broods are started while the previous brood is still in attendance, again always a single egg, unlike other coursers, and they appear physically incapable of incubating two eggs (Maclean 1967).

The long pointed wings of the pratincoles enable a flight described as swallow-like despite their greater size. Utilizing their wide gapes expertly, they usually capture insects and termite alates on the wing, but are prepared to take prey off the ground, such as locust hoppers before they fly. Apart from the problematic Australian Pratincole, there is a small pratincole in India, and another, the pale-

*The Red-winged Pratincole* (Glareola pratincola) *(top) is almost identical to the Black-winged Pratincole* (G. nordmanni) *(bottom) but has reddish axillary feathers (the 'arm-pits') to the latter's black axillaries. The two bibs and 'collars' are identical and it is plain silly to call one species 'collared' for it does not distinguish between them.* (Photos: Peter Ginn (top); Warwick Tarboton (bottom))

coloured Grey Pratincole of West Africa, beyond our limits. The remaining four species are dominated by the large numbers of Red-winged (Collared) Pratincole, a migrant which also breeds sporadically with us, and of the Black-winged Pratincole, which only reaches us as a migrant. Both these Eurasian sibling species have creamy throats bounded by identical thin black collars.

Tree (1989d) has emphasized that the differing underwing coverts are not always well differentiated in flight, with the underparts more useful. The Black-winged has a yellow-buff breast which merges abruptly into the white of the belly, whereas the buff breast of the Red-winged merges gradually into the belly colour. Both typically have the long forked tails of pratincoles, but the Black-winged's is shorter and less deeply forked. The Red-winged has white tips to the secondaries, forming a terminal bar. Huge numbers of Black-wingeds pass through western Zambia to spend the non-breeding season spread over the vast area of the Kalahari, a reduced range compared to the past, and possibly correlated with former widespread locust control. Thousands of Red-wingeds may follow migrating swarms of locusts or feed on insects disturbed by game or domestic herds, and a flow of 30 000 was observed between 3 and 5 April moving north through Juba in the southern Sudan (Urban *et al*. 1986). Red-wingeds breed as far south as KwaZulu-Natal on a sporadic basis, and chicks are capable of flying before attaining full size, following their parents for considerable distances from the breeding colonies.

Of the two remaining pratincoles, the smaller Rock Pratincole has declined considerably in southern Africa according to Tree (1989e), who points out a severe decline in the rock islands utilized by these specialist breeders to actually lay their eggs on bare rock, or sometimes in small potholes filled with gravel or sand (Tarboton 2001). Tree (1989e) ascribes this decline to dam-building, with such islands submerged, and also poor agricultural practices, with rivers silting up, raising water levels and slowing surface flow, so that other rocky islands are also submerged. He estimates that our southern populations now total fewer than 1 800 of these specialist nesters.

Finally there is the Madagascar Pratincole, which breeds there but migrates to the east coast of Africa, at least as far down as near the Zambezi (Van Perlo 1999). It was placed on our bird list by McLachlan & Liversidge (1957) on a Kirk specimen from the lower Zambezi, which Benson suggested came from Anjouan Island (McLachlan & Liversidge 1978). The South African Ornithological Society List Committee (1969) however rejected the species, amazingly because 'there have been no subsequent records'. Madagascar Pratincoles are especially abundant in coastal Kenya, e.g. Sabaki 'where up to 800 regularly rest, sometimes as many as 9 000 or more' (Urban *et al*. 1986). Hundreds are sometimes seen on Lake Victoria. Surely our birders should rather be encouraged to look out for this pratincole? Numerous vagrant seabird species have been added to our list with careful observations. Relatively plain-coloured, its folded wing-tips extend 50 mm past the clearly shorter tail, and under-wing coverts are a pale chestnut with a more rufous belly. A white eye-stripe extends from under the eye backwards toward the nape, prominent against darkish lores. The Madagascar Pratincole is present on the African coast from March to September.

*The Rock Pratincole* (Glareola nuchalis) *is endangered by soil erosion silting up their rock nest-islands or dams submerging them.* (Photo: Peter Ginn)

# Skuas, Skimmers, Gulls and Terns
## Family Laridae

Following the new Roberts VII systematic order in the case of this over-enlarged family is done with considerable reservations. Whether the terns are treated as a subfamily of the Laridae or a family of their own (Sternidae) is not too critical. Regrettably, the inclusion of the skuas and skimmers here, and not in their own families (Stercorariidae and Rynchopidae), is another matter. I would far prefer to follow various authorities like the *The birds of Africa* (Urban *et al*. 1986) and *Seabirds: an identification guide* (Harrison 1983), and retain them in their own families as more realistic.

The skuas comprise probably seven species of largish piratical seabirds, mostly brown in colour, with strongly

**Top:** *African Skimmers* (Rynchops flavirostris) *only resemble terns superficially. The amazingly shaped skimmer bill is clearly shown here. Found only in Africa, apart from two non-overlapping sibling species found in the Americas and Asia respectively. Skimmers have been shown not to be as closely related to gulls and terns as previously thought.*
**Bottom:** *A skimmer in flight shows the characteristic high wing action to avoid colliding with water when fishing.*
(Photos: Tony Heald)

hooked bills, unlike gulls. They obtain most of their food by agile bullying of other seabirds into disgorging their food (kleptoparasitism). Also, unlike gulls, their bill structure is divided into four separate plates, one a raptor-like cere across the base of the upper mandible. The four largest and most thickset skuas are classified in the genus *Catharacta*, but of these, two species do not reach us. The South Polar (with light to dark morphs or colour phases) and Antarctic Skuas breed in the Antarctic and on sub-Antarctic islands. Then there are three smaller, faster skuas, classified in *Stercorarius*: the Pomarine, Arctic and Long-tailed Skuas, also called jaegers. They have longer tails, and up to three distinguishable morphs each. All three species breed in the Arctic regions, but winter further south at sea, including our waters. To generalize, they fly like falcons, and the *Catharacta* skuas like eagles. Ryan & Sinclair (2001) indicate the complexities of skua taxonomy, including new genetic evidence that the Pomarine Skua may have originated as a hybrid between a *Catharacta* skua and a *Stercorarius* skua.

The skimmers comprise only three specialized and non-overlapping species, with a wide distribution in the Americas, Africa and Asia. They are clearly not as closely related to gulls and terns (Sears *et al*. 1976) as once thought. Their knife-edged mandible is unique in birds by fitting into a matching groove in the maxilla above. Even more remarkable, the mandible grows longer at a late stage in chick development, so that it extends clearly and incongruously past the maxilla tip. This results in the lower bill being obviously longer than the upper, enabling the unique skimmer feeding method. Skimmers will rarely stand in shallow water and sift for food with their bills. However, their classical feeding method is to skim flying low over preferably calm water, with their long mandible extended into it: ploughing through the surface water. The main prey is small fish up to 8 cm long, and other aquatic organisms such as shrimps.

Encountering any such prey in the highly productive uppermost layer of water causes the bill to snap shut on the prey item. The organism is then swallowed without even a wing-beat being missed. To withstand the undoubted shock of such encounters, extra skull and vertebra attachments with linked strong muscles suffice. The long wings have a deliberately high flight action, so that the wing-tips remain above the water surface and do not collide with it. Particularly in seawater, where the plough-strip becomes phosphoretic, and especially attracts plankton, the skimmer deliberately comes back exactly along the same glowing strip to capture small fish attracted to the plankton concentration. This has been described as the most remarkable bait in the animal kingdom. At dusk and dawn the surface plankton are at their most prolific, so the skimmer's hunting peaks are timed to coincide with these. Another remarkable unique skimmer characteristic found in no other bird is an adaptation to the dazzling white sandbanks on which skimmers usually nest. This is a vertical slit-pupil like that of a cat, enabling efficient glare control with more rapid opening when required.

The gulls are a familiar group of about 40–45 species world-wide, often erroneously referred to as 'seagulls', since they are primarily coastal scavengers or also inland species. They are not pelagic apart from exceptions like the Black-legged Kittiwake, usually classified in the small genus *Rissa*. Gulls originated in the northern hemisphere, and are much less common in the southern hemisphere. We have 10 species in southern Africa. Harrison (1983) wisely stated that 'field identification of gulls represents one of the greatest challenges to be found in any sphere of birding'. This is because of the criteria involved, with doubtful species possibly better classified as subspecies, resulting in regular 'hybridization', and often an inability even by experts to distinguish young gulls to species level. However, no other group of birds has a monument erected in its honour, as at Salt Lake City, where the grateful Mormons expressed their appreciation of the gulls which saved their first crop from insect pests. With rare exceptions like Sabine's Gull, also probably meriting classification in *Xema*, gulls lack forked tails.

Gull classification is far from finalized, with our 'old' Southern Black-backed Gull again separated as a full species from the Kelp Gull, although now named Cape Gull. However, I specifically studied Lesser Black-backed Gulls in Europe as far north as Scandinavia in the hope of seeing one at Barberspan, but like Capt. Shewell only recorded Cape Gulls. It is therefore most irritating when flashes of misguided hindsight by observers never present blithely reclassify these carefully observed inland records erroneously as Lesser Black-backed Gulls. The origin of the word 'gullible' is obscure, but one wonders. Gulls are loath to dive underwater, although terns do. To me, the most interesting aspect of dealing with gulls is being simply able to reach out from a boat and lift swimming Grey-headed Gull chicks off the water surface for ringing purposes, in direct contrast to many other waterbird chicks I know. Even though escaping from an island, they remarkably make no attempt whatever to dive.

Terns are an extremely attractive and uniform group, about 42–43 species in number world-wide. All have

**Top:** *The Damara Tern* (Sterna balaenarum) *is a most attractive tern, endemic to the Namib Coast.* (Photo: Fanie Hendriks)
**Bottom:** *The Caspian Tern* (S. caspia), *the world's largest tern, breeds on a small scale in South Africa.* (Photo: Geoff McIlleron)

forked tails, though only slightly forked in the largest tern, our Caspian Tern. Most aberrant is the Gull-billed Tern, also here. This also looks rather tern-like, but has longer legs, a more gull-like bill, and a very different voice to *Sterna* terns. On balance, it should be classified in its own monotypic genus, *Geochelidon*. The Large-billed Tern should similarly be classified in *Phaetusa*. There are 31 typical terns which should be classified together in *Sterna* (with 15 species here), three lake terns in *Chlidonias* (all present with us), the Inca Tern with its facial plumes in *Larosterna*, the Grey Noddy in *Procelsterna*, two or three dark noddies in *Anous*, of which the Brown Noddy and Lesser Noddy reach us, and the only pure-white tern in *Gygis*. This last-mentioned species is better known to us as Fairy Tern, but another 'Fairy' Tern occurs around Australia, so the alternative name of White Tern is a good compromise. Unlike gulls, terns are prepared to plunge into water after their fish prey.

Terns deserve more attention than is possible here, like our little endemic Damara Tern and the world's greatest traveller, the Arctic Tern. Remarkably it breeds in the Arctic and flies south for the Antarctic summer, an annual round-trip of up to 35 200 km, enjoying more daylight hours than any other bird species (Harrison 1983).

*Whiskered Tern* (Chlidonias hybrida) *alighting on its floating nest.*
(Photo: Cyril Laubscher)

ORDER FALCONIFORMES

# Hawks, Kites, Vultures, Buzzards and Eagles

## Family Accipitridae

No fewer than 212 species of diurnal birds of prey are grouped in this large family, on which even valuable single-species monographs have been written, like those on the Black Eagle (Gargett 1990) and African Fish Eagle (Brown 1980). Southern Africa is richly blessed with raptors, and for a basic study of predation pressure I established that we had 68 diurnal raptors in comparison with North America's 28 species and Eurasia with 47 species. Most diurnal birds of prey are classified in this family.

First on our list of 54 'typical' raptors in southern Africa is the cosmopolitan Osprey, now deprived of its own monotypic family, despite many anatomical differences to other raptors. Then come some aberrant kite-like raptors like the African Cuckoo-Hawk; the strange Honey Buzzard specializing in wasp larvae; and the even stranger specialist Bat Hawk, which gulps down whole bats in the limited time they are available to hunt. We have one *Elanus* kite, the Black-shouldered, a rodent specialist; and definitely two generalist *Milvus* kites, the Yellow-billed and the Black Kite, still clearly deserving species status. Next comes our well-known African Fish Eagle, better known for emitting 'the characteristic call of Africa'. It is one of seven species in this genus, including a close relative in Madagascar and the American Bald Eagle.

Then come the Old World vultures, not close relatives of the New World vultures which can actually scent

**1:** *The Bateleur Eagle* (Terathopius ecaudatus) *shown here with wing-tips extending past the tail, typical of a master-flyer.* (Photo: John Wesson)
**2:** *An African Hawk-Eagle* (Aquila spilogaster) *holding out her wings to shade her chick from the hot sun.* (Photo: Lorna Stanton)
**3:** *The African Fish Eagle* (Haliaeetus vocifer) *feeding on a dead fish. Its ringing call is considered characteristic of Africa.* (Photo: John Wesson)
**4:** *A Crowned Eagle* (Stephanoaetus coronatus) *feeding its chick.* (Photo: Garth Batchelor)
**5:** *A Rufous-breasted Sparrowhawk* (Accipiter rufiventris) *feeding her chicks. Note the alien tree which has allowed it to expand its range.* (Photo: Nico Myburgh)

carcasses under dense vegetation. Our vultures include the strange Palmnut Vulture, which eats carrion and catches fish itself (Chittenden & Myburgh 1996), but prefers the fruits of the Raphia Palm, and consequently is most likely to be found in Zululand. The spectacular bone-breaking Lammergeier or Bearded Vulture extends from the Drakensberg beyond our limits to Europe. Depicted on the pyramids, the Egyptian Vulture formerly nested on our cliffs, but was nearly eradicated here after the rinderpest with arsenic cattle-dips. Fortunately vagrants appear to be increasing in the Lowveld and Bushveld, as are the Palmnut Vulture and Lammergeier. Egyptian Vultures are remarkable for tool-using, actually repeatedly throwing stones with their bills at ostrich eggs to break the shells. Our other vultures include Hooded, White-backed, Rüppell's (relatively recently), the endemic Cape Vulture, the 'king' Lappet-faced Vulture and the aggressive White-headed Vulture, which reportedly still occasionally kills prey.

Two snake-eagle species are regularly seen here, the Black-chested and Brown Snake-eagles, and two are marginal with us, the Southern and Western Banded Snake-eagles. The length of snakes which snake-eagles can produce from their crops to feed chicks is remarkable. The Bateleur Eagle is a beloved bird here, and has greatly benefited from the increase in game farms. It appears now to have survived the serious irresponsible threat of carelessly strewn strychnine-poisoned meat-blocks which drastically reduced its numbers and range. We have five harriers,

**1:** *The Egyptian Vulture* (Neophron percnopterus) *was eliminated in South Africa as a breeding species, but stragglers indicate a possible slow comeback.* (Photo: Clem Haagner)
**2:** *The White-headed Vulture* (Aegypius occipitalis) *possibly still kills occasional prey.* (Photo: J. Delport)
**3:** *Flight pattern of the Yellow-billed Kite* (Milvus aegyptius), *typical of the* Milvus *kites looking for prey.* (Photo: Fanie Hendriks)
**4:** *The Yellow-billed Kite is a valid species distinct from the Black Kite.* (Photo: Fanie Hendriks)
**5:** *The Lammergeier* (Gypaetus barbatus) *extends from the Drakensberg to the Alps.* (Photo: Geoff McIlleron)

the African Marsh and Black Harriers which breed here, and the Pallid, Montagu's and Western Marsh (formerly European) Harriers which are Palaearctic migrants. The bare yellow cheeks of our Banded Gymnogene interestingly flush scarlet under hormonal control, actually while one watches in the breeding season, and its apparently double-jointed foraging antics are always amusing. The Lizard Buzzard is a strange little thickset raptor, easily identified by its unique under-chin pattern.

The Pale Chanting Goshawk with its western distribution and the Dark Chanting Goshawk in the east are decidedly similar long-legged sibling species. However, the Gabar Goshawk is a very different raptor, mainly notable to me for the *Stegodyphus* colonial spiders which they deliberately 'transport' alive in the spider nests to disguise their own fresh nests so that they are soon festooned and appear ancient. This is in agreement with Tarboton (1997a), who reviews possible reasons for this bizarre habit. Malan (1998) considers the use of these spider nests in both chanting goshawks to be nest-lining, which it may well be. However, the Gabar Goshawk is no chanting goshawk, and should continue to be classified in *Micronisus*, not *Melierax*, even though its origins may be traced back to a common ancestor.

Other typical shortwing accipiters include our most unobtrusive in the elusive African Goshawk, the Shikra Goshawk (an Urdu Indian term implying 'hunter', an improvement on 'Little-banded'), and our bird specialist sparrowhawks, the Little, Ovambo, Rufous-breasted and Black, the latter female large enough to take guineafowl with ease. Then come five true buzzards: our migratory Steppe and much rarer Long-legged; the Forest Buzzard similar to Steppe, but breeding with us; our Jackal Buzzard with the evocative jackal-like call; and the white-breasted Augur Buzzard, which replaces it north of the Limpopo. Then come true eagles: the Steppe and Lesser-Spotted as migrants; the Tawny Eagle, powerful but inclined to carrion; and our well-known Black Eagle, also most regrettably and obscurely called Verreaux's Eagle, when 'Black' Eagle is extremely apt for the only black eagle in the world (the so-called Indian Black Eagle is no eagle, but only a nest-robbing aberrant kite, lightly built with weak feet).

**1:** *Our endemic Cape Vulture* (Gyps coprotheres) *is facing a gradual decline in numbers in which illegal poisoning is clearly implicated.* (Photo: Geoff McIlleron)
**2:** *The Palmnut Vulture* (Gypohierax angolensis) *is facing a brighter future due to the foresight of a man like Ian Garland at Mtunzini.* (Photo: Hugh Chittenden)
**3:** *Our remarkable Bathawk* (Macheiramphus alcinus), *a superb flyer which snatches bats with ease, and swallows them whole.* (Photo: Ron Hartley)

Then there are two dashing hawk-eagles, the African and Ayres', not usually classified in *Aquila*; the similar Booted Eagle formerly considered a Palaearctic migrant, but which now also breeds with us; our commonest eagle, the Wahlberg's, which lays only one egg, and appears unable to raise two chicks; our largest eagle, the Martial, which is long-toed and prefers monitor lizards (leguaans) as prey; the mild Long-crested Eagle which prefers rodents; and finally our 'helicopter', found mainly in forest, the short-winged, long-tailed Crowned Eagle, easily Africa's most powerful eagle, capable of killing Bushbuck with pair combination. With monographs already written on species like the Black Eagle and African Fish Eagle as earlier emphasized, all aspects of this family cannot possibly be covered here. For example, one fascinating aspect is the murderous so-called Cain and Abel syndrome, of which Simmons (2004), himself one of a twin, gives an excellent synthesis.

# SECRETARYBIRD

## FAMILY SAGITTARIIDAE

Our remarkable Secretarybird is well known and aptly described as a terrestrial eagle. Less well known is that it is classified in its own monotypic family, has no close relatives, and that even a monotypic order was proposed for it by an expert. It is currently found only in sub-Saharan Africa; two fossil species are reported from the Eocene and Miocene of France.

Its eagle head is decorated with strange loose feathers, universally accepted as resembling the quill-pens of old-time clerks habitually stuck behind their ears, augmented by black knickerbocker breeches and a grey jacket. It is consequently given the name of 'Secretarybird' in many languages. Its tail-feathers are graduated, but the central pair of tail-feathers extends about 25 cm past

*Secretarybird* (Sagittarius serpentarius) *attacking a snake: it offers its wings for the snake to strike at harmlessly.* (Photo: Clem Haagner)

the other rectrices, giving it a characteristic silhouette. Standing about 1,3 m tall, its very long legs are correlated with a relatively weak grip by the feet (Brown 1976). Secretarybirds consequently use their bills to seize small prey, to kill, dismember and to carry nesting material. They and the New World vultures (Family Cathartidae) are apparently also the only raptors to roost squatting on their nests, but Secretarybirds do have the excuse of long legs. Their feet are remarkable. Not only are their legs three times the length of those of an eagle of equivalent size (Brown 1976), but their sturdy toes are only one-fifth the length of an equivalent eagle's toes. The claws are obviously blunt: striding all day over the veld would wear sharp claws down rapidly. The front three toes are joined by a basal web, and the hind-toe is short and rudimentary.

They are not a sociable species. Apart from their families, groups are encountered only at veld fires, or at watering-points in arid areas, where Maclean (1993) indicates that up to 50 may be encountered. Although Secretarybirds do not eat carrion, Brown & Amadon (1968) describe them collecting small burnt mammals and insects from veld fires. Like ground-hornbills, they are prepared to eat any prey small enough, from birds' eggs to small tortoises. Tiny chicks are carefully fed regurgitated liquid, but when chicks are large enough, the whole 'mixed bag' of prey is simply regurgitated into the nest for them to gobble down. Whole clutches of gamebird eggs like those of partridges and guineafowl are regurgitated simultaneously into the nest, together with numerous grasshoppers and locusts (probably the main prey), rodents, small birds, lizards, snakes, chameleons, frogs, beetles, etc.

Their predilection as snake-killers appears to be exaggerated, although they certainly kill reasonably sized snakes when encountered. Lacking the teamwork of a ground-hornbill flock, they put up a spectacular individual attack, offering their invulnerable flight-feathers for the snake to strike against, and then stomping it when off-balance with their feet in lightning-fast kicks until incapacitated. They make sure that snakes are dead before swallowing them. Anecdotes of their carrying large snakes aloft to drop them from a height onto a hard

**1:** *Secretarybird feeding chick; addled egg also visible.* (Photo: Clem Haagner)
**2:** *Secretarybird challenging a Black-backed Jackal.* (Photo: Geoff McIlleron)
**3:** *A Secretarybird in flight or coming in to land.* (Photo: Tony Heald)
**4:** *A Secretarybird in silhouette showing the long two central tail feathers and tiny feet.* (Photo: Tony Heald)

surface, as a Lammergeier drops bones or a raven drops tortoises, appear to be charming fables as Secretarybirds simply seem incapable of this. However, they do cache prey items for later use, as a female (slightly smaller than the male) was observed to cache a mouse under a bush, and return later for it (Brown & Amadon 1968).

It seems possible that Secretarybirds may have become a little too terrestrial. Despite nomadic aerial movements, and spectacular aerial display-flights in the mating season, during which the normally silent birds utter hoarse growling calls, as well as being recorded at an altitude of 3 600 m, a chase described by Haagner & Ivy (1923) makes one wonder: 'It requires a considerable run before it can rise on wing, and seldom flies either high or far. We on one occasion ran a bird down on horseback with a pack of greyhounds, the bird running with the fleetness of an antelope, with outstretched wings, occasionally rising into the air, but its flight was of short duration, the bird invariably descending and continuing its course on foot, using its wings as propellers. This alternate rising and settling kept on till the bird was too tired to rise, and the dogs eventually brought it to bay against a bank, where it pluckily defended itself with wings and beak. Calling the dogs off, we let the bird go on its way unmolested, having experienced the best run with the hounds we had had that season, and the bird's staying powers having had the effect of putting our horses into a foamy lather from head to foot.' Why did the Secretarybird not simply fly away from its pursuers?

The Secretarybird obviously chooses open terrain and avoids long grass, not choosing forested or densely wooded areas, or hilly, rocky country (Tarboton *et al.* 1987). Here it moves on an irregular course with measured tread of 120 paces per minute at about 2,5–3 kph (Maclean 1993). Brown & Amadon (1968) state 5 kph, and over 33 km/day. Secretarybirds can walk faster than a man can run. Given a choice, Tarboton (2001) indicates that this bird prefers to construct new nests annually, but this obviously depends on available nest-sites. The ideal appears to be a lone-standing thorny flat-topped tree, preferably an acacia. A large nest is made of sticks and regularly lined with grass. Eggs usually number two, rarely four. The fledging period is about 85 days (up to 106), and further parental dependence 62–105 days (Tarboton 2001). In a good rodent year, Secretarybirds are double-brooded (Brown 1972). The first sign of nest occupation is a roosting pair, for up to six months before egg-laying, and roosting commences an hour or more before dark (Brown & Amadon 1968).

# TRUE FALCONS
## FAMILY FALCONIDAE

Superficially it is not easy to separate these raptors from those of the preceding Accipitridae. There are constant differences though, so that some experts consider that these should be recognized at a still higher level, such as a sub-order. There are various internal anatomical differences, but these compact powerful birds with long pointed wings and feathered plus-fours above their bare legs can be separated externally by the clear notch in their upper mandibles just behind the hook of the bill, together with the associated 'tooth'. The order of flight-feather moult also differs considerably, and the excretions of adults fall simply under the perch, while those of other adult raptors are powerfully squirted a distance away. Falcons also do not build their own nests, either occupying natural sites or taking over other suitable old nests. They often have a characteristic black moustache streak on their cheeks.

Three subfamilies are recognized, two extralimital in South America, so only the third will be considered, the widespread subfamily Falconinae. *Falco* is the second-largest raptor genus. First, however, is our Pygmy Falcon, the only one of our 16 southern African falcon species not classified in the genus *Falco*, but *Polihierax*. Often mistaken for a shrike, it is a bold tiny raptor only 20 cm long. It is grey above with white underparts, but has black flight- and tail-feathers, finely spotted with white. Both sexes have a white rump, and the female a chestnut back. Most South Africans only think of Pygmy Falcons as occurring in the Kalahari, utilizing

Sociable Weaver nests, and scoff at the occasional Lowveld records. However, there is another Pygmy Falcon population in East Africa, where no Sociable Weavers occur. Here the falcons use nests of the Red-billed and White-headed Buffalo-weavers, and this breeding population occurred as far south as the Rust-der-Winter Bushveld, where the family of General Smuts recorded them for years in an enormous buffalo-weaver colony on their farm Rooikoppies. Regrettably these and other recorded locals disappeared with extensive pesticidal use on the Springbok Flats after the Second World War. They have been recorded breeding near Gorongosa by José Tello (warden). Occasional vagrants still reach the Mpumalanga and Limpopo Lowveld.

The remaining 15 true falcons in southern Africa are conveniently divided into two groups: the seven kestrels which hover over relatively open vegetation, preying mainly on rodents and insects, and eight falcons which do not hover. The Grey Kestrel does occasionally hover, but is little-known, occurring along the Cunene River at the extreme edge of its range. Three Palaearctic kestrels occur here in large numbers, though regrettably declining, and all three also breed in the northern hemisphere. The Lesser Kestrel is currently the subject of a conservation peace initiative in Jerusalem (Jenkins 2003). Up to 13 500 occurred in De Aar in 1997 (Taljaard 2003), more than 10% of its world population. My sisters never forgot such kestrel concentrations from their boarding-school days at Potchefstroom. They had to pass in groups under the roosting kestrels at night. Wakened kestrels do what comes naturally, but the girls solved the problem by sheltering giggling under their umbrellas.

The Western and Eastern Red-footed Kestrel males are almost identical except for slate-grey and white underwing-coverts respectively, although the females differ considerably, and the juveniles can also be distinguished. They often form mixed flocks, hovering together in their winter quarters. The Rock Kestrel is territorial and less common, fond of rodents. It not only occurs as a breeding species over most of southern Africa, but extralimitally into northern Africa right across Eurasia to the East Indies. The Greater Kestrel with its characteristic pale iris is visibly larger than the foregoing kestrels, and although widespread and solitary, appears to

*A male Pygmy Falcon* (Polihierax semitorquatus) *with a* Nucras *lizard as prey.* (Photo: Tony Heald)

*An adult Greater Kestrel* (Falco rupicoloides), *note the pale iris.*
(Photo: Fanie Hendriks)

**Left:** *Western Red-footed Kestrel female* (F. vespertinus).
**Right:** *Lesser Kestrel male* (F. naumanni).
(Photos: Fanie Hendriks)

avoid a strip along our eastern and south-eastern borders. Dickinson's Kestrel is marginal in South Africa, found solitarily in our north-eastern corner, and does not seem to hover much, though feeding on arthropods.

The uncommon Red-necked Falcon is a small but dashing falcon, almost solely a bird-killer, and which often shows an association with *Hyphaene* palms, in which it readily nests. The Sooty Falcon breeds in the northern hemisphere in extremely arid conditions, and breeding is remarkably timed to coincide with the southward migration of passerines and their fat chicks, as well as larger migrants. It is a deceptive and also much overlooked species (Milstein, Jones & Steyn 2000). Eleonora's Falcon is basically similar, but both more sociable and considerably larger than the Sooty. It also raises its chicks on bird migrants when breeding along Mediterranean coasts. The bulk of both these migratory falcons tend to spend the winter in Madagascar, subsisting on invertebrates rather than bird prey.

Both the rare resident African and migratory Eurasian Hobby Falcons are long-winged fast-flying falcons, subsisting mainly on birds and flying insects. The Lanner and Peregrine Falcons are two of the finest and most exciting falcons in the world, used for up to 3 000 years by falconers mainly for gamebird hunting due to their undoubted abilities. They are considered to approach the ideal of falcons, with only the considerably larger Gyr Falcon of the Arctic regions sometimes higher rated. Finally there is our little Taita Falcon, which closely resembles a miniature Peregrine, also an exceptional flyer. It is possibly the rarest falcon in the world, with only a tiny population in the Transvaal Drakensberg, and other tiny populations in Zimbabwe, Zambia and Kenya, preying on birds like swifts and martins.

Many people consider the falcons, and the Peregrine Falcon in particular, to be the epitome of flying birds, to strike with the hind-talon at incredible speed, and return to seize the falling carcass. One question is always asked: how fast? This is particularly because they are predatory birds. Some large swifts and the closely allied spinetails are probably the fastest of all birds, but it is the falcons that have caught the imagination of man for many centuries. Various claims have been made, like the aeroplane which measured the speed of a diving Peregrine Falcon (not after prey) at 290 kph. In a typical excellently reasoned objective article, Ryan (1999) has discussed this problem. He pointed out that large falcons, assuming even a moderate drag coefficient, should be able to attain speeds of 400 kph with a stoop of 1 000 m. But do they achieve this? He considers not, with accurately measured Peregrines up to 184 kph, and a Gyr Falcon at 209 kph. Why should falcons only reach half their potential? He points out three problems: the risk of injury which increases with speed, the possibility of mechanical stresses at such speeds, and the most likely: manoeuvrability, which I unhesitatingly agree is the key. The faster the stoop, the greater the recovery turning radius, and probability of missing the intended prey due to even slight evasive action. So by reducing their speed to well below their potential, falcons greatly increase their hunting success and reduce other potential damage.

**Far left:** *The Peregrine Falcon* (Falco peregrinus)*, to many the finest of all flying birds.*
**Left:** *The tiny Taita Falcon* (F. fasciinucha)*, probably the rarest falcon in the world.*
(Photos: Ron Hartley)

ORDER CICONIIFORMES

# Grebes

## Family Podicipedidae

Grebes belong to an ancient family, at least 80 million years old. Although we know little of their remote ancestry, it is obvious that they evolved from a distinctive parental stock, which must have been well established all over the world before the Tertiary Period (Austin 1962). Except for the penguins, they are better adapted than any other birds for an aquatic life, unquestionably the best of all flying birds. They are found on every continent except Antarctica, the stronghold of the penguins. It is clear that, despite their smaller size, they occupy the niche of the penguins over most of the world, as well as that of the similar divers or loons (Gaviidae), an arctic family of only four species that do not reach us. This is an example of convergence, but not close relationship.

Grebes tend to have patchy distributions, which vary with expansions and contractions, and our Black-necked Grebe has a wider distribution than any other grebe. In contrast, three species of grebe are confined each to a single Andean lake. Up to 23 grebe species are accepted, with some of the rarest already threatened with possible extinction. Only one grebe species has unstriped chicks, the strange Western Grebe, which is also the only grebe to impale fish underwater. All grebes eat fish, tadpoles, aquatic larvae and basically any suited form of aquatic animal life. Grebes are primarily freshwater species, but some utilize the sea seasonally.

Anatomically the positioning of their legs is most unusual, placed remarkably far back on their bodies for optimal foot-propulsion while swimming underwater, and an almost exclusively aquatic life. Unlike penguins they cannot even walk properly, only climb on and off their nests. They are also one of the only four bird families in the world to have lobed rather than webbed feet, but the lobes have evolved separately, and do not indicate any common relationship. Although, with one flightless exception, grebes tend to fly fast and well with a high wing-loading, they must patter over the water to become airborne. A concerned farmer near Barberspan telephoned me one morning about a helpless baby bird unable to fly, and unattended by its parents. His description left me puzzled. On investigation I found a magnificent adult Black-necked Grebe in full breeding plumage, which had tipped a cattle fence while flying at night. Although uninjured, it was lying helpless on the grass, totally unable to take off. Except for the concerned farmer, it would have died there, but

**Left:** *A Black-necked Grebe* (Podiceps nigricollis) *on its nest with stained eggs visible.* (Photo: Geoff McIlleron) **Right:** *A helpless Black-necked Grebe adult unable to take off from the ground due to its leg placing after tipping a cattle fence at night (see text).* (Photo: Peter Milstein)

ringed and released at Barberspan it was once more in its element. Grebes apparently prefer to fly at night, particularly moonlit nights.

Correlated with the extreme rearward leg placements are the tails of grebes. Unlike most birds, their tails are vestigial, comprising soft feathers with no stiff rectrices. In other words, grebes lack a functional tail, with short soft feathers and only rudimentary quills. These are useless for steering, so both in the water and in the air, grebes steer with their feet, which trail behind them, conspicuous in flight. Despite their nominal tails, grebes have more feathers per bird than any other bird group: 15 000 or more. These soft dense feathers, particularly the lustrous belly-feathers, were much sought-after a century ago to decorate women's hats. This cruel fashion was responsible annually for the slaughter of millions of beautiful birds, preferably when breeding, especially for their nuptial plumes. It was eradicated 100 years ago, giving rise to the establishment of the nature conservation organizations. Feather-hunters became most frustrated by grebes, which would dive with remarkable agility at the flash of a firearm, and evade the flying lead. This brilliant evasion earned the grebe insulting names like 'water-witch' and 'hell-diver'. Another remarkable aspect of grebes is their unique habit of eating their own feathers, and feeding these even to tiny chicks a few days old. Balls of many whole and disintegrating feathers in grebe stomachs must have some digestive function. Since these feathers have little or no nutritional value, the most plausible theory seems to be that they temporarily hold back the passage of sharp fish-bones until these are softened by digestion.

We have three grebes in southern Africa, all of widespread distribution, but which breed with us: the Great Crested, the Black-necked, and the Little (Dabchick). Particularly the Great Crested is known for one of the most spectacular mutual breeding displays in the animal kingdom (Simmons 1964). Huxley's (1914) paper on this was one of the classic foundation papers on animal behaviour. All three of our grebes make nests of sodden aquatic vegetation protruding 5–10 cm above water-level. They cover their eggs with aquatic vegetation when disturbed at the nest, as well described by Steyn (1996). However, the Black-necked Grebe often does not do so. The chicks are transported on their parents' back, even diving with them. Dislodged chicks simply pop up to the surface. Dean (1989) describes fascinating aspects like colonial Great Crested Grebes having to swim underwater to reach their own nests, and Little Grebes pulling leeches off hippos underwater. Tarboton (2001) details various aspects of grebe nests and breeding.

Finally, lest we forget, grebes were one of the early alarm-bells when persistent organochlorines and other hazardous pesticides were carelessly inflicted on our environment. Halliday (1978) indicated how the pesticide DDD was applied to Clear Lake in southern California to counter a plague of gnats. Accumulating in microscopic plankton and passing through the food-chain to small fish eaten by grebes, it 'all but wiped out' the grebes, with DDD concentrations in their tissues at levels of 80 000 times greater than the level at which the pesticide was applied to the lake.

# Tropicbirds

## Family Phaethontidae

The tropicbirds are a small family of only three medium-sized species, but probably the most beautiful of all seabirds. They have a world-wide distribution in tropical and subtropical waters, avoiding colder waters. They are not gregarious, except when nesting on oceanic and offshore islands. It is only in the vicinity of such suitable nest-sites that they are reasonably numerous. Otherwise they are recorded as being silent birds, seen singly or in pairs, often many hundreds of kilometres from land, easily the most pelagic of their order. However, several may join large flocks of feeding terns and shearwaters.

Tropicbirds fly relatively low (about 10–17 m up), gracefully over the ocean surface like large white doves. They feed by first hovering and then plunging into

*An exceptional photo of a Red-tailed Tropicbird* (Phaethon rubricauda), *taken hand-held by Allan Batchelor.*

the sea with half-opened wings like gannets, their close relatives, after fish or squid. Sometimes spiralling slightly, they plunge in with a slight splash, reappearing in a second or two with prey in their bills. On surfacing, they float buoyantly with long tails cocked at an angle. They may then shake the water from their plumage, and fly off again. Flying fish are a favourite prey in the Atlantic. Like gannets, tropicbirds have a system of air-cushions under the skin on their chests to protect them from the impact of striking the water surface.

Although tropicbird sexes are similar, the streamers of males average longer. The largest tropicbird dimension-wise is the Red-billed Tropicbird, up to 50 cm in length, with its elongated tail extending another 50 cm. The characteristic strong and slightly decurved coral-red bill, with blackish-barred upperparts in both adults and juveniles, together with the long white tail-streamers and some black primaries, are diagnostic for the Red-billed. The next-largest tropicbird is the Red-tailed, which is the whitest of the tropicbirds, with a length just under 50 cm, but with red tail-streamers only 33 cm in length, together with a scarlet bill. However, in addition to the proportionately shorter tail, Harrison (1983) also emphasizes that the Red-tailed has a heavier jizz, that its flight is rather ponderous and laboured in comparison with that of the other two tropicbirds. Finally, the White-tailed Tropicbird is the smallest and lightest of the three, only 40 cm in length and with 40 cm white tail-streamers. It has an orange to yellow bill, a diagnostic upper-wing pattern of black tertial stripes, and some black primaries with white tips. Each of the tropicbird species has a different pattern of black eye-stripe on their white heads. Juvenile tropicbirds tend to be barred with blackish, but only the Red-tailed juvenile has a blackish bill. All first-years lack the elongated central tail-feathers.

Despite the wide-ranging pelagic movements of tropicbirds when not breeding, it is interesting that the Red-tailed Tropicbird is absent from the Atlantic Ocean except for barely rounding the Cape of Good Hope in South African waters. Inland records (Pretoria, Free State) of storm-driven specimens are recorded (Maclean 1993), and Sinclair (1989) records two spending several weeks on an Eastern Cape cliff ledge, of which possibly one returned the following year. In contrast, the Red-billed and White-tailed Tropicbirds occur in all the major oceans. Apparently the flight of the White-tailed Tropicbird is buoyant with much gliding (Maclean

1993), while the flight of the two larger tropicbirds appears to be characterized by regular wing-beats and short glides.

Various authorities describe how tropicbirds approach ships, often being heard before seen even in bright sunlight. They fly over the vessel, announcing their arrival with shrill calls also described as screams, circle it once or twice, and then disappear as mysteriously as they came. The call is also noted as a high-pitched trill, and British travellers in particular compare this to a boatswain's whistle, calling them 'bo'sun birds'. However, the more amenable White-tailed Tropicbird appears exceptional, often following ships, even inclined to perch in the rigging (Harrison 1983). A bird of the lovely golden-washed subspecies from Christmas Island was found on a ship in Durban (Sinclair 1989). Red-billed Tropicbirds occasionally follow ships, but Red-tails seem least interested.

Because the short legs of tropicbirds are set far back, Stonehouse (1964b) emphasizes that they cannot support the weight of their bodies on land. Their webbed feet are therefore used for paddling, shuffling over the ground, and for digging a shallow nest-scrape. Consequently, tropicbirds nest optimally high on steep cliffs or other nest-sites where they can take off without walking or springing. Courtship involves excited flying by close groups near nest-cliffs, even depressing and undulating their tail-streamers. On low-lying islands, they may be obliged to ground-nest under a shrub. They prefer to nest in cavities or under overhanging rocks, sites which provide shade and can be defended against conspecific intruders. Stokes (1968) describes the long tail-feathers bent into a hoop to fit into small cavities. Mating takes place at the nest-sites, and tropicbirds fight over them and mates, attempting to seize intruders and eject them from the nest-sites.

A single egg is laid, and incubated by both parents in sessions of 2–5 days. Interestingly, the egg colour varies from deep to pale purplish-brown, actually becoming paler during the course of incubation as pigment is rubbed off (Stonehouse 1964b). Incubating tropicbirds are amazingly tame, squawking and pecking at humans, but having to be lifted off their eggs. Native South Sea islanders value Red-tailed streamers for decorative purposes, plucking them from incubating birds, which are otherwise not harmed (Austin 1962). Newly hatched tropicbird chicks are covered in thick grey or fawn down, and are left alone in the nest shortly after hatching when both parents hunt for food. With the extended breeding season over many months, many chicks are killed at this critical stage by intruding adults seeking nest-sites (Stonehouse 1964b). Chicks develop slowly, and leave the nest 11–15 weeks after hatching. Like petrels, they are deserted by their parents, and must fend for themselves (Austin 1962).

# Gannets and Boobies
## Family Sulidae

These large seabirds have long pointed wings, wedge-shaped tails, strong straight serrated bills, and are usually white in colour, with sexes alike. The classification of this family is not yet finalized. The main problem is the three widely spaced temperate gannets, often placed in the genus *Morus*: the Northern, Cape and Australasian Gannets. In addition, there are another six more tropical species, known as boobies and classified in the genus *Sula*. This generic splitting may be more traditional than justified, and Thomson (1964) describes the genus as 'sometimes rather unnecessarily split into two'. In general, three separate gannet species appear justified in terms of both Biological and Phylogenetic Species Concepts, together with the six booby species. However, there are a tiny number of gannets with intermediate characters, which will be briefly discussed, with a clear case of successful Cape Gannet × Australasian Gannet hybridization in Australia (Harrison 1983).

Our Cape Gannet is distinguished by a black tail and secondaries, unlike the white Northern Gannet tail and secondaries; the slightly smaller Australasian Gannet also has dark secondaries, but only the four central

*Massed breeding of the Cape Gannet* (Morus capensis). *Note that the gular stripe (down from the bill, extending down throat) is considerably larger than in the other two species of gannet.*
(Photo: Allan Batchelor)

tail-feathers black. Both the Australasian and Northern Gannets have a short gular stripe on the throat, whereas the Cape Gannet has a much longer one. Furthermore, the distinctly yellowish head of all three species distinguishes them from the white-headed boobies. However, a few Australasian tail-patterns have been observed in the Cape Gannet, and a few black tails in the Australasian Gannet. A few Australasian vagrants have been observed on Marion Island, the Crozets and South Africa (Harrison 1983). Rare here, the Australasian Gannet can also be located in South African colonies by a more high-pitched call (Sinclair & Ryan 2003), as well as the tail, a darker eye, and a more golden wash, while some Cape Gannets also have white outer tail-feathers. These few aberrations may possibly be ascribed to the rounding-off of species isolating mechanisms or introduction of genes from rare hybrids. There are wide gaps between the species breeding ranges, and no significant intergradation. Cape Gannets (chiefly yearlings) range as far as the Gulf of Guinea in the west and Kenya in the east after breeding.

The more sedentary boobies are so named because some people think they 'look stupid and act stupid', and Austin (1962) emphasizes that they cannot seem to learn that man is their enemy. Landing on sailing ships, they sat quietly on the rigging for a hungry sailor to grab. Stokes (1968) describes their defiantly standing their ground to man and not flying, so being easily caught. Of the six booby species, only two are accepted with us, the Red-footed Booby and the Brown Booby. The wide-ranging Masked Booby can easily be confused with Cape Gannet and Northern (extralimital) Gannet sub-adults, and has been removed from our list. The Brown Booby is erroneously thought to be common in our waters, but only a very few records are accepted. The Red-footed Booby shows much polymorphism, at least four morphs, which readily form mixed pairs. It also nests in trees, not on the ground like our other species.

In general, this family comprises magnificent flyers despite being heavily built birds with thick necks of moderate length, and large heads. A small bare throat pouch indicates their relationship to the pelicans. External nares (nostrils) are sealed in gannets and adult cormorants, and partially blocked in pelicans. All four toes are joined together by webs like the others of their order, and the well-vascularized feet are carefully wrapped around their eggs since no brood patches occur in the order. Larger species usually have one egg, smaller up to four, but usually produce only one chick. When grown, chicks are abandoned to slim down, and then fend for themselves. With Cape Gannets up to 1 000 in a flock (Brown *et al*. 1982), it is remarkable to see them diving from 30 m perpendicularly into the sea at a shoal of pilchards or maasbankers in rapid succession, chests protected by air-cushions like tropicbirds, and causing splashes up to 3 m high. It is alleged that fish up to 2 m deep are stunned. They can also swim well underwater, and have been caught in nets at depths of 28 m. Boobies dive from lesser heights, and particularly Red-footeds wait at the bow of a moving ship to seize flushed flying fishes with masterly timing. Brown Boobies are sometimes piratical.

When in 1833 Audubon first saw the Bird Rock gannetry in the Gulf of St Lawrence, he assumed that it was several feet of snow. The flat top of the rock held at least 100 000 pairs of Northern Gannets, and the side-ledges another 50 000. The Canadian Government built a lighthouse on Bird Rock in 1869. The access thereby provided enabled fishermen to club the defenceless nesting gannets for bait. By the turn of the century, they had wiped out the gannets on top, and only a few thousand of the most inaccessible ledge-nesters survived. Protection then by the Canadian Government turned the tide, and the populations are still increasing (Austin 1962). Compared to this incredible slaughter, the considerable killing by fishermen off South Africa and particularly off West Africa as described by Brown *et al*. (1982) is hardly serious. However, conservation measures should undoubtedly be implemented here as well. Gannets are not pelagic, but they concentrate on the continental shelf and are vulnerable.

# DARTERS

## FAMILY ANHINGIDAE

People have been greatly puzzled when what seems to be a bird's head with a long sharp bill and a much longer slender neck comes swimming casually past, remarkably showing no sign of a body. The small head characteristically jerks forward and backward again repeatedly. No snake can swim extending so high above water, but it is not surprising that this bird, for bird it is, has been called the 'snakebird'. Its proper name is the African Darter, one of probably four closely related species in a family with a world-wide distribution in tropical and subtropical climates, from Australia to South America. It is of ancient lineage, going back

**Left:** *African Darter* (Anhinga rufa) *hanging its waterlogged wings to dry.* (Photo: Martin Goetz) **Right:** *The snake-like head of the African Darter.* (Photo: Geoff McIlleron)

at least 80 million years to pre-Tertiary times (Austin 1962). Although some authorities have classified this little family together with cormorants, this is a regrettably superficial appraisal as clearly indicated by Brown *et al*. (1982), who mention considerable differences between them. One example (Thomson 1964) is that it has only one carotid artery, whereas cormorants have two. Another is a peculiar lining in its stomach, with a mass of hair-like processes of unknown function. This may serve the same function as the mystery feather-balls in grebes, possibly slowing down the passage of fish-bones till partial digestion takes place. A more impressive modification is to the eighth and ninth cervical vertebrae, enabling the kinked neck to be drawn back so that the bill can be shot forward (Brown *et al*. 1982). The darters have been dubbed the first underwater spear-fishermen, for this articulation permits the bill to become a triggered spear (Thomson 1964).

Not only does the darter have heavy bones to work against gravity, and no air-sacs, but the external nares are completely closed in adults (Austin 1962). The belly and back plumages absorb water quickly to reduce buoyancy. With this reduction, darters can remain submerged in water longer than cormorants, able to slowly swim submerged among vegetation when searching for prey (Brown *et al*. 1982). When swimming underwater, feet are used together, but on the surface, used alternately. Underwater, darters swim with the wings partly opened, and use them for steering (Winterbottom 1952). Fish form the main prey, but also crayfish, frogs, salamanders and even water insects. Fish are expertly speared, impaled on the bill. On the surface they are frequently beaten and pounded to stop struggles. When subdued and shaken free, they are caught in mid-air, and always swallowed head-first to prevent damage from fish spines.

Darters characteristically build their nests in trees standing in water, preferably in a high forked branch. Tarboton (2001) considers darter colonies to be usually 10–50 pairs, but he points out that elsewhere in Africa colonies numbering thousands of nesting pairs have been recorded. Darter-only colonies are rare, and he points out that most colonies are shared with herons, cormorants and spoonbills. Both sexes build, with the male gathering nest-material, and the female constructing an untidy platform of sticks and reeds, usually lined with twigs and grass. Apparently it can be completed in a day, and four eggs are the usual clutch. Although chicks hatch blind and naked, by two days they are covered with an attractive coat of white down like little lambs, and later develop a buff head and throat. At two weeks, chicks are prepared to abandon the nest if danger threatens, climbing back later using wings and bill.

Brown *et al*. (1982) describe the attractive courtship displays including neck intertwining, which also forms part of the relief ceremony. Above the colony, darters may soar on thermals, with long necks and tails forming a perfect cross. Flying involves a few wing-flaps and then gliding. The contrast between the handsome nuptial plumes and the later dishevelled flight-feather moult is considerable, but the tail is not moulted simultaneously. Although distribution is indicated as being confined to Africa (Brown *et al*. 1982; Sinclair & Ryan 2003), it is clearly stated by Moreau (1966) that a relict population of *rufa* still occurs in the Jordan Valley, presumably via the Nile long ago.

# CORMORANTS
## FAMILY PHALACROCORACIDAE

The cormorants are the largest and most successful family of their order, found world-wide. They form a relatively uniform group of about 31 species, with black the dominant colour. It is interesting that most of the southern hemisphere cormorants have white underparts. Their bills are characteristically narrow and long, but the upper mandible has a sharp hook, which often penetrates into their fish prey when they grasp it firmly. Although it can be said that they vary in length from a metre to half a metre, this is a deceptive description, for some have long tails, and some short. The most plentiful species is the Guanay Cormorant of South America's west coast, which occurs in many thousands. The rarest species is the large Galapagos Cormorant, which has developed much reduced wings in isolation, and is quite unable to fly. It is only found on two of the Galapagos islands, Fernandina and Isabela, seldom venturing as far as 1 km to sea, returning to roost at night. Their population consists of fewer than 1 000 pairs (Harrison 1983).

Of our five species of cormorant, the two smallest are long-tailed: the Reed and the Crowned Cormorants. Although they are distinguishable, despite even being considered conspecific by some, their similarity might have been a problem if the Reed was not an inland freshwater cormorant, while the Crowned is marine and found off the west coast, mainly on islands. Next is our largest cormorant, the White-breasted, but if hybridization is as rife as reported from north-east Africa, with black-throated birds mated with white-throated birds, etc. (Brown *et al*. 1982), it is difficult to accept the validity of this species assessment. Then comes our most numerous, the Cape Cormorant, and the Bank Cormorant, both marine species, with leucistic (dilute pigmentation) individuals reported as often encountered (Harrison 1983) in the latter species. All our cormorants are classified in the genus *Phalacrocorax*, which has been in existence for 40 million years, although the family, with 21 fossil species, is at least another 10 million years older (Austin 1962). With cormorant identification, always remember the wise words of Harrison (1983): 'Identification of all cormorants complicated by seasonal variation in plumage and several transitional plumage stages before juveniles reach full maturity.'

Cormorants nest in trees, reeds and on the ground. Extremely large numbers of nests are built on especially suitable sites, from sticks, reeds, weeds and whatever materials are to hand. The Bank Cormorant builds its nest from wet seaweed, plastering it firmly to the site, and taking much longer to build than other cormorants (Tarboton 2001). Cormorant nests sometimes touch each other on favoured sites like islands. The pale-blue chalky eggs vary from as few as one or two, to five or six. Newly hatched chicks look like reptiles or spacemen, but develop rapidly and become covered with black down. When threatened, chicks regurgitate their food to lighten themselves before fleeing. They flee to water, and return to their nests later. One of the saddest sights at a breeding colony is an adult hopelessly entangled with nylon fishing-line, but still barely able to waddle and swim. Even such a tragic bird cannot be easily caught to free it by cutting the line, and if it reaches the water, it dives in panic instead of being helped. If the long-line anglers who so carelessly leave hundreds of metres of this nylon death-sentence on the shore could see the results of their handiwork, they might be a little more considerate and less lazy.

**1:** *Reed Cormorant* (Phalacrocorax africanus) *in juvenile plumage.* (Photo: Charles Barrett)
**2:** *White-breasted Cormorant* (P. lucidus) *adult in breeding plumage (note white thigh-patch).* (Photo: Martin Goetz)
**3:** *Reed Cormorant in adult breeding plumage drying its wings.* (Photo: Geoff McIlleron)

Like darters, cormorants regularly hang out their wings to dry, but in the early mornings this cannot be necessary, and it must be habit or thermoregulation. The important thing is that, as with darters, this soaked plumage is not an oversight by the Great Architect, but an asset, enabling them to lose buoyancy rapidly and swim more efficiently underwater to hunt their prey. This matches their lack of air-sacs and use of heavier bones to counteract gravity. Fish are seized and usually brought to the surface so that the cormorants can ensure that they are swallowed head-first. It is said that cormorants can catch fish in murky water by utilizing their sense of hearing. This is probable, because a blind cormorant was found in good condition, obviously still capable of fishing well. Cormorants dive deep underwater, but do not dive in from the shore. From the water surface they spring in the air to dive, sometimes nearly emerging from the water. Depths of up to 31 m are achieved, proven by cormorants caught in nets. Cormorants deliberately select slower-swimming fish. At Barberspan it was proven that they fed almost solely on mud mullets (moggel), a fish which is rarely caught on a hook (Milstein 1975b), so actually aiding the angler instead of competing with him, as often alleged by disgruntled anglers. Some anglers have short-sightedly actually smashed cormorant eggs in the breeding colonies, most regrettable and working against their own interests (Milstein 1975b).

Finally, cormorants are of great commercial value for two reasons. The first is their importance as guano producers, where they are one of the most significant contributors to this valuable fertilizer. Artificial nesting platforms for breeding and guano production have been built along our west coast since 1927. The second is their actual use in commercial fishing in Japan and China, a centuries-old practice maintained for cultural and tourism purposes. Cormorants are fitted with a leather collar to which a leash is attached. Each fisherman handles up to a dozen trained cormorants. The collar prevents the cormorants swallowing all but tiny fish. When their throats are full of fish, they are individually hauled in, and regurgitate their prey into the boat. After a shift, the fishermen give their cormorants a throatful of fish, and then have to replace the collar above the fish, otherwise the habituated cormorants will disgorge their fish again.

# HERONS, EGRETS AND BITTERNS
## FAMILY ARDEIDAE

This is a well-known family, which is not only the largest of its order, but also the most widespread. World-wide there are about 61 species, with 22 recorded in southern Africa, more than a third of the world total. They are characterized by long necks, usually long straight bills with long slit-nostrils, and mostly long legs. Some people superficially confuse them with storks and cranes. However, due to a modification in the sixth cervical vertebra, which helps the heron shoot out its bill when hunting or frightened, herons always fly with their necks bent into an S-shape. Storks and cranes fly with their necks straight. Heron toes are long and narrow, with the middle toe pectinated, or grooved for grooming.

Primarily fish-eaters, herons have significant tracts of powder-down feathers to assist removing the fish slime when grooming. Power-down feathers differ considerably from normal contour feathers in that they are never moulted, but continue growing throughout the bird's life. The feather tip degenerates progressively into a talc-like powder, with particles measuring about a micron in diameter, used for dressing the contour feathers. Bitterns even rub their heads into the powder-down patches, so that after a meal of eels for example, such a clean-up results in the powder-down particles being visible on the bittern heads. Although most herons have three pairs of powder-down patches, bitterns only have two pairs. Herons have powder-downs most highly developed, although they are found less concentrated in various other birds too.

By coincidence the first heron listed in our sequence, the Slaty Egret, was for a century considered conspecific

**Top:** *The Slaty Egret* (Egretta vinaceigula) *was not accepted as a full species for exactly 100 years, but considered to be immature plumage or aberrations of the Black Heron. However, it never canopies like the Black Heron, but fishes like an egret. The rufous throat is regrettably not visible here.* (Photo: Sharon Heald)

**Bottom:** *Black Heron* (E. ardesiaca)*: note the yellow feet and toes. After erecting its unique canopy, the toes are wiggled to attract small fish within striking distance.* (Photos: Geoff McIlleron)

with the second, the Black Heron. This was from its discovery at Potchefstroom in 1871 (Gurney 1871) to its acknowledgement as a full species in 1971, and not juvenile plumage or an aberrant variety (Benson, Brooke & Irwin 1971). The Black Heron is our most interesting species, one of eight mainly small herons classified in *Egretta*, and which has developed a unique fishing method. While America's Reddish Egret in particular frightens fish by 'parasolling', suddenly spreading one or both wings briefly, our Black Heron makes an incredible sophisticated un-birdlike dome with its wings, holding the pose in shallow water of suitable depth, and striking unerringly with its unseen bill from the

**1:** *A Common Squacco Heron* (Ardeola ralloides) *explodes into beauty by opening its concealed white wings.* (Photo: Fanie Hendriks)
**2:** *Goliath Heron* (Ardea goliath), *simply the world's largest heron.* (Photo: Eliot Lyons)
**3:** *Great Egret* (Egretta alba), *the largest of the egrets and with a seasonal change in bill-coloration.* (Photo: Geoff McIlleron)
**4:** *A Grey Heron* (Ardea cinerea) *which has captured a fish, holding it prior to swallowing it head-first.* (Photo: Eliot Lyons)
**5:** *The Rufous-bellied Heron* (Ardeola rufiventris), *a rare species supposedly closely related to the Squacco Heron.* (Photo: Fanie Hendriks)

created darkness. The Black Heron strikes at small fish seeking shelter under the dome, or attracted by its long wiggling orange toes (Milstein & Hunter 1974). To sandwich this remarkable species between the similar but unspectacular Slaty and Little Egrets is puzzling indeed. The American vagrant Little Blue Heron is next, then the Yellow-billed Egret, and then the larger Great Egret with a significantly longer neck, and a bill which changes seasonally from yellow (non-breeding condition) to black (breeding). Next follows the vagrant largely coastal Western Reef Heron in two colour-phases from both West and East Africa, and another American vagrant, the Snowy Egret.

Then come the larger more typical *Ardea* herons: headed by our widespread Grey Heron, which I was privileged to study in England (Milstein, Prestt & Bell 1970), and was fascinated to find, for example, that although the whole British population had been censussed since 1928, the way the chicks were fed was not accurately known. The much less aquatic Black-headed Heron feeds on invertebrates, often also rodents, birds as large as Laughing Doves, and even moles. Our

**1:** *The Green-backed Heron (*Butorides striata*) makes up for size in intelligence – it actually floats bait downstream repeatedly (porridge, insects) to lure small fish within reach.* (Photo: Charles Barrett)
**2:** *Green-backed Heron with fish prey, preparing to swallow.* (Photo: Fanie Hendriks)
**3:** *White-backed Night Heron (*Gorsachius leuconotus*): largely nocturnal; incubating on a low tree nest.* (Photo: Will Nichol)
**4:** *Dwarf Bittern (*Ixobrychus sturmii*), an attractive, shy species.* (Photo: Geoff McIlleron)

Goliath Heron is the largest heron known, but I have recorded it rarely killing such a large carp that it was abandoned, too large to swallow. The Purple Heron is medium-sized, but a master of camouflage. Our Cattle Egret is probably the most successful heron, colonizing Europe, Australia, North and South America in recent times, always in association with grazing livestock, which flush grasshoppers for it.

The Common Squacco Heron simply opens its white wings and explodes from a camouflaged nondescript into a thing of beauty. The decidedly similar but more heavily marked Madagascar Squacco Heron is a vagrant to Mozambique, Zimbabwe and Zambia. The interesting Rufous-bellied Heron is currently placed with the two squaccoes in *Ardeola*, but merits further study. This probably applies even more to the Green-backed Heron, currently being treated as a widespread conspecific on probably inadequate evidence. The most fascinating aspect of this heron is the actual use of bait to catch fish, allowing it to drift downstream, and retrieving it to release it higher upstream again. Success was filmed with an apparent fly, capturing a small fish (Q. Coetzee, pers. comm., who also reported bits of rusk utilized and filmed), while Brown *et al.* (1982) report bits of maize porridge utilized. Criticisms of limited success are ridiculous when compared with the even lower success rates of human anglers, and large fish are understandably ignored.

Our widely distributed Black-crowned Night-heron has the unique distinction of being elevated to the 'go-i' rank of the Japanese peerage by the tenth-century Emperor Diago, who was greatly impressed by its beauty and tameness in a new water-garden. It is still known today by Japanese everywhere as the 'goi heron' (Austin 1962). The *Gorsachius* night-herons are, together with the bitterns, our only solitary-nesting herons. I knew instantly, when observing my first beautiful down-coated White-backed Night-heron chicks in a rock-cleft on Lake Kyle, that this species could not be congeneric with the Black-crowned as classified at the time. To conclude with the bitterns, the Little and Dwarf Bitterns are most attractive small herons. Wishing to photograph a Little Bittern at Barberspan, I put it in a glass enclosure, and was amazed to see it take up the full bitterning vertical reed-like posture completely in the open, and hold the stretched pose. The booming Great Bittern has declined considerably in numbers here for no apparent reason (Tarboton 2001). Although it was a favourite delicacy of King Henry the Eighth, his example has fortunately never been widely followed, and can be discounted as a cause.

Municipalities too often ignore the sometimes tremendous potential of wetland sanctuaries within their boundaries, and the undoubted attraction of the Austin Roberts Bird Sanctuary in Pretoria in its heyday was an excellent example. Another stunning example is the remarkable Black Heron. Tarboton (2001) correctly indicates that the first nesting of the Black Heron in the whole of southern Africa was in the Durban Bayhead mangroves in 1961 and the following summer. However, both these attempts were unsuccessful. The first successful breeding of the Black Heron in southern Africa was incredibly in the urban sanctuary of Westdene in Benoni (Schmitt 1971)!

# Hamerkop

## Family Scopidae

The Hamerkop is a rather plain brown bird about 50 cm long, with an attractive barred tail often overlooked. The rather heavy bill is balanced in profile by a heavy crest, likened to a hammer in appearance: the source of its name. Hamerkops are unusual in that crest feathers are the earliest to develop (Liversidge 1963). More remarkable indeed is the nest. Tarboton (2001) describes it simply and effectively as the largest domed structure built by a single pair of birds. It is built of sticks, other plant material and mud. The small snug nest-hole is strategically placed in the least accessible part of the nest. This special nest-hole demands special flight techniques.

*Hamerkop* (Scopus umbretta) *fishing in a fast-running torrent.* (Photo: Martin Goetz)

*The nest of a Hamerkop pair nearing completion. Tarboton (2001) aptly describes it as the largest domed nest built by a single pair of birds.* (Photo: Clem Haagner)

These have been best described by Kahl (1967) and Steyn (1996). Although taking off from level ground is achieved by a single upward leap, the preference to take off from an elevated perch is clear. When launching from such a perch, the Hamerkop makes a forward leap slightly upward, diving from the perch at a steep angle with wings closed, and only beginning to flap when a short distance away. Such diving is well suited to departure at speed from the nest-hole, and may have originated in this connection (Kahl 1967). When entering the minimal-sized nest-hole, the bird folds its wings just before arrival, and in effect dives upward into the nest-hole (Kahl 1967). This is in agreement with Steyn (1996), who likens the entering movement to a dart, and the exit to a cork from a popgun. The upward-sloping entrance tunnel to the chamber is important, and Steyn (1996) correctly emphasizes the invariable mud-plastering of this tunnel to provide smooth passage.

Although most nest data comes from Mali (Wilson & Wilson 1986), where a smaller subspecies occurs, it is clear that South African nests are larger. These West African nests ($n=169$) measure $0,7 \times 1,0$ m in diameter, and 1–1,5 m in height (Wilson & Wilson 1986). However, South African nests measure up to 2 m diameter with roof 1 m or more thick (Maclean 1993), or total height of 1,5–2 m with depth 1,6 m from entrance to the back of the nest (Steyn 1996). West African chambers measure $60 \times 50 \times 40$ cm, while South African chambers are about 80 cm in diameter, and 30–40 cm high (Steyn 1996). The snug nest-hole in West Africa is 10–15 cm in diameter, on a ramp sloping upwards at 15–20°. South African nest-holes range from 13 cm diameter (Liversidge 1963) to 13–15 cm (Steyn 1996). Basal nest height for the 169 West African nests was 2,0–13,8 m (mean 8,18 m). No geographical orientation had any significant effect, the nest-hole almost invariably facing the direction towards which the chosen fork inclined.

Siegfried's (1975) nest hypothesis based on an inadequate or elusive food-supply was rejected by Wilson & Wilson (1986) with no support from their study, including fast-growing chicks and a larger clutch-size (4,8) than the maximum of 3,4 in 22 other ciconid species in Africa. They also rejected roosting in nests throughout the year, exaggerated fidelity to nests in successive years, and nocturnal foraging activities. Similarly, reported communal nest-construction by up to seven Hamerkops (Gentis 1976) is doubtful, with not a single case of communal building other than by breeding pairs in their large sample over nearly five years. Careful analysis of this interesting account by myself and others indicates that it was a typical practice play-session by a fledged brood of four Hamerkop youngsters, pestering their probable parents who were attempting to construct a nest. Another Hamerkop, probably adult, was not involved. Wilson & Wilson (1984) also dispute the claims for *Xenopus* frogs (platanna) as its main diet, despite even the remarkable aerial success rate of 79% with *Xenopus* tadpoles (Kahl 1967), stating that the food observed by them was almost entirely fish, generally *Tilapia* fingerlings, including all regurgitations from regularly weighed chicks. Despite amphibians being very abundant in their study area, only two frogs were recorded as prey. Hamerkops are versatile feeders: ranging from perching on hippo backs to catch frogs (Thomson 1964), stamping on soft mud to see what emerges, also even following ploughs (Winterbottom 1952), and increasingly feeding on road-casualty carrion (Milstein 1983).

Courtship is bizarre, often involving a group, running around each other, crests rising and falling, bowing and indulging in repeated false mountings, sexual role reversals, sometimes even facing the wrong way, with what Steyn (2000) calls maniacal calling. The building peak by both birds is clearly in early mornings, also late afternoons, best described by Liversidge (1963), Steyn (1996, 2000) and Wilson & Wilson (1986). The latter describe a basal platform (in four days), nest cavity (in 13 days), with nest-hole depression visible, and this hole complete in 16 days. At this stage roofing commences, and the pair then co-operate on the roof, one inside, one out. Corner-building is best described by Liversidge (1963), then large sticks are laid across with a 'typical' rafter 65 cm long, diameter from 2,9 to 1,9 cm, and weight 56 g. Wilson & Wilson (1986) describe one stick weighing 232,5 g (with adult Hamerkop only weighing 470 g), and completion by 20–25 days, Liversidge (1963) 40 days.

The apparent male continues to build up and decorate the roof even after egg-laying. He also apparently does the mud-lining, shuffling a mass of spirogyra-like algae into a muddy heap, then picking it up and flying to the nest, up to 30 trips of two minutes each per session (Liversidge 1963). Wilson & Wilson (1986) state no lining to the egg-depression, but Liversidge (1963) a thin grass-layer. Lydekker's (1895) fable of a three-compartmented nest-chamber appeared in the literature as fact for nearly 70 years. A remarkably constant micro-climate results in the nest, negating Liversidge's (1963) efforts to distinguish incubation changes with sophisticated temperature-recording apparatus. The final exterior decorating includes almost invariably a blue cloth (Wilson & Wilson 1984), and a remarkable materials list by Lorber (1985) includes six bicycle tyres and 56 scraps of tin-foil. These desirable nests are often taken over by other animals ranging from bees to large pythons, but chiefly Barn Owls. Two geese species and our largest owl often nest on top, and Egyptian Geese regularly enlarge the nest-hole with their bills to gain access.

Apart from its enormously strong, truly remarkable nest, unique among birds, the Hamerkop has always been a puzzle to bird taxonomists: whether it is an aberrant heron, a stork, or something else. Hamerkops lack the powder-down feathers common in herons, and except when transporting heavy nest-material, fly with neck only slightly hunched, extended like a stork (Austin 1962). Yet it has heron-like voice organs, a variety of calls, the middle-toe claw grooved heron-like for preening purposes, while its hind-toe is level with the three other toes. There are no stick-exchange displays, found in both herons and storks (Kahl 1967). Hamerkops never excrete on their legs to cool them as storks do. Even when subjected experimentally to high environmental temperatures, they still never attempted to cool their legs (Kahl 1967). Conservative host-specific bird-lice that infect Hamerkops are closest to those of certain plovers (Austin 1962).

Hamerkops have an unusual way of sitting on horizontal tree branches. Standing on the branch, they lower their legs until their breasts rest on the branch. Kahl (1967) emphasizes that this has no counterpart in either storks or herons. He concludes that Hamerkops show no close behavioural ties to either herons or storks. Kahl (1967) considers it probable that the Hamerkop is a specialized descendant from a very ancient line, and does not believe that present behavioural evidence indicates a particularly close relationship with any living bird so far studied. To conclude, many birds have bills modified to facilitate feeding. However, Liversidge (1963) makes a strong case for the Hamerkop's deep strong bill to have developed 'as an ideal structure to manage the large and heavy material for its nest', not for obtaining food where a much flatter bill would have sufficed.

# FLAMINGOES
## FAMILY PHOENICOPTERIDAE

World-wide, generations of children have grown up knowing exactly what a flamingo looks like, though many never saw a real flamingo. This is due to outstanding illustrations of the most celebrated croquet match ever, created by the whimsical genius of Lewis Carroll in his children's classic, *Alice in Wonderland*. Here flamingoes, tucked firmly under an arm, with their long graceful necks and unique bills extended forward, were used with aplomb as the croquet mallets. Compared to body-size, flamingoes have the longest necks and legs in the world. Their remarkable bills are sharply decurved about halfway down their length. Equally remarkably, these bills are used upside-down to filter minute organisms from brack and salty water. The more like an organic soup the water is, the better it is suited to flamingoes.

Indeed, flamingoes only enjoy fresh water to drink and bathe in, even uncomfortably hot thermal springs (Weaving 1989). Their efficient filtering system has its only counterpart in vertebrate animals with the baleen whales (Mysticeti). Flamingo filtering systems are detailed in Brown (1969), Brown *et al.* (1982) and other specialized references, powered by a thick fleshy tongue which would be the envy of any mother-in-law, and a favourite delicacy of Roman emperors. Flamingo mandibles are also unique: the upper mandible is only a lid, described as 'deep-keeled' or 'shallow-keeled' according to the amount of filtering lamellae present. However, the large lower mandible houses the strongly developed tongue in a groove where it can fulfil its piston-like function of forcing water through the filters.

**Below:** *An adult Lesser Flamingo* (Phoenicopterus minor) *feeding in shallow water.*
**Right:** *An adult Greater Flamingo* (P. ruber). *Note the two-colour bill compared to the Lesser's.* (Photos: John Wesson)

Interestingly, the still-developing bill of newly-hatched flamingoes closely resembles the ancestral bill of ancient fossil flamingoes from the Miocene Period.

Flamingoes occur eastward from the Galapagos to the former eastern limit in Sri Lanka (now extinct there), and south to Tierra del Fuego, tip of South America. It is estimated that there are about 6 million flamingoes in the world, and of them about 4,5 million are the deep-pink Lesser Flamingo, endemic to the African continent (Brown 1964). Next most common is the large Greater Flamingo, our other species, pink with scarlet and black wings, found from the Americas to the Indian sub-continent and down to our tip of Africa. Then there is the Chilean Flamingo, and two smaller species which lack the back-toe (genus *Phoenicoparrus*), the Andean and James' Flamingoes. The latter is the rarest in the world, considered almost extinct until more were discovered in the Bolivian Andes. The other three have elevated hind-toes, and are controversially classified here as *Phoenicopterus*. The Lesser, with its quite different voice and much more specialized algae-feeding (mainly blue-green), was long-classified as *Phoeniconaias*, and there is dissatisfaction among flamingo experts over this lumping together (Brown *et al*. 1982).

Greater and Lesser Flamingoes coexist well, according to Brown (1965). The former is a bottom-feeder, even up-ending in deep water to eat larger prey like small molluscs, crustacea, organic particles in mud, as well as algae and diatoms. The Lesser is an algae and diatom specialist in the uppermost layer of water, with many more sieving lamellae than the Greater. It can therefore not feed by swimming in rough water, and prefers to feed regularly at night when the surface is calm. Weaving (1989) indicates that 100 000 Lesser Flamingoes consume some 18 tons of these particularly tiny algae per day. They are worked onto the tongue, and swallowed.

Despite indications like waterfowl, and especially geese (webbed feet, closely related mallophaga, similar voice, similar chicks, calls during flight, gabbling, etc.), there are also indications of relationship to storks, ibises, herons and gallinaceous birds. However, flamingoes achieved their present form early, before the dawn of the Tertiary era, and their systematic position remains obscure (Brown 1964).

In southern Africa predation is fortunately not noteworthy, although in East Africa flamingoes are terrified by Marabou Storks (Steyn 1996). Brown *et al*. (1982) indicate that more than 6–8 Marabous can cause wholesale desertions of colonies of 4 000–6 000 flamingo pairs. Similarly our disease problem in southern Africa is apparently also negligible, unlike a somewhat sensational report for Kenya by Balfour (2001). The regular East African fluctuations at individual sites and ongoing research with monitoring are indicated by Owino (2002), while more objective comments than those of Balfour (2001) are made by Johnson (2002). A well-balanced assessment of these bacterial deaths is made by Simmons (2002), who points out that the oldest flamingo in captivity is a still-breeding Greater aged 62 years old, while another in the wild died aged 40, and correctly emphasizes the episodic nature of the unfortunate mortality.

Flamingoes are opportunistic and erratic breeders. Steyn (1996) gives details of recent successful breeding attempts in southern Africa. Breeding appears to be initiated by males, and Greater and Lesser displays are rather similar, except that the Lessers pack so tightly that the inner birds cannot even open their wings. Displays are described by Brown *et al*. (1982), Steyn (1996) and Weaving (1989). Nest-mounds are scooped up by both sexes, and measure about 15–36 cm high, with a slightly hollow top where the single white egg with its blood-red yolk is laid. Steyn (1996) describes in detail how the legs are alternately shaken clean of mud before the flamingo settles on them. He also indicates how a large breeding colony of 500 000 pairs of Lessers has been estimated to move about 15 000 tonnes of mud. The raised nest-mound is important in hot environments, and Etosha nests are 2–8°C cooler than the surrounding pan, while in the extreme conditions of Lake Natron (Tanzania), the nest-cup was a remarkably 25°C cooler than the mud below.

At hatching the parent keeps trumpeting high-pitched calls to achieve the essential imprinting of both chicks and adults on each other. In less than a week, vast crèches are formed, where the imprinted chicks can then answer their parent's call to be fed. The chicks are fed on liquid, first a red fluid rich in blood corpuscles, fats and glucose, which is carefully dripped from the parent's bill into the chick's open bill (Steyn 1996). Newly hatched chicks have swollen rubbery coral-red legs, which rapidly slim down to blackish. Chicks peck up bits of egg-shell for calcium needed for their rapidly-growing legs (Steyn 1996). Particularly in the Lesser Flamingo, chick crèches can build up to thousands. A relatively few adult 'nurse-maids', which are almost certainly non-breeding adults, accompany the grey army of chicks.

Sometimes these 'nurse-maids' are called upon to play another essential role. Rarely the waters dry up early. Not yet able to fly, the chicks then have the choice to march or die. An additional hazard then also comes into play: soda-mud hardening on their lower legs, forming what Steyn (1996) aptly calls 'anklets of death', causing a pitiable mortality. At Etosha in 1971, 30 000 chicks marched off in a solid mass. First they headed northerly for 30 km, reaching the nearest water. When this also dried, they marched on westwards for another 50 km to adequate water this time. The essential imprinting had enabled the chicks and their faithful parents bringing food to find each other, mainly at night when flamingoes prefer to fly. A combination of 'nurse-maids' and chain of parents showed the way. The research conservationists who monitored the 30-day epic march estimated that approximately 27 000 chicks survived the incredible ordeal (Steyn 1996). Although some chicks died on the way, the mortality was lower than expected. Without their parents commuting with nutritive liquid food between the chicks and the nearest food-supply, probably most or all would have died. At Makgadikgadi some 20 years later, Lesser Flamingo chicks again trekked 80 km to water, and it was estimated that three-quarters of the chicks survived according to Steyn (1996). He stated that there was no doubt that this trekking was most remarkable in the annals of avian survival.

*Greater Flamingo taking off, well-illustrating the proportions and colour of this remarkable bird species.* (Photo: Fanie Hendriks)

# IBISES AND SPOONBILLS
## FAMILY THRESKIORNITHIDAE

The ibises and spoonbills are an interesting bird family, with a fossil record that goes back 60 million years to the Eocene, and at least 15 extinct species are known. Even more remarkably, human history records go back 5 000 years to ancient Egypt. About 27 ibis species exist, and six spoonbills, found throughout the world's warm temperate and tropical regions with the exception of Oceania (Austin 1962). The more successful ibises have long narrow bills which are strongly decurved, while the spoonbills have a characteristic flattened nerve-rich spoon-ending to their bills. Obviously these differences result in considerable differences with regard to their feeding habits. The ibises can select prey, chiefly invertebrate, and probe into soft ground and mud, while the spoonbills slop vulgarly through shallow water, seizing and swallowing whatever small vertebrate and large invertebrate prey they encounter. A characteristic of both groups is a bare face, but one group of ibises has the entire head and neck bare as adults. All ibises and spoonbills are gregarious when feeding, and most breed colonially. Like storks, they lack powder-down patches, but have a pectinated middle claw like the herons. Tarboton (1989a) well describes the way a flapping ibis flock suddenly all glide, while spoonbills flap steadily on.

The first ibis on our list of five species is the well-known Glossy Ibis, spread over five continents. Previously a Palaearctic migrant, it suddenly started nesting in the East Rand marshes in 1950. I independently stumbled on these nests as a schoolboy soon after this hush-hush discovery, and will never forget the exciting sight of the beautiful deep blue eggs in under-storey nests in a large heronry. Glossy Ibises have a handsomer breeding plumage than most ibises, for example iridescent glossy plumage and a distinctive white line from maxilla around the eye and back to the mandible.

Next is our tree-nesting, only solitarily breeding ibis with a long-term pair-bond: the grey-green Hadeda Ibis, known for its raucous cries although most of the family do not have voice-boxes. Not only has it become an urban bird, much overlooked when slyly nesting soundlessly in quiet back-gardens, but it has more than doubled its distributional range in the past century. It expanded into the south-western Cape in the early 1960s. Nesting on a horizontal fork so flimsily that the eggs can often be seen from below, it has even nested on a telephone pole, apparently in an old Black Crow nest (Steyn 1996). Hadedas fly in a ragged group, never in formation.

Third is our most interesting ibis, also our only endemic, the Bald Ibis. It nests usually on cliffs or in suitable pot-holes (Tarboton 1989). Such a pot-hole colony in a giant finger of rock near Polokwane (Pietersburg) is the only dryland colony to have survived man's persecution. Most of the Karoo colonies are

**Top:** *The Bald Ibis* (Geronticus calvus) *is calling here from its cliff-cavity nest in a small colony.* (Photo: Niels Jacobsen)
**Bottom:** *This particular Hadeda Ibis* (Bostrychia hagedash) *has a peculiar 'white' iris like a Sombre Bulbul, first recorded and photographed by Dr Fanie Hendriks in the Okavango.* (Photo: Fanie Hendriks)

**Left:** *Adult Sacred Ibis* (Threskiornis aethiopicus) *with bald head and neck.* (Photo: Fanie Hendriks)
**Right:** *Adult African Spoonbill* (Platalea alba) *showing the spatulate bill well.* (Photo: Fanie Hendriks)

extinct, indicated only by their names today (Milstein 1973). Regrettably ibises are edible, and when hard-pressed on commando during the Anglo-Boer War in the Karoo, my grandfather like other hungry crack-shot Boer cavalry was delighted to dine on tasty Bald Ibises.

For its sibling species in North Africa and the Middle East, Thomson (1964) correctly uses the names Hermit Ibis (from the scientific name *eremita* or hermit) and Waldrapp (the German-Swedish name) for this ibis which made its last stand in central Europe inhabiting ruined castles in the forests. The Hermit Ibis is now possibly extinct in Morocco, and teetering on extinction's brink in Turkey, its last stronghold. It is frankly silly to unnecessarily double the length of the names of both species to 'northern' and 'southern', when the Hermit Ibis is not really bald, but has an erectile ruff at the back of its head spread forward in display, as well as two raised black patches on its crown (Cramp *et al*. 1977), like the scarlet crown-patch on the Bald Ibis.

At the previously mentioned pot-hole colony, a total of 155 buttons were picked up directly under the pot-hole nests but not elsewhere, clearly shown to have passed through the digestive tract (Milstein 1973, 1974). The only reasonable explanation is that the buttons match a prey image in the Bald Ibis's relentless search for beetle prey. Tarboton (2001) mentions several reports in the 1990s of Bald Ibis tree-nests. If valid, since these nests are usually made of non-durable soft vegetation, take-over of nests of other species may be involved. Bald Ibises are usually colonial nesters, but confusion between this species and the Hadeda is most unlikely.

Fourth is the Sacred Ibis, deified by ancient Egyptians as the embodiment of Thoth, scribe of the gods and god of wisdom, magic and medicine, who was always depicted as ibis-headed. It is alleged that the ancients knew that this bird played a role in controlling bilharzia, a disease that medical evidence has proved even the pharaohs suffered from. This possible role would most likely have involved breaking the parasite's life-cycle by eating the intermediate snail-hosts. Tarboton (2001) indicates that large colonies may contain up to 1 500 pairs, and that such large colonies are always in reeds. Males initiate breeding and fetch the nest-material, but females build. Both sexes incubate and care for the chicks, which insert their bills into those of the parents to obtain food. Sacred Ibises were so venerated long ago that their carcasses were embalmed and buried with pharaohs and in temples. Remarkably, probably as the result of a cult, hundreds of thousands of such embalmed Sacred Ibises were wrapped in grave-cloths and interred row on row in catacombs at Saqqara. Obviously common breeders in Egypt until about 1800, they had almost completely vanished by 1850 (Cramp *et al*. 1977).

Last member of the family here, the African Spoonbill, makes a nest very similar to that of the Sacred Ibis. The white eggs with reddish spots are equally similar, so that extreme care should be taken to avoid errors. One clue is that spoonbill eggs tend to be more pointed. Newly hatched spoonbill chicks can be distinguished by their bills showing clear indications of the spoon to come. Sacred Ibis and African Spoonbill displays are similar, and they have hybridized in captivity successfully (Steyn 1996).

To conclude, ibises and spoonbills got off more lightly than the herons and egrets in the appalling slaughter for beautiful feathers to decorate women's hats a century ago. However, from Florida southwards two of the world's most beautiful birds, the Scarlet Ibis and Roseate Spoonbill, have never fully recovered. Large areas of mangrove swamps where they once thrilled observers with their beauty remain barren.

# PELICANS
## FAMILY PELICANIDAE

Described as 'very large to enormous waterbirds', pelicans are among the largest flying birds (Brown *et al*. 1982). The largest pelican is our Great White Pelican, with a maximum wingspan of 3,6 m, followed by the Dalmatian Pelican with a maximum wingspan of 3,45 m, but no other pelican species exceeds 3 m in wingspan (Harrison 1983). In all there are seven species of pelicans worldwide, and the largest subspecies of the Brown Pelican, *Pelecanus occidentalis thagus*, of the Humboldt Current off Peru and Chile is clearly a large subspecies and nothing more. There are 10 fossil species of pelican known, and Oligocene fossils as old as 30–40 million years are so similar to modern birds that they are classified in the same genus (Austin 1962). The origin of the name 'pelican' is unknown, and both the ancient Greeks and Romans used it in this form. The well-known rhyme that the pelican's beak can hold more than his belly can is true, but not that it uses its bill as a storage facility. On the contrary, it is used solely as a fisherman's landing net, and once the surplus water has been tipped out, the fish are swallowed immediately.

The strangest of all the superstitions concerning the pelican is that it supposedly fed its chicks on its own blood after it had deliberately injured its breast with its bill. This fable has been somehow linked to Jesus Christ's suffering on the cross. In the heraldry of the Middle Ages, the pelican therefore became regarded as a symbol of mercy and piety. The origin of this strange fable is said to have arisen from the way the pelican's scoop-bill is rested on its chest. It is clear that the scholars of the Middle Ages made no attempt to study the biology of the pelican, or they would have reached quite different conclusions. Pelicans start incubating with the first egg, and lay the rest of the clutch at staggered intervals. This means that the oldest chicks have an unfair advantage over their siblings, and they mercilessly attack the younger ones until they succumb. Seldom indeed does a younger chick survive Big Brother's attacks, just like cainism, the Cain and Abel syndrome of a number of eagle species.

We have two species of pelican in southern Africa, the Great White and the Pink-backed Pelicans, with largely overlapping African ranges. The Great White extends into southern Europe, the Middle East, up to the Indian sub-continent, Malaysia and as far as China. The more uniform, less contrasty Pink-backed Pelican reaches the Middle East and Madagascar. These ranges are made possible by considerable powers of flight, and pelicans sometimes have to fly at least 160 km per day, a round-trip to feed chicks, at sites like North America's Great Salt Lake, or East Africa's Great Rift Valley. Although pelicans struggle to take off, they are decidedly different once in the air. Pelicans sit high on the water, and this is the clue. They are light-boned, and an amazing system of air sacs links through their bones and under their skins. The Brown Pelican found off North and South America has this best developed, for it is the only diving pelican, and has special air sacs like those of gannets to cushion the shock of their successive 10 m dives into the sea. They are too buoyant to disappear under the surface, but seize their prey as gannets do. The shock of the impact can be heard a kilometre away, and apparently stuns fish.

When fishing, the Great White Pelicans have a precision team-work operation, driving fish ahead of a horse-shoe formation until they can attack them simultaneously in the shallows, with a success rate of about 20%. Brown *et al.* (1982) describe the simultaneous flipping wings open and plunging their bills in among the trapped fish at intervals of 15–20 seconds, sometimes longer. A Great White Pelican was found freshly dead at St Lucia, choked by a Spotted Grunter fish weighing 3,8 kg, one-third of the pelican's weight (Cyrus 1989). The Pink-backed Pelican occasionally fishes communally, but habitually fishes singly (Brown *et al.* 1982). It swims with head held high above the water, looking for fish. When some are spotted, it draws its head down to almost between the wings, and advances very slowly till within range to strike the prey (Ginn 1989).

Great White Pelicans breed on islands, with rudimentary nests, but Pink-backed Pelicans make substantial stick-nests in tree colonies, though small for the size of the bird (Steyn 1996). Tarboton (2001) indicates all regular pelican breeding sites in southern Africa, few indeed. Great White Pelicans appear to have minimal displays, but those of the Pink-backed are impressive. The male selects a nest-site and has two advertising displays: the first involves rapid clappering with the bill, and the second is displaying the red interior and yellow exterior of the bill to other pelicans (Ginn 1989). Pink-backed chicks which fall from nests

**Left:** The *Pink-backed Pelican* (Pelecanus rufescens) *is duller than the Great White Pelican.* (Photo: Fanie Hendriks)
**Below:** *White Pelicans* (P. onocrotalus) *becoming restive on a close approach.* (Photo: Nollie Zaloumis)

are never fed on the ground by their parents, but are preyed on by large predators like lions. Great White Pelican nest-sites should be left strictly alone, as the pelicans are very nervous (Steyn 1996). They have the same nest-site requirements as flamingoes, and have recently become a serious threat to flamingoes in Kenya, not actively, but simply by their passive presence causing desertions.

# STORKS

## FAMILY CICONIIDAE

One of the most charming fables of all time involves one of the world's favourite birds: the White Stork. We all know that it doesn't actually bring babies, but we enjoy pretending it does. France is the exception to the rule, as the White Stork is there not a favourite bird. Although White Storks were prolific breeders in France, as commonly as in the Netherlands, Germany, Poland or Denmark for example, they no longer breed in France, and France is the poorer for it. Storks have an ancient fossil history, at least 50 million years. World-wide, there are at least 17 species of storks still living, although with one decidedly aberrant species, 18 species are probably valid, and one of our leading experts considers there to be 19. In comparison, there are more than 20 extinct stork species (Austin 1962).

Storks in general have long straight bills, sometimes slightly bent upwards (recurved), or slightly bent downward (decurved). Their legs are typically long,

**1:** *Saddle-bill Stork* (Ephippiorhynchus senegalensis) *pair fishing in fast-flowing stream.* (Photo: Martin Goetz)
**2:** *Saddle-bill Stork flying over Moremi grassland.* (Photo: Clem Haagner)
**3:** *White Stork* (Ciconia ciconia) *dusty in winter quarters.* (Photo: Eliot Lyons)

**1:** *Nearly adult Marabou Stork* (Leptoptilos crumeniferus) *showing 'whitewashing'. This is deliberate defecation onto its highly vascular legs to assist in cooling its body temperature.*
**2:** *Black Stork* (Ciconia nigra) *fishing while wading in shallow water.*
**3:** *Woolly-necked Stork* (C. episcopus) *wading in mud and shallow water.*
(Photos: Eliot Lyons)

with three forward-pointing toes still joined by a partial web, and a back-toe which is at a higher level than the front three. They have no comb on the middle toe like herons, nor patches of powder-down feathers, the only family in their order to lack these. Due to muscles in their syrinx being either absent or poorly developed, as a family they tend to be mute, but most make up for it by clappering their bills. Storks fly with both neck and legs outstretched, except for the Marabou Storks, which only fly with neck outstretched for short distances, otherwise retracted as in the case of the Shoebill Stork, which probably justifies its own family. The Marabou's long bill is 'surprisingly light' (Brown *et al.* 1982).

First, according to Kahl's new stork classification as adopted by Brown *et al.* (1982), is our Yellow-billed Stork, with bill slightly decurved, and face and forehead bare. Its bill is highly tactile, capable of extremely rapid reaction when encountering prey in muddy or opaque water. It is one of our stork species with an annual pair-bond, and nests colonially in trees. Two close relatives occur in Asia and one in America.

Next is our African Open-billed Stork, blackish-brown in colour, glossed green and purple in breeding plumage, with a black-and-white relative in Asia. Since Livingstone's visit in the 1850s, it is known to nest in enormous colonies on the Zambezi. Both openbill species develop a large matching gap midway in the mandibles, so that one can see right through the bill from either side. The function of this gap is not clear, for contrary to its appearance it does not seem to be used to open or hold its snail or mussel prey (Masterson 1989a). These molluscs are held in the bill tips, and opened underwater, where the details cannot be seen. It appears that the snail is pinned down with the tip of the upper mandible, while the blade-like lower mandible is inserted between the operculum and shell, cutting the columellar muscle so that the snail is removed with the shell almost intact. When feeding on freshwater mussels, the lower mandible is inserted near the hinge to cut the adductor muscle, so that the mussel can be easily eaten, shell again almost intact (Brown *et al.* 1982). Supposed leaving of mussels in the sun to open is doubted.

Our Black Stork appears to be more plentiful than

previously suspected, though declining more in Europe (Brown *et al*. 1982, Tarboton 1989c, 2001). It is primarily a shallow-water fisherman, nesting solitarily on cliffs, and once on a Hamerkop's nest, but regularly on large raptor nests, most often building its own stick-nest. Unlike the White Stork, the Black Stork shuns the haunts of man (Thomson 1964). A nest discovered in 1941 in Botswana was still in use in 1978 (Steyn 1996).

Abdim's Stork is clearly smaller but similar to the Black Stork, and an inter-African migrant which does not breed with us. Its food is large insects like grasshoppers, locusts and crickets, as well as army worms. One Abdim's Stork, captured near Harare for ringing, had survived being shot through the body with an arrow of central African manufacture, over 1 000 km away (Masterson 1989b). The arrowhead had a blade about 2,5 cm wide and about 7,5 cm long, with a shaft another 7,5 cm long. The arrow had entered the stork's back, and the point was protruding from next to the breast-bone. The stork also carried an airgun pellet in its pectoral muscle, but was in good health, and after arrow-removal flew off none the worse for its experiences.

The attractive Woolly-necked Stork is a rare breeder in southern Africa, first recorded at Mtunzini in 1953 (Tarboton 2001), and in Zimbabwe in 1970 (Steyn 1996). Its scientific name *episcopus* is derived from the soft curly neck-feathers, reminiscent of the rabbit fur trimming used to adorn the robes of French bishops (Masterson 1989c). The small solitary nest is well concealed inside a densely foliaged tree (Tarboton 2001), and there is apparently no sibling aggression, runts being fledged up to 10 days after other chicks have flown (Brown *et al*. 1982).

White Storks have an ancient association with man, and probably the earliest reference is the Biblical comments on its African migrations. Since at least the early Middle Ages they have been encouraged to nest on houses in Europe (Austin 1962) and huts in North Africa (Brown *et al*. 1982). There is even an ancient breeding record for Scotland, but regrettably a marked twentieth-century decline in Europe (Thomson 1964). Some nests have been used for centuries: one in use in 1549 was still occupied in 1930, and another nest removed from a cathedral weighed 800 kg (Steyn 1996). With the convenience of nesting on houses, many nestlings have been ringed and valuable data obtained (Milstein 1982). A genetic migrational divide from Kempen in the Netherlands to the Bavarian Alps was determined, with western storks flying south-west to Gibraltar, and eastern storks flying south-east to Suez. Nestlings transposed experimentally over this line migrated in the 'wrong' direction, for example flying into the Alps instead of to Suez. Large soaring birds like storks fly overland if possible to benefit from thermals.

**Right:** *Open-billed Stork* (Anastomus lamelligerus) *wading. Note the gap between mandible and maxilla.*
**Below:** *Yellow-billed Stork* (Mycteria ibis) *laughing, or is it a yawn?*
(Photos: Eliot Lyons)

Tarboton (2001) documents the first South African nest near Oudtshoorn (1933–1941), and subsequent nests from 1961 at Bredasdorp and in the southern Cape. Steyn (1996) describes an injured female at Tygerberg Zoo, which successfully mated with a wild male. A Bredasdorp-hatched chick was recovered on the Tanzanian border, at least 3 300 km away (Brown *et al*. 1982), which ended speculation over what such chicks would do. Fidelity to winter quarters is also proven, with a known White Stork which responded to specific calls visiting a farm near Kadoma, Zimbabwe for at least six successive years (Masterton 1989d).

Saddle-billed Storks are large and spectacular, and sexes can be distinguished by a brown iris in the male and yellow in the female. They are described as 'the tallest African stork ... as large as a Marabou' (Brown *et al*. 1982), but this is doubtful as the Marabou Stork is longer and with a greater wingspan. Probably the handsomer, slimmer and more graceful Saddle-bill gives a misleading size impression. They appear to be completely silent, although their close relative, the Black-necked Stork (Asia to Australia), is reported to clapper. Lack of spectacular displays or breeding coloration is probably due to a permanent pair-bond. It nests singly right on top of tall trees. A fisherman, it is capable of swallowing at least a 500 g catfish, snipping off the sharp spines before swallowing (Brown *et al*. 1982).

Our largest stork, the Marabou, has a diet ranging from termite alates to elephant carcasses (Brown *et al*. 1982). They breed only at one locality in southern Africa, the Okavango, where they occupy mixed tree colonies, taking up the highest positions. Because they have an annual pair-bond, they develop spectacular plumage and 'soft parts', with displays like inflation of the large air sacs. The attractive white undertail coverts, 'marabou down', were in commercial demand (Steyn 1996) for the iniquitous millinery trade. Marabous join vultures at kills and steal scraps, but are careful not to rob the 'king' Lappet-faced Vultures. In turn, piratical eagles like the Tawny Eagle rob Marabous. These storks walk along the water's edge, causing panicking flamingoes to bunch tightly together. Then, after a short flight, a flamingo is stabbed in the back. The disabled flamingo is then drowned, and torn to pieces in 3–4 minutes by one or more storks. As discussed under flamingoes, mass colony desertions readily take place.

The unmistakable Shoebill Stork appears to be more closely related to storks than any other bird. Although it should probably be classified in its own family immediately after the storks, in view of pending finalization and what appear to be puzzling doubts as to a perfectly valid sighting in suitable habitat of two Shoebills by Mathews (1979) in the Okavango's Moremi, I am including this species here in the Ciconiidae for the present and as a reminder to birders.

Finally, Masterson (1989b) describes an interesting habit unique to storks. This is the deliberate release of excrement alternately onto their highly vascularized legs to cool their body temperature. Dependent on the application frequency of this excretion, the legs become 'white-washed', though obviously soon washed off wading storks. I admit to having missed this remarkable habit until Phil Kahl pointed it out to me many years ago at Barberspan.

# FRIGATEBIRDS
## FAMILY FREGATIDAE

Described by experts as the most easily recognized of all seabirds as a family, the five species of frigatebirds are remarkably similar, and all classified in the same genus. They are characterized by long slender bills clearly hooked, short necks and a slender body with remarkable wings of up to 2,44 m in wingspread (Harrison 1983). These disproportionately long and sharply pointed wings are excellently adapted for dynamic flying, with only occasional deep wingbeats, and aided by unusually deeply-forked tails for steering and braking. Their flight is described in superlatives by experts like Harrison (1983), describing their remarkable aerial manoeuvres, and Austin (1962) assessing this as 'little short of miraculous'. Audubon, the famous early American

*A male Frigatebird* (Fregata minor) *on his territorial perch, with gular pouch partly blown up. He sits displaying there until a female accepts him, and commences bringing him sticks.* (Photo: Tony Heald)

ornithologist, considered them to be in the same class as the Peregrine Falcon as exceptional masters of flight.

Frigatebirds soar ostensibly motionless by the hour, hanging effortless and steadily in the sky, but then in an instant are able with bursts of unbelievable speed to fly rings around other seabirds, intimidating victims by various bullying techniques into disgorging their fish prey as indicated by Austin (1962), Stonehouse (1964c) and other observers. Brown *et al.* (1982) indicate that part of the answer is the decidedly long wings sharply bent at the carpal joint with a high aspect ratio. Together with adaptations like their powerful pectoral muscles, their extremely light bones and linked air-sacs, frigatebirds are remarkably suited to prolonged effortless soaring or swift attacks. Although Austin (1962) and others have indicated that the frigatebirds have lower wingloadings than any other bird, it is probably safer in the relative dearth of comparable studies to restrict this to 'any other seabird', following Brown *et al.* (1982).

It must be emphasized that the remarkably versatile frigatebirds are not obligatory 'pirates' or klepto-parasites, but that this is only one aspect of their prey spectrum. One leading authority on the family has pointed out that frigatebirds are found in tropical and subtropical oceanic areas where flying fish are abundant (Stonehouse 1964c). When their shoals are attacked by schools of predatory fish like tuna or mammals like dolphins, fleeing flying fish take to the air, and are masterfully snatched by the hovering frigatebirds. Additional prey items include various fish species, stranded fish, jellyfish, squid, hatchlings of sea-turtles, etc. Refuse is also expertly snapped up from the sea (Stonehouse 1964c), as with sticks and feathers for nests, and Austin (1962) stresses how neatly this is done without even a ripple, or getting a drop of water on their plumage. Even the chicks of other frigatebirds become prey if not zealously guarded. Consequently, Harrison (1983) has ample justification for his statement that, while obviously conceding piracy, this may be overstated in the literature.

The price paid by the frigatebirds for this superlative flying ability involves less mobility on the ground, with relatively puny legs and feet, and reduced waterproofing of plumage (Stonehouse 1964c). Even buoys are utilized to compensate for this ineptitude, permitting easier take-off from their nests, and Austin (1962) emphasizes that they can only shuffle along clumsily, or climb to a high-enough place to take off. Their feet are not well-suited to swimming, but more to perching, with only remnants of webs joining all four toes, and sharp claws. Obviously little inclined to the possibility of fossil formation by their life-styles, these web remnants are now controversial, though generally still accepted as evidence of their inclusion in the Pelecaniformes. Ryan (2002) has queried this classification as incorrect on recent molecular evidence, suggesting that frigatebirds are more closely related to albatrosses, petrels, divers and penguins. Further controversy occurs with their reduced waterproofing. Wanless (2002) states flatly and erroneously that they 'have no waterproofing', exaggerating this to state that 'if they land in the sea, they drown'. A proper assessment is for example Stonehouse (1964c), who states that they 'seldom settle on the water as their oil-glands are small, and their plumage rapidly becomes saturated'.

Although they nest in trees and shrubs by preference, they can and do nest successfully on the ground if this vegetation is not available. The incubation period is also controversial, 44–55 days according to Brown *et al.* (1982), but most doubtfully 'around three months' (Wanless 2002). Stonehouse (1964c) stresses that frigatebirds, unlike most seabirds, tend to remain close to their breeding grounds throughout the year. Although single wanderers have been reported well over 800 km from the nearest land, he points out that the presence of several frigatebirds together has long been recognized by sailors as a sign that land is near. Although they are almost constantly airborne, Stokes (1968) agrees, stating that they 'are not in any way pelagic birds, seldom seen away from the tropical islands they frequent'. Harrison (1983) stresses that they are strictly diurnal, roosting on islands at night. Yet in contrast, Wanless (2002) unacceptably states that frigatebirds 'travel vast distances from their roosting sites', and even that they 'are capable of sleeping on the wing over the sea', without any evidence indicated. This is still a puzzle even with the much better-known swifts.

Harrison (1983) emphasizes that at sea identification of frigatebirds is notoriously complex, and 'represents, perhaps, the most difficult identification challenge in any seabird group'. He gives tips on their identification well worth consulting, and largely lacking in field-guides. Even a spectacular glossy black male with grossly distended scarlet gular pouch, sitting guarding his nest-site and displaying until a female accepts him and commences bringing him sticks, is not easily distinguished to species level. Males are always smaller and darker than females. Young frigatebirds are particularly difficult, with intergrading age groups.

In conclusion, it is little known that, on some of the archipelagos in the central Pacific Ocean, frigatebirds are tamed for a specific purpose. They are used, like homing pigeons, to carry messages from island to island (Stonehouse 1964c).

# PENGUINS

## FAMILY SPHENISCIDAE

The group name 'penguin' was transferred by sailors about 200 years ago from the extinct flightless Great Auk of the northern hemisphere, which disappeared due to a combination of volcanic explosions in its core area and merciless butchering of the survivors by man. Austin (1962) points out that the scientific name is derived from the Greek, and refers to the narrow flipper-like wings: useless for flying, marvellous for swimming, and quite effective for battering the shins of human visitors to their nest-grounds. Confined to the southern hemisphere, the centre of penguin abundance is the southern oceans between South America, Africa, Australia and the Antarctic pack-ice, from the Galapagos south to the icy realms of the Emperor and Adèlie Penguins.

Their lack of flight-feathers is unique among birds with keeled breastbones, but these and the brief appearance of wing-quills early in their embryonic life prove undoubtedly that they are descended from flying ancestors about 100 million years ago. The flippers are joined only at the shoulder and the lack of an 'elbow' is also unique (Austin 1962). Fossils show that penguins were well established and differentiated similar to today over much of their present range 50 million years ago. This was by the early Tertiary period, when modern birds had only recently started to develop. Austin (1962) indicates that over 20 fossil species similar to modern penguins are known, but with proportionately longer wings and legs. The plant and invertebrate fossils found with them indicate that these ancestral penguins lived under warm, possibly subtropical, conditions. Some of these early penguins were over 20% larger than the Emperor Penguin.

Penguins have amply compensated for their loss of flight by their superb swimming skills, which rival those

*Jackass Penguins* (Spheniscus demersus) *at their nests, one of our six 'African' penguins.* (Photo: Allan Batchelor)

of seals and dolphins, and are unquestionably the most truly marine of all birds, ideally adapted for pelagic life (Austin 1962). Harrison (1983) emphasizes their high degree of specialization, including that they differ from most seabirds in their layer of blubber and the thick coat of modified feathers. Their stiff closely-packed feathers grow all over the body, instead of the usual clearly-demarcated feather tracts, to form a thick insulating mat with a smooth shiny surface that is impervious to water, and offers little resistance to the bird's passage through it. Harrison (1983) endorses Austin's (1962) description of high speed under water: 'literally flying through the water, often at great speed, when they porpoise out of the water to breathe'. Austin (1962) emphasizes that they get all their motive power from their short powerful flippers, and that their sturdy webbed feet, placed at the extremity of their bodies, are used for steering (endorsed by Gill (1945): 'chiefly'), but must also supply some motive power as when tobogganing.

Austin (1962) watched Adèlie Penguins easily outdistance a ship cruising at 16 knots, and states that the underwater speed of penguins has been estimated to be well in excess of 40 kph. Penguins prefer swimming underwater to on the surface, where they swim with heads just visible, and sometimes the back exposed or tail cocked. When a ship approaches, they dive (Harrison 1983). Penguins can propel themselves so fast that they are able to shoot out of the water and land on an inaccessible rock or ice-pan 2 m and more above the surface. Yet, when underwater, feeding penguins dart among schools of fish and shrimps with the ability of bats in the air (Austin 1962). The remarkable Emperor Penguin can dive to depths of 265 m, and remain submerged for up to nine minutes (Harrison 1983). Penguins do not know how to feed on land, feeding mainly on fish, squid and shrimps underwater, and those captured for zoos or rehabilitation have to be force-fed for weeks before learning to pick up fish thrown to them.

*A Jackass Penguin on his nest viciously threatens an intruder.*
(Photo: Darrel Plowes)

They leave the sea only to breed and moult, and subsist then on stored blubber.

Harrison's (1983) classification of 16 species divided into six genera is followed here, all typical stocky penguins with dark upperparts and white (to pale in the smallest species) underparts. He regards them as most closely related to the petrels and shearwaters of the family Procellariidae, but as highly specialized species in their own right. The first penguin on our list is the King Penguin, rarely reported here, at 95 cm the second largest penguin, but more brightly coloured than the Emperor Penguin, together comprising the genus *Aptenodytes*. Then we have two of the three *Pygoscelis* penguins: the 81 cm Gentoo with white head-markings, and the plain black-and-white Adèlie (70 cm). Of the five *Eudyptes* penguins, we have the circumpolar species, the Rockhopper and Macaroni Penguins, both crested 'hopper' penguins.

Finally, we have two of the four *Spheniscus* species: one our Jackass Penguin (known by this name without exception from the very first South African bird-books), and the other one almost certainly a ship-assisted immigrant to the Cape Town Docks. This is the Magellan or Magellanic Penguin, similar to the Jackass Penguin but clearly distinguishable. This small genus is the best-adapted of all penguins to a warm climate; the closely related Galapagos Penguin is even found near the equator. Our Jackass Penguins breed where possible in a hole excavated in the ground, and usually lay 2–3 eggs. These eggs were formerly collected commercially on our guano islands for gourmets, but with the greatly increased threat of catastrophic oil-pollution by supertankers, particularly to non-flying seabirds which must swim through this curse to breathe, has been wisely discontinued. Illogically, the internationally accepted and apt name of Jackass Penguin must now suddenly give way to a brand-new name, African Penguin, at someone's silly whim, because, of our six species of African penguins, it is the only one which breeds here. So whenever you hear the loud donkey-like braying of the Jackass 'African' Penguin, particularly at night (Sinclair, Hockey & Tarboton 2002), please ignore it and be fashionable rather than sensible, you have your wires crossed.

To conclude with fascination rather than frustration, the account by Austin (1962) is still one of the best of a remarkable breeding event: the breeding of the Emperor Penguin in the howling blizzards of the Antarctic winter. Like the King Penguin, the Emperor makes no nest at all, but incubates standing vertically upright, with the single egg held under a fold of insulated belly-skin on its feet. However, the Emperor Penguin is probably the only bird never (or very rarely) to set foot on dry land. Off the icy coast of the Antarctic continent, it spends much of its time feeding in the krill-rich waters of the broken off-shore icepack. It commences its breeding cycle in autumn rather than spring, coming ashore in late March, which is autumn in the southern hemisphere, and heading over the ice for the precise spot where the colony bred the year before. Here they go through their courtship displays, and in May, just as the sun is setting for the long Antarctic winter, the female lays her single egg. The male takes over immediately, and the female heads off to feed, having spent some eight weeks on the barren ice.

The abandoned males, gathered together into large 'pods', each still holding his precious egg, prepare for winter's onslaught. Ambient temperatures during June and July fall to –60°C, with the cold intensified by winds of up to 160 kph, where any slip means a dead embryo. For nine weeks, without any relief, the male incubates his egg in pitch darkness. As soon as the chick hatches, with incredible timing as the male only has sufficient food exudate in his stomach to feed the chick for the first day or two, the female returns. Sleek, glossy, fat and full of food, she comes tobogganing over the ice faster than a man can ski. She then takes over from her mate, while the male in turn sets off for open water to feed, having lost one-third of his weight, about 11 kg. This takes him only a couple of weeks to replenish, and by the end of August he comes back in turn to help feed the chick for the next three months. Finally the young Emperor Penguin must fend for itself at the most favourable time of the year: in early December when the shore ice is melting and the Antarctic summer just commencing.

ORDER PROCELLARIIFORMES

# STORM-PETRELS

## FAMILY HYDROBATIDAE

In the new Roberts VII classification followed here, the storm-petrels are now placed first of the four families in the order Procellariiformes, and the former family name Hydrobatidae retained in preference to Oceanitidae. Authorities like Harrison (1983) and Maclean (1993) rejected the name Hydrobatidae in favour of Oceanitidae for the storm-petrels. The Hydrobatidae are the smallest family of their order, with eight genera and about 20 species. In general they form two main groups, corresponding with subfamilies, one in each hemisphere, with some overlap in the tropics. The southern group comprises the genera *Oceanites*, *Garrodia*, *Pelagodroma*, *Fregatta* and *Nesofregatta*, characterized by long legs, short toes, rounded wings and square tails. The northern group includes *Hydrobates*, *Halocyptema* and *Oceanodroma*, with short legs, long toes, forked tails and (usually) longer, more pointed wings.

The plumage of both groups is generally black or dark brown, some with white on rump or underparts, paler below. Storm-petrels consequently provide one of the greatest identification challenges. The slight distinguishing characteristics between species are hard to see at any distance, although the group is well known to sailors. They often follow in the wake of ships, feeding on tiny marine life brought to the surface by propellers: plankton and even galley scrapes, particularly if fatty. Some storm-petrels are abundant and found in several oceans, while some are confined to one area where they are locally abundant. Some are migratory, for example Wilson's Storm-petrel breeds in Antarctica, and migrates to sub-Arctic oceans of the northern hemisphere. Seven storm-petrel species figure on the southern African list, but due to the aforementioned

*Wilson's Storm-petrels* (Oceanites oceanicus) *flying extremely low over the sea and patting the water surface with their feet.* (Photo: Allan Batchelor)

identification problems, this is probably incomplete. Brown *et al*. (1982) consider nine species probable.

Storm-petrels definitely incorporate the smallest seabirds in the world: of the 20 species the largest is only 25 cm long, and the smallest has a wing-span of only 30 cm, little larger than a swallow. Yet they are typical pelagic seabirds, and only return to their nest-islands to breed. For the rest of the year, they roam the open seas. When storm-petrels rest on the ocean surface, due to their buoyancy they sit high in the water. Usually, however, they flutter restlessly around, close to the water surface with irregular bat-like wing-beats, and apparently are capable of sustained flight over considerable distances. Even in severe storms, the storm-petrels choose to fly continuously and challenge the elements. Amazingly they shelter in the hollows of the waves themselves for protection. Regrettably, sometimes in exceptionally severe storms, large numbers of storm-petrels are dashed against the shore in so-called 'wrecks'. In misty weather these birds are also sometimes dazzled by the lights of ships, and 'rain' in large numbers onto the decks. In general, however, it is clear that these tiniest of seabirds are outstandingly adapted to their stormy environment, and are aptly named. They appear to be as active by night as by day.

Austin (1962) emphasizes that probably no seabirds are the subject of more folklore, legends and myths than the little storm-petrels. They are so-called from the ancient sailor superstition that their presence presages a storm. This is not precisely true, but they do suddenly appear around ships at sea at the onset of windy weather, whether day or night, seemingly from nowhere. The sudden influx can involve large numbers, and is accompanied by their soft twittering. The name petrel is thought to be a diminutive of St Peter, who walked on water with the Saviour's help. This is derived from their habit of snatching tiny food particles from the surface of the sea without alighting. When they do this, they flutter close to the water's surface and pat the water with their feet, sometimes both feet together, but more often alternately which gives the illusion that they are walking. Infrequently but occasionally, they dip under the surface of the sea for a morsel. Sailors collectively call storm-petrels by the unusual name of 'Mother Carey's chickens', derived from 'Mater Cara' the Virgin Mary, guardian of all seafarers.

Despite their tiny size, storm-petrels are outstandingly adapted for marine life with their manoeuvrability and utilization of the sea's rich plankton resources. They sometimes occur in enormous numbers where such food is plentiful, especially near their breeding grounds, but also singly or in small groups. One authority has even alleged that the Wilson's Storm-petrel is the most plentiful single bird species in the world. However, their size makes them particularly vulnerable to predators like skuas and gulls, and they consequently spend the day silently in their tiny burrows or rock crevices on their breeding grounds, or stay out at sea. However, at dusk a dramatic change takes place. Under one's very feet, thousands of storm-petrels may stand twittering at the mouths of their burrows. This is to guide their incoming mates to their home burrows by their calls, so that they can be relieved from incubation duties and go off to feed. Incubation sessions last 2–4 days. Only one small egg is laid, but remarkably long incubation periods of 5,5–7 weeks are the norm (Austin 1962). The contrast between this dusk peak of activity continuing less frantically until dawn, and the silence and unobtrusiveness during daylight hours is staggering. Storm-petrels have relatively weak legs, so that they walk on their full tarsi aided by their wings. Similarly, without wind they may struggle to become airborne.

In conclusion, this order Procellariiformes consists of 23 genera and about 93 species, ranging in size from large albatrosses to the storm-petrels. All have nostrils extended in two tubes either together on top of the mandible or singly along the sides ('tube-noses'). The bills are always hooked, divided into plates separated by grooves (Harrison 1983). One family, the Pelecanoididae, comprising one genus and four species, is border-line with us, but will receive brief mention. The reason is that the Common Diving-petrel *Pelecanoides urinatrix*, the most widespread of this basically Antarctic genus, was formerly on the southern African list but has been removed. Since it appears to be only a question of time before it is re-admitted, its existence merits attention. It bears a striking resemblance to the Little Auk *Alle alle* (Alcidae) of the Arctic, glossy black dorsally and white ventrally, with a short bill and tail, and flies fast with whirring wings. Harrison (1983) considers this to be an excellent example of convergent evolution.

# ALBATROSSES
## FAMILY DIOMEDEIDAE

Almost a 'traditional' classification of all albatrosses into two genera, *Diomedea* (11 species) and *Phoebetria* (two species) has been expanded under strong phylogenetic influence in Roberts VII to 15 species in South African waters alone: a split to four *Diomedea* species for the great albatrosses, with the smaller albatrosses (mollymawks) placed in *Thalassarche* (8 species), except for the Laysan Albatross split into *Phoebastria*. A good example may be the Chatham Albatross (Ryan 2001) – possibly a species phylogenetically on far better grounds than most, or a clear biological subspecies or even species dependent on data. The albatross family has been known generally to seafarers for centuries, at least since the fifteenth century, when the Portuguese navigators commenced sailing southward along the coast of Africa. They called these strange long-winged birds 'alcatraz', Portuguese for 'large seabirds'. Corrupted into English as 'albatross', it has been used in this form ever since.

Albatrosses are undoubtedly the best gliders in the world, with their long narrow wings supremely adapted to the up-draughts from the waves (Austin 1962). However, they are not suited to flapping flight, and may

*Wandering Albatross* (Diomedea exulans): *generally credited with having the largest wingspan of living birds.* (Photo: Allan Batchelor)

be hampered by a flat calm. He also emphasizes that, given sufficient wind, they travel in any direction, upwind as well as down, with hardly a wingstroke. Contrary to public opinion, it appears that the Wandering Albatross, the world's largest albatross species, may not have the world's largest wingspan, being slightly exceeded by the Great White Pelican at 3,60 m (Harrison 1983), 9 cm longer. However, a proper statistical analysis would be necessary to decide the issue. With these remarkably shaped aerofoil wings, the albatrosses obviously prefer windy weather. Their appearance in large numbers, particularly at the onset of stormy weather, has made sailors decidedly superstitious concerning albatrosses, which were regarded as the spirits of drowned sailors.

Stretching across the Atlantic and Pacific oceans at the equator is a broad strip of sea that is relatively windless, known as the doldrums. This has been proved to be a formidable northward barrier to albatrosses in general. Albatross distributions have been largely governed by the prevailing wind patterns over the world's oceans. Too few southern albatrosses have penetrated this barrier in recent times to establish themselves north of it. Yet a Pliocene fossil albatross from England has proven that albatrosses were found there previously, prior to the last ice age. The greatest concentration of albatrosses is found in the southern latitudes with some circumpolar including the largest species, three found in the northern Pacific, and one found breeding in the Galapagos and extending seasonally to equatorial South America. A strong indication of the southern hemisphere origin of these north Pacific albatrosses is the fact that even these three species nest during the southern hemisphere spring and summer (Harrison 1983), which is October to April. Recent sightings of both Yellow-nosed and Black-browed Albatrosses suggest that some at least reach the northern Atlantic (Harrison 1983), but he points out that assisted passage cannot be ruled out. A Black-browed Albatross first seen in 1860 in the Faroe Islands travelled annually with a flock of gannets to winter off Britain, returning to the Faroes each spring (Austin 1962) till stupidly shot in 1894, and is now gracing a Copenhagen museum.

All the Procellariiformes lay a single white egg in burrows or clefts, except for the albatrosses, which nest in the open. In the southern albatrosses the egg is laid on a concave mound of mud or soil lined with grass or feathers, but in the northern Pacific representatives the nest is little more than a hollow scraped in the ground. In the great albatrosses the breeding cycle can extend to longer than a calendar year, so that they breed every second year. Incubated by both sexes, the egg is not replaced should anything happen to it, and the pair will only breed again the following year. Their strange courtship antics continue throughout the breeding season. The great albatrosses commence breeding only in their ninth or tenth years, smaller species probably in their sixth or seventh years. Harrison (1983) describes how both sexes incubate, and emphasizes the remarkable way both also feed their chick. Albatross parents are able to convert their squid and other prey into a rich oily substance to be later regurgitated from their stomachs, without deterioration. This tremendous advantage gives them an immense foraging range. He states that some parents have been found 3 200 km from their chicks, which are capable in turn of swallowing 1,8 kg of regurgitated oil in one meal. This long-lived species can fly incredible distances. At 40° S the distance around the world is about 30 400 km, so a projection assuming non-breeding would enable the Wandering Albatross to fly 181 times around the world in its lifetime. This amazing feat explains how this species can follow even fast ships for days without any visible effort.

Albatrosses had few enemies until the late nineteenth century, when man's greedy profit motive reared its ugly head. Limited 'fishing' for albatrosses with baited hooks had taken place since the days of sailing-ships by hungry or bored sailors, but this was minor. Ships replenishing provisions from isolated large colonies took both albatrosses and their large eggs, but these were sporadic raids, not the purposeful eradication which came later. Albatrosses with their fearless, trusting and amusing behaviour became great favourites among the armed forces stationed on Pacific island bases like Midway. Here the troops had to be forced to destroy eggs and as many as 30 000 albatrosses which caused collisions with war-planes and later jet aircraft in particular. On the other hand, starving Japanese troops eradicated all the albatrosses before being dislodged from the famous Wake Island colony, so that for at least 15 years none bred at this key site (Austin 1962). Today albatross populations are threatened by modern long-line fishing techniques, and may be heading for extinction (e.g. Petersen 2003, Ryan 2004). Not yet conclusively proven, helpless albatross chicks may even be eaten alive by introduced mice (Cooper 2004).

However, undoubtedly the most shocking episode in the albatross saga remains the incredible slaughter for the feather trade, the decoration of women's hats in the late nineteenth century. Literally many millions of breeding albatrosses were killed for this purpose. The flight-feathers were utilized for hats, and the body-feathers called 'swan's down' to stuff mattress and cushions.

The great numbers of Short-tailed Albatrosses were only discovered in 1740 by Steller on his journey with Bering across Siberia to the Pacific, yet by 1933 they were already considered extinct. To widespread delight, a small group of Short-tailed Albatrosses appeared in 1953 out of the blue, and commenced breeding on Tori Shima, a small volcanic island 580 km south of Tokyo. These albatrosses were declared a national monument, protected by the Japanese weathermen stationed on the island. Tori Shima was formerly the site of the largest colony of Short-tailed Albatrosses, and is still the only certain breeding site, although another site is suspected but requires confirmation. According to calculations, 5 million Short-tailed Albatrosses were slaughtered on Tori Shima between 1887 and 1903 alone (Harrison 1983).

# Petrels and Shearwaters
## Family Procellariidae

This is the largest and most diverse family of the Procellariiformes, the last family of this order. Hereafter remain only the numerous perching birds of the final order Passeriformes. Bill structure differs from the albatrosses with the nostrils united in a single tube placed on top of the culmen. All members of this order have a distinctive musky body odour, which clings to preserved museum specimens for decades. These and other anatomical and behavioural features distinguish this family from all bird groups, and they have no near relatives (Austin 1962). Their fossil record goes back to the Eocene, and Austin suspected Cretaceous ancestors up to 100 million years and more ago.

This family shows a wide range in size, from the giant-petrels, which are the size of small albatrosses, to the little prions or whale-birds, only 25–30 cm long, and usually less than 60 cm in wingspan. Harrison (1983) stated that prion taxonomy is not fully agreed on: they were formerly treated as 5–6 species, but hybridization may indicate only three species of *Pachyptila*. However, with only two undoubted sibling species of giant-petrel (up to 99 cm in length), one monomorphic and the other with a 10% white morph, even sympatric occurrence occurs. Correlated with the large size of these two species, they are the only petrels to feed on land though with a clearly different jizz, and Harrison (1983) aptly describes them as 'ungainly and uncouth scavengers'.

Apart from the two giant-petrel species already mentioned, next on the southern African list is the Southern Fulmar, congeneric with the Northern Fulmar found north of our limits and which showed remarkable proliferation in recent times. Then come two monogeneric species, first the Antarctic Petrel, larger and duller than the handsome spotted Pintado Petrel. Next is the world's only small white petrel, the monogeneric Snow Petrel, confined to pack-ice and adjacent Antarctic seas. This is followed in our waters by 26 or 27 species of *Pterodroma* petrels, often referred to as the 'gadfly' petrels, and which may link the fulmars to this group. Then comes the Kerguelen Petrel, now classified in Roberts VII as *Lugensa* rather than *Pterodroma*, and which has even been suspected of being a melanistic form of Gould's (White-winged) Petrel. Next is the Blue Petrel, resembling the prions but larger, and the only petrel with a white-tipped tail.

The prions have been briefly mentioned; all five have now been accorded species status in Roberts VII. They get their more apt alternative name (whale-birds) from

*Southern Giant-Petrel* (Macronectes giganteus) *on nest.* (Photo: Allan Batchelor)

their habit of squirting water through their bills, where a sieve holds back the tiny live organisms which sustain them. There are also three large *Procellaria* petrels listed: White-chinned, Spectacled and Grey. A valuable update on the Spectacled Petrel has been provided by Ryan (2005). This species has shown a remarkable comeback after near-extinction caused by feral pigs on their island a century ago before the pigs died out naturally. Finally there are 10 shearwaters listed from our waters: the two *Calonectris* shearwaters (intermediate between *Procellaria* and *Puffinus*) and eight *Puffinus* shearwaters. One of the latter group, the Balearic Petrel, was provisionally treated as a subspecies by Harrison (1983).

Two shearwaters are of particular interest. The first occurs as a breeding species in the northern Atlantic, and has its main wintering grounds off eastern South America, with a secondary wintering ground off South Africa. It is still known as the Manx Shearwater although it has not nested on the Isle of Man since about 1800 (Austin 1962), and may consist of more than one closely related species (Harrison 1983). Ringing studies show these shearwaters to be remarkably tied to their breeding sites, with an 'uncanny ability to return' (Austin 1962). One Manx Shearwater taken from its nest off Wales, and transported by air to Boston where it was released there over unfamiliar waters, was back in its nest-burrow 5 472 km away in 12,5 days. Another Manx is the probable holder of the world long-distance record: about 19 200 km from Britain to Australia via the shortest sea-route.

The Short-tailed Shearwater or 'Muttonbird' of Tasmania is the best-known of the family because of its great economic value, which has resulted in it being carefully studied by the Australian government (Austin 1962). Hundreds of thousands of these shearwaters nest on islands in the Bass Strait, between Australia and Tasmania, with peak counts off New South Wales of 60 000 per hour (Harrison 1983). Incubation sessions are 12–14 days before mate relief. Despite the size of the relatively small egg, the incubation period is as long as 52–55 days, and the fat chicks rapidly outweigh their parents, being abandoned to slim down at 14 weeks. It is at this stage that hundreds of thousands of the fat oily chicks are pulled from their burrows, slaughtered, hung up to drain the valuable oil, and canned as 'Tasmanian Squab', a notable delicacy. They are succulent and not 'fishy' flavoured. It must be emphasized that the harvesting is based on careful scientific research and monitoring, so that enough chicks are allowed to fly away each year to balance the annual adult mortality, and immense flocks of adults blacken the water of Bass Strait annually before going ashore to breed. The fledged chicks follow the adults by instinct on an invariable figure-of-eight route covering the north and south Pacific basins, and based on prevailing winds. They do not return for 3–4 years while they behave as non-breeding adults, and breed thereafter, usually on their natal island.

## ORDER PASSERIFORMES

*Not only is this the last order of birds, but it is also the largest, unquestionably containing the largest number of species per family in a number of cases. They include many of our best-known and most familiar birds. The passerines are also known as 'perching' birds, with a 'standard' foot: three toes pointing forward and one, the first toe or 'hallux', pointing backward, all on the same level.*

*The purpose of this book is not to discuss complicated taxonomic aspects within a basic scientific classification. However, it is essential that the global importance of the Passeriformes must be emphasized. In short, this order dominates the entire bird kingdom with approximately 60% of all bird species, and includes more than one-third of the recognized bird families. This reflects a tremendous proliferation of the bird fauna, starting about 70 million years ago. With such historically young groups, the relationships are in addition regrettably less clear.*

*Although it was possible to undertake treatment even of single species per family thus far, where the numbers of bird species per family were manageable, it was decided to modify the treatment of the families from this point. It is basically because of the comparatively large numbers of passerine bird species inevitably allocated per family. Consequently, because the passerines also tend to be better known to birders than the non-passerines, shorter discussion has also been implemented. With more illustrations also available, these images have likewise been increased in number with shorter captions.*

# PITTAS

## FAMILY PITTIDAE

Superficially the pittas resemble thrushes with extremely short tails, but are clearly distinguishable by the peculiar attachment of the syrinx and by the formation of the tarsus (Mackworth-Praed 1964). The main centre of distribution is also in the Old World tropics, with three species extending to Australia and two in Africa. In some species there is a high degree of sexual dimorphism, but in others male and female are virtually indistinguishable. Their shape, appearance and habits are remarkably constant, and all are placed together in the genus *Pitta*: 23–26 smallish, exceedingly colourful species with bright patterns.

They are a good example of an ancient family which formerly enjoyed a pan-tropical distribution over the Old World as far as the Solomon Islands. Their uniformity is exceptional: all are thick-set birds with a large head, short neck, short rounded wings, of which the outermost primary is always the longest, and 12 retrices, with some hardly recognizable as such due to their degeneration. They are

*An Angola Pitta* (Pitta angolensis) *being released after flying into lighted buildings at night.* (Photo: Darrel Plowes)

basically ground-dwellers in dense vegetation, but roost low down. They scratch among leaves in dense cover for insects, although some specialize in millipedes and others in termites, while one Australian species is even a snail-eater, and selects a particular anvil-stone to break the shells on. For most of the year, pittas are found singly or in pairs. Some are sedentary, others like our Angola Pitta are definitely migratory and attracted to powerful lights at night. Our second African pitta, the even handsomer Green-breasted Pitta, is not easily seen, and would be frequently overlooked but for its calls. All known pitta calls have some similarity, either trilling or a short series of distinct whistles. Nests are similar: large, oval, rough but with finer lining, placed low down in vegetation or actually on the ground with a side entrance. Contrary to the variable pittas themselves, egg coloration is very constant for the family: background white or cream, with reddish or purple markings underlain by speckles of lilac or grey.

# BROADBILLS
## FAMILY EURYLAIMIDAE

Whereas the pittas are largely terrestrial, and found in the forest understorey, the broadbills are rather like sluggish flycatchers which tend to perch low down in forest, and hunt aerially like flycatchers from a perch, requiring a tail to manoeuvre. Otherwise there are similarities, like the beautiful coloration so often found in forest birds, and their unusual attachment of plantar (equivalent to the sole) tendons, differing from other local passerines. Broadbills have a syrinx controlled by only one pair of muscles, and also partly-joined toes. Fourteen species are known, mostly brightly coloured, with a similar distribution to the pittas, in the Old World tropics from Africa to the Philippines.

In Africa we have four broadbill species, three of which are considered plain-coloured and aberrant. The African Broadbill is the plainest-coloured despite its white back which is puffed out during display. It tends to avoid climax forest when there are competing broadbill species (Sinclair & Ryan 2003). The similar-sized Rufous-sided Broadbill male has a more uniform black head and rufous sides, while the Grey-headed Broadbill is more similar in coloration but a larger bird. The most recently discovered broadbill in Africa, the African Green, is as green as those from Borneo except for its pale blue throat.

The African Broadbill extends further south than the brighter broadbills: to at least Port Shepstone. I have watched it push a surprisingly long even hank of nondescript plant material into a chamber through a chosen side entrance, and then build a protruding porch above this entrance. This broadbill is the probable host of the enigmatic Barred Long-tailed Cuckoo, which lays immaculate white eggs, but which however do not seem to be readily ejected from the darkish nest-chamber. Most fascinating to me is the short looping display flight while uttering a loud distinctive call described by Ginn (1989). This impressive display makes the African Broadbill unlikely to be overlooked in the breeding season. Otherwise it sits mostly slightly hunched silent on a perch, sluggishly watching for insect prey to wander into easy striking distance.

*African Broadbill* (Smithornis capensis) *clinging to its nest.* (Photo: Peter Steyn)

# Old World Orioles
## Family Oriolidae

The name 'oriole' is well known for two reasons. It is derived from the word 'aureolus', from the brilliant golden or yellow plumage of some prominent members of a small Old World family of 28 or 29 uniformly starling-sized sturdy birds, with duller dimorphic females but no unique attributes. Strikingly combined with black, this colour pattern extends to the extreme of pitch-black with the Black Oriole of Borneo. The other reason is that this name has also been applied to a much larger, less uniform family of about 87 New World species derived from bunting origins, all with nine primaries instead of 10, which will not receive further attention as they are not 'true' orioles. Only four orioles of Old World origin are not classified in *Oriolus*, due to bare skin around their eyes and markedly shorter bills. They are called 'fig-eaters' (*Sphecotheres*), and they are known for their flimsier nests.

The best-known oriole is the handsome Eurasian Golden Oriole, which is the greatest migrant in the family, with the longest wings. All Eurasian Golden Orioles migrate to south of the equator, including some to India. The African Golden Oriole shows much less black, and its overwhelming golden coloration makes it clearly the most beautiful of the 'true' orioles. The Black-headed Oriole has several similarly coloured sibling species, but is conceded to be the best songster and mimic in the family. The Green-headed Oriole is the scarcest of our four. It is most unusual in having green coloration dominating: green head and breast, green mantle and tail. It occurs only on Gorongosa Mountain in southern Africa and also a few forested localities farther north. The rarest oriole species is probably the tiny population on São Tomé Island in the Gulf of Guinea, with hardly any yellow coloration. However, Moreau (1964) has pointed out that oriole speciation has been most active in the eastern portion of the oriole distribution, which is still largely unknown. In conclusion, orioles enjoy a varied diet: insects such as hairy caterpillars, which they clean of bristles, and fruit. This applies particularly to the migratory Eurasian Golden Orioles, gorging themselves on figs. Orioles tend to spend much time in the canopies of tall trees where they are not readily seen despite their bright colours. However, their attractive clear whistles and sweet fluting are a clear indication of their presence.

*Black-headed Oriole* (Oriolus larvatus) *carrying food to its nearby chicks.* (Photo: Peter Ginn)

**Left:** *African Golden Oriole* (Oriolus auratus) *pair at their nest, male at left.* (Photo: Peter Ginn)
**Right:** *A* Black-headed Oriole (O. larvatus) *perched on an* Aloe *inflorescence, drinking nectar.* (Photo: Darrell Plowes)

# DRONGOS

## FAMILY DICRURIDAE

The drongos comprise a small family of 20–23 species from the Old World tropics, usually black in colour. They range from Africa to Australia and China, and penetrate into the Palaearctic in the east. All drongos are classified in *Dicrurus* with one New Guinea exception: the most primitive species placed in a monotypical genus (*Chaetorhynchus*) with 12 instead of 10 tail-feathers. There are five African species, including one from the island of Principe off West Africa, but only two species reach southern Africa. The first is the well-known Fork-tailed Drongo and the other is the poorly named Square-tailed Drongo, with a shallowly-forked tail. Field guides show various distinguishing criteria like red iris and prominent rictal bristles. The various species of drongos are fine flyers, with pointed wings and forked tails; 'a magnificent "flier", turning and twisting with extreme speed and skill' (Whistler in Vaurie 1964).

One characteristic of the drongo that is universally admired is its total fearlessness when it comes to protecting its home range and nest in particular. I have many times been highly amused when our most powerful eagles, like the Martial and Crowned Eagles, ostensibly sailing along as monarch of all they survey, suddenly commence a panic-stricken evasion routine, ducking and diving. At a distance one sometimes needs binoculars to home in on one or two little black specks fearlessly strafing the supposed kings of the air. Usually one is close enough to readily identify the culprits: almost always none other than an incensed drongo shooing the mightiest of birds away from the vicinity of the drongo nest. Often, adding insult to injury, one clearly sees a feather plucked from the eagle's back, immediately and disdainfully dropped to drift away on the air currents. Effective counterattack by eagles or even more manoeuvrable falcons or crows is out of the question. The best but still futile retaliation is for the eagle to turn spectacularly on its back and brandish its talons longingly in the air at the cheeky little black tormentor.

Many authors have commented on this common interaction, also emphasizing that this aggression is not merely nasty-natured as drongos do not bully smaller birds near their nests. Many little birds have actually nested in the same tree as the drongo does for the blanket protection offered by the true king of the air. Drongos are famous for diving at intruders approaching their nests: cats, dogs, their owners, even a leopard. A related example of one-upmanship took place near a game farm I established when for several years a pair of Fork-tailed Drongos built their nest in an incredibly vulnerable site. This was actually in a series of single coil-springs holding up a live cable on an electrified railway-line. Although it was not possible to monitor progress due to the risk of a possibly shocking experience, repeated usage showed clearly that these particular drongos had pioneered a remarkable nest-site. Subsequently I have asked many birders which bird could possibly nest successfully in such a vulnerable site, but few indeed had the right answer.

Drongos also sing well when they wish to, and are not restricted to their series of harsh attacking squawks. They are excellent mimics in addition, sometimes so good that many calls have to be checked out to see who, if anyone, is mimicking. The call of the Pearl-spotted Owlet is one of those calls which cause the mobbing instinct of persecuted small waxbills and other little birds to surface. Once, when my wife played back a recording of a Pearl-spotted Owlet to the presumed source, she was markedly unimpressed when a Fork-tailed Drongo flew in at speed, and almost landed on her lap. Which of the two possibilities had she been listening to?

**Above:** *The Square-tailed Drongo* (Dicrurus ludwigii), *with tail not particularly square, but squarish.* **Left:** *The Fork-tailed Drongo* (D. adsimilis) *is decidedly aggressive in the vicinity of its nest.*

(Photos: Peter Ginn)

# Monarch Flycatchers
## Family Monarchidae

There is a fairly sharp zoogeographical division between the Old World flycatchers and the monarch flycatchers which number about 365 species, mostly from North America. The Old World flycatchers will be briefly discussed later, in their place in the systematic order. However, we have two of the spectacular monarch flycatcher groups present in South Africa, each with a single representative here. The first is the Blue-mantled Crested-Flycatcher, with both male and duller female crested. The male has the upper breast dark and sharply demarcated from its white belly, while both show a prominent white wing-bar. Another closely related similar species is found further north of here. Our Blue-mantled is one of the greatest show-offs in the bird world: except when at rest both males and females flare and flirt wings and tail almost continuously. The second is the well-known but beautiful African Paradise Flycatcher, with another 12 sibling species elsewhere in the Old World; males long-tailed, females less so, ranging in colour from black to white, as well as red-orange as found in Africa.

**1:** *African Paradise Flycatcher* (Terpsiphone viridis) *female spangled with raindrops.* (Photo: Nico Myburgh)
**2:** *Female African Paradise Flycatcher feeding chicks.* (Photo: Martin Goetz)
**3:** *Blue-mantled Flycatcher* (Trochocercus cyanomelas) *female displaying.* (Photo: Cyril Laubscher)
**4:** *Blue-mantled Flycatcher male on nest.* (Photo: W.T. Miller)

# Bush-shrikes, Puffbacks, Tchagras, Boubous, Helmet-shrikes, Batises and Wattle-eyes

## Family Malaconotidae

The monograph on shrikes by Harris & Arnott (1988) provides a well-arranged grouping of the bush-shrikes, involving communication, background, and various other biological components, linking the group in a logical sequence based on extensive field knowledge. First is the solitary or monogeneric Brubru Shrike, then the Southern (Black-backed) Puffback Shrike, the only puffback to reach South Africa. Then comes the slightly aberrant Marsh Tchagra *Tchagra minuta*, with our three commoner tchagras: Black-crowned, Brown-crowned and Southern.

Next comes our three boubous, *Laniarius*, then the Crimson-breasted Shrike and five spectacular *Telephorus* bush-shrikes, from the Bokmakierie to the Gorgeous Bush-Shrike, succeeded by the powerful Grey-headed Bush-Shrike.

Now follows what is often considered an endemic family, but in the classification followed here is treated

**1:** *White Helmet-Shrike* (Prionops plumatus) *with large hungry chicks.* (Photo: Cyril Laubscher)
**2:** *Gorgeous Bush-Shrike* (Telophorus viridus) *– normally rather shy and reluctant to pose.* (Photo: Martin Goetz)
**3:** *Retz's Helmet-Shrikes* (P. retzii) *sometimes form mixed groups with White Helmet-Shrikes.* (Photo: Peter Ginn)
**4:** *Grey-headed Bush-Shrike* (Malaconotus blanchoti) *at nest.* (Photo: Peter Ginn)

as members of the bush-shrike family: our three helmet-shrikes. There is regrettable confusion here, because what was called the Black Helmet-Shrike became unwisely named Red-billed Helmet-Shrike, and then Retz's. This blundering continues with *Prionops caniceps* now being 'known' as Red-billed. How can any sense result when, in a small endemic family, five out of eight helmet-shrikes have red bills (particularly when the taxonomy does not appear to be finalized)? Most birders seem to make sense of the old 'black' and 'white' as in the two best-known storks, neither of which are 'purist' black or white.

The rather unusual *Bias musicus* or Vanga Shrike should be classified here, following Harris & Arnott (1988). The isolated White-tailed Shrike from Namibia is an aberrant endemic shrike which has been linked to the bush-shrikes since its discovery in 1837, and confirmed as such by Harris & Arnott (1988). The batises and wattle-eyes also appear to merit classification here as miniature shrikes.

1: *Cape Batis* (Batis capensis): *female incubating, male on the left. Our most attractive batis.* (Photo: R.E. Viljoen)
2: *The Chinspot Batis* (B. molitor) *(male shown) is widely distributed in the Bushveld and Lowveld.*
3: *The Black-throated Wattle-eye* (Platysteira peltata), *of a group closely related to the batises and the only wattle-eye to reach us.*
4: *The Southern Boubou* (Laniarius aethiopicus) *has become a garden bird in many localities.*
5: *The Crimson-breasted Shrike* (L. atrococcineus) *is the handsomest of the boubous. Due to its spectacular red, white and black coloration, the colours of old Imperial Germany, it was known in early Namibia as the 'Kaiservögel' or 'Reichsvögel'.*
6: *The Olive Bush-shrike* (Telophorus olivaceus) *(male shown) utters one of the typical forest bird-calls.*
7: *The Black-crowned Tchagra* (Tchagra australis) *is the largest and handsomest of our three usual tchagras.*
8: *The Southern (Black-backed) Puffback* (Dryoscopus cubla) *female. The male has a large white rump, which is puffed up in display.*
(Photos 2–8: Geoff McIlleron)

# CROWS AND RAVENS
## FAMILY CORVIDAE

The crow family has been regarded by many ornithologists as the high point in the bird kingdom because of their alleged intelligence, though this may have been somewhat overestimated. The family comprises about 103 species, and there is a tendency to split it into the true crows with their croaking calls, and the more colourful smaller corvids like jays, magpies and jackdaws, etc. The crow family includes the largest birds in the Passeriformes. Crows are found all over the world except New Zealand, some islands in the Pacific, and the polar areas. Their origin is apparently the Palaearctic, with fossils known up to 25 million years old. It is interesting that the crows reached the New World late in time and have no specific representative in South America. Furthermore the smaller crows reached Africa after the long-term separation south of the Sahara, so that only six *Corvus* crows bridged the gap and only three reached us in the south. The most recent crow arrival in southern Africa, the House Crow, is most regrettable, having used ships to travel down Africa's East Coast since 1972. An urban nest-robber also observed to be fond of pecking the eyes out of vulnerable mammals like lambs, calves and kittens, it deserves total eradication. After the Second World War, the Pied Crow was studied advancing westward on tar roads in the Western Transvaal, feeding on roadside carrion. The Black Crow with its slender bill does feed on agricultural crops, but far less than the Pied Crow,

**1:** *The Pied Crow* (Corvus albus), *our commonest crow, is easily distinguished by its broader white collar and white fore-belly.*
(Photo: Fanie Hendriks)
**2:** *The White-necked Raven* (C. albicollis) *occurs mainly in mountainous terrain.*
(Photo: Peter Ginn)
**3:** *The Black Crow* (C. capensis) *is a useful species, beneficial on balance to man.*
(Photo: Fanie Hendriks)

which does damage in large flocks at groundnut heaps. Fortunately this does not compare with the damage caused by flocks of American Crows up to 40 000 strong that used to fly up to 64 km to feed. Our White-necked Raven with its more powerful bill is no longer tied to montane country.

Some of the extralimital smaller crows are fond of nuts, and one fascinating case is how the Common Jay's habit of storing acorns up to 4 km away increased the northern spread of the oak forests by up to a remarkable 1,5 km per year after the last ice age in Europe. Interestingly, our Black Crow is the only crow in the world to lay eggs with a pink background speckled with red-brown and brown, while all other crow eggs have a blue background speckled with black and grey. Furthermore, in tree-less habitat where their normal nest-sticks are not available, there are nests on record in which every scrap of building material is a piece of wire, except for the hair lining.

# TRUE SHRIKES

## FAMILY LANIIDAE

Although the shrikes in general are not a particularly popular group of birds to the general public, they are an interesting group of the Passeriformes because they are the only birds of prey of the order. This refers to the true shrikes rather than to the bush-shrikes or the helmet-shrikes. The broad classification of the shrikes is often controversial. There is no doubt that they are closely related, an ancient group with at least seven fossil species dating back to the Early Miocene. The true shrikes consist of a family of 24 species, with 22 in the genus *Lanius* of which at least four reach us. The remaining species is more aberrant, and classified as *Corvinella melanoleuca*, now named Magpie Shrike (formerly Long-tailed Shrike). From East Africa, *C. aequatorialis* is probably conspecific with *C. melanoleuca*,

*White-crowned Shrike* (Eurocephalus anguitimens) *with her chicks in their most attractive cob-webbed nest.* (Photo: Peter Ginn)

and has a shorter tail. Similarly the White-crowned Shrike *Eurocephalus anguitimens* is probably conspecific with the paler-rumped *E. rueppelli*. The origin of the true shrikes is clearly in the Old World. Only the powerful Great Grey (or Northern) Shrike occurs right around the Arctic regions, and a single endemic shrike, the Loggerhead, has reached North America. Shrikes apparently never reached some large areas like South America, Australia and Pacific islands.

In general, the true shrikes are whitish below, grey or brown above, with black and white in the wings and on their heads.

**1:** *The Lesser Grey Shrike* (Lanius minor)*, a summer migrant to South Africa but in much smaller numbers than the next species.* (Photo: Eliot Lyons)
**2:** *Red-backed Shrike male* (L. collurio)*. A common summer migrant to South Africa.* (Photo: John Wesson)
**3:** *The black-and-white Magpie Shrike* (Corvinella melanoleuca) *resembles the European Magpie.* (Photo: Geoff McIlleron)

They tend to have an upright stance, long tails, reasonably sturdy legs, and a powerful bill with a hook and a notch like the raptors proper. However, they use their bills to kill, not their legs, flying low to peck at larger prey like mice, and descending to the ground for smaller prey. One of the most interesting true shrike habits is their 'pantry', hanging up surplus prey on thorny branches or barbed wire fences. For example, Austin Roberts found four Quail Finches impaled together. The idea of a 'pantry' or prey-store has been doubted in times of plenty when shrikes may not return to their larder. However, there is sufficient evidence of use of such a pantry which has been entirely consumed by such shrikes over periods of time. Furthermore, they tear piecemeal at such impaled prey rather than holding it in their feet and tearing at it with their strong bills as a raptor does. Another suggestion has been that the larder attracts insects, probably unimportant.

Many thousands of Red-backed Shrikes migrate from Europe and Asia to partake of our annual summer surplus of suitable food, as does the Lesser Grey Shrike, but in considerably lower numbers. Another migrant to Africa is the Woodchat Shrike, which usually remains north of the equator. An experienced bird-ringer captured, ringed and released an immature Woodchat Shrike in Bryanston, but regrettably he did not consult anyone on the identity, an unfortunate oversight, so that the record has never enjoyed the status it possibly deserved.

# CUCKOOSHRIKES
## FAMILY CAMPEPHAGIDAE

The cuckooshrikes are an Old World family of relatively primitive insectivorous birds with hooked, toothed bills like true shrikes, while in general appearance and grey coloration reminding one of cuckoos. However, there is no close relationship. The family consists of 72 species in 10 genera, but only 13 species in Africa of which three reach us, including the only white-breasted species.

Long pointed wings and a long rounded tail increase the misleading resemblance to cuckoos. Bristles at the

base of the bill partially cover the nostrils. However, the most interesting characteristic of the family is felt rather than seen. These are the rump feathers, peculiar because the base is soft, but the shaft hardens and ends in a sharp point which is easily felt. Furthermore, these exceptional rump-feathers are loose like those of doves. It is suggested that they serve the same purpose: to facilitate escape from a possible attacker by staying behind in the grasp of the attacker.

It is interesting that only one of the 72 cuckooshrikes has an eclipse plumage, an Australian species in which the male exchanges his black-and-white breeding plumage for brownish resembling the female. The largest cuckooshrike, also Australian, spends much of its time foraging on the ground, not moving quietly through the canopy like other cuckooshrikes. However, it still nests in typical cuckooshrike fashion in an attractive shallow flimsy cup built in a fork, well camouflaged with lichens, and the chicks have well-camouflaged whitish down.

Our Black Cuckooshrike has black males with either yellow or no shoulder-patches and a yellow gape to the bill, helpful with identification when present. Originally the yellow shoulder-patches were described as indicating a different species, while the handsome strongly dimorphic female also looks like a different species. Our other two *Coracina* cuckooshrikes are only slightly dimorphic in plumage. Most cuckooshrikes, and certainly our three species, live up to their scientific name of 'caterpillar eaters', but also consume fruit on a much lesser scale. I was surprised to see a Grey Cuckooshrike gobbling down the small fruits of the Common Strangling Fig as it is supposed to be insectivorous, feeding on hairy caterpillars in particular.

**1:** *Black Cuckooshrike* (Campephaga flava) *female feeding chicks.* (Photo: Cyril Laubscher)
**2:** *Black Cuckooshrike male feeding a chick. Note the yellow gape.* (Photo: Geoff McIlleron)
**3:** *White-breasted Cuckooshrike* (Coracina pectoralis), *the only cuckooshrike with a white breast.* (Photo: Geoff McIlleron)

# Rockjumpers
## Family Chaetopidae

Two endemic bird species aptly named 'rockjumpers' are separated by several hundred kilometres, one in the southern and south-western Cape Province and the other in a high-lying basically Eastern Province strip lying north-eastward to the Lesotho massif. Erroneously assumed for many years to be aberrant thrushes, they have now been shown to be aberrant babblers, classified in their own family. Apparently they are reluctant to fly unless disturbed, when they fly to the nearest rock-outcrop to seek cover, sometimes reappearing some distance away. They are normally found singly or in small groups (probably family parties). Tarboton (1989) described them aptly as 'bounding agilely across rocks rather than flying', also 'entirely terrestrial in their habits, digging up or picking up insects', and Martin (1989) as 'hopping from rock to rock, examining cracks and crannies for insects'. Apart from insects, they will opportunistically feed on small vertebrates like lizards. Their loud excited calling indicates their presence in the vicinity, even at a distance.

In some high areas of Lesotho, up to 3 000 m, they are the most numerous birds to be seen (Tarboton 1989). At the other extreme, in the south-western Cape, they occur right down to sea-level, and remain there throughout the year. Apart from minor constraints such as the Drakensberg Rockjumper not reaching sea-level, or the Cape Rockjumper being slightly larger than the Drakensberg Rockjumper, Tarboton (1989) points out the close resemblance in call-notes, habitat, breeding behaviour, general habits, plain white eggs, and female plumage. The two species are easily distinguished in the field, however, by the considerable difference in the male coloration of breast and belly: warm chestnut in the Cape Rockjumper, lighter orange-rufous or alternatively lemon-yellow in the Drakensberg Rockjumper. Interestingly, Martin (1989) recorded what appears to be the first male helper helping feed chicks of the parental pair of Cape Rockjumpers, later repeated several times at other nests near Sir Lowry's Pass. Finally, a birder desirous of finding a historic Rockjumper nest, dozed off in the warm sun, and woke up with immaculate timing, opening his eyes to see the sought-after rockjumper disappear under a small rock where its nest was situated.

**Left:** *Cape Rockjumper* (Chaetops frenatus) *male.* (Photo: Will Nichol)
**Above:** *Drakensberg Rockjumper* (C. aurantius) *male.* (Photo: Garth Batchelor)

# Tits and Penduline-Tits
## Family Paridae

This family appears far from a stable classification, lumping together approximately 55 species of tits, and sometimes even including the American Verdin. The European Penduline-Tit is probably closely related, but doubtfully congeneric, with a different type of nest. This nest has the unique distinction of having placed the species on the Netherlands National List after the nest was discovered by Dutch ornithologists subsequent to the chicks having fledged, but without a sighting of the parents or chicks. Our six species of *Parus* tits are typical tree-hole nesters and insectivores, congeneric like the other tit species found in the Holarctic, Oriental and Afrotropical regions, and therefore not requiring discussion. Americans tend to call their 10 species 'chickadees'. In contrast, however, the nests of our *Anthoscopus* penduline-tits are simply one of the wonders of the bird world and it is more than likely that their classification will revert to their own family.

It has an anti-predator structure which is fascinating. Made of vegetable down or sheepswool or both, the nest is felted together to form an exceedingly strong structure, which when fresh is reported torn with difficulty. The true entrance to the nest is in the roof of a little porch, directly above a carefully integrated decoy entrance pocket intended to lure questing predators. Despite it being even possible to hear the chicks, due to the structure of the nest the predators cannot reach them. The penduline-tits use a foot to pull down the lower portion of the entrance. Then from the inside they will butt and pinch to seal the entrance spout. When the true entrance is sealed up, and the double-layer porch 'roof' is pinched together with butting, with a few actual bill pinch-marks possibly visible, then it is almost impossible to detect the true entrance.

I cut a cross-section through an old Grey Penduline-Tit nest on a hunch, and found that the decoy pocket was clearly an integral part of the nest, much thicker-walled than anyone would reasonably expect (Milstein 1975c).

**1:** *Grey Penduline-Tit* (Anthoscopus caroli) *male carrying a tick about to enter its nest.* (Photo: Peter Ginn)
**2:** *Cape Penduline-Tit* (A. minutus) *with food about to enter the nest after opening the 'secret' entrance.* (Photo: Peter Ginn)
**3:** *Nest of Cape Penduline-Tit.* (Photo: Peter Milstein)

The obvious reason for the considerable thickness was to prevent predators breaking from the decoy pocket into the nest-chamber, so that the lower half of the nest was almost solid reinforcement, and the nest contents – up to a dozen tiny white eggs – were placed unexpectedly high up in the nest. In the non-breeding season, the special little nest is used for communal roosting by up to 18 penduline-tits.

*Southern Black Tit* (Parus niger) *male, closely related to the tits of Europe, at its tree nest-hole.* (Photo: Geoff McIlleron)

# Swallows and Martins
## Family Hirundinidae

The swallow family differs from all the other 4 000 members of the Oscines sub-order by their nearly completed windpipe rings, whereas all the rest have half-completed rings with membranes in front. The swallows are the most uniform group in the Oscines, comprising 74 species with only one rather aberrant member, the large Congo River Martin. There are 38 swallow species in Africa, of which 29 are endemic. The swallows are a beloved group, particularly in the East, where they are considered as luck-bringers when they nest on houses. They have nested on man-made structures for centuries, but some are more inclined to use artificial nests than others. The peak is probably the swallow tower in Griggsville, Indiana, which housed 3 000 swallows, and eliminated a mosquito plague.

A more modern example here is where our colonial-breeding South African Cliff Swallows have utilized grain silos and road bridges to expand their breeding territory in flat Highveld areas. There are even numerous examples of swallows nesting on working boats, with one

*Blue Swallow* (Hirundo atrocaerulea) *female at the nest feeding chicks.* (Photo: Peter Ginn)

well-known example involving a daily round-trip of 290 km, where the parents accompanied the boat to feed their chicks, and raised brood after brood under these unusual conditions.

Swallow species form natural groups according to the type of nest they utilize. We lack the relatively primitive swallows which nest in tree-holes. Our Brown-throated and Banded Martins are regular breeders in earth burrows, but Sand and Mascarene Martins are non-breeding migrants. The Grey-rumped Swallow carries lining down vacant rodent-holes. Cup-shaped mud nests (involving about 1 000 building flights) are built by Angolan, White-throated, Wire-tailed, Blue, Pearl-breasted and Barn Swallows. The Barn Swallow (formerly named European) is a large-scale migrant into southern Africa, shown by ringing data to originate from Britain right across to Siberia.

Nests with an extended tunnel entrance (involving 5 000 or more building flights) are built by Greater, Lesser, Red-breasted, Mosque and Red-rumped Swallows, and readily taken over by White-rumped Swifts, which then have feathers protruding from the entrance. South African Cliff Swallows build closed tunnel-less nests adjoining each other. Precisely such nests are built by House Martins, but mainly in the northern hemisphere,

**1:** *Pearl-breasted Swallow* (Hirundo dimidiata), *easy to distinguish from the White-throated.* (Photo: Nico Myburgh)
**2:** *Lesser Striped Swallow* (H. abyssinica) *fanning its tail.* (Photo: Fanie Hendriks)
**3:** *Greater Striped Swallow* (H. cucullata) *starting to build the entrance tunnel.* (Photo: Geoff McIlleron)
**4:** *Wire-tailed Swallow* (H. smithii). *Despite the chestnut crown and thin tail streamers, not easy to distinguish from the Pearl-breasted Swallow at a distance.* (Photo: Martin Goetz)
**5:** *The Brown-throated Martin* (Riparia paludicola) *is closely related to the Sand Martin of Europe.* (Photo: Fanie Hendriks)
**6:** *White-throated Swallow* (H. albigularis), *closely related to the migratory Barn Swallow.* (Photo: Geoff McIlleron)

rarely in South Africa. House Martins have unique attractive feathered feet. The Rock Martin builds a rather shallow cup. Finally, there are three saw-wings: the Black Saw-wing, which breeds with us in earth-bank burrows, and the White-headed and Eastern Saw-wing, which are migrants. The ridiculous belief of Aristotle that the restless millions of swallows ready to migrate disappeared into the mud at the bottom of pools to hibernate was scientifically disproved by the first great ornithologist, Emperor Frederick II of Hohenstaufen. However, this fable persisted until the eighteenth century with Linnaeus, for example, as one of its staunch supporters. Frederick (1194–1250) was excommunicated and his brilliant findings suppressed until 1788.

# Bulbuls and Nicators

## Family Pycnonotidae

The bulbuls are a well-known Old World family of about 120 species, found over Africa and Asia. They do not reach Australia naturally, though one well-known bulbul species has been successfully released there. Africa is considered to be the centre of bulbul distribution, with only two small genera of the 15 bulbul genera not represented. Bulbuls are closely related to the babblers, but in general are far less terrestrial and possess less sturdy legs. They are also smaller, ranging in size from about a sparrow to a thrush. Regarded as relatively primitive, the bulbul family is fairly clearly defined. Two characteristics are a strange patch of hairy feathers on the hind-head, and bristles at the bill.

They are not in general good flyers, with short rounded wings. Often dull-coloured, bulbuls have brownish, greenish, greyish, whitish, and blackish feathers, even with yellowish bellies. Various patches of bright feathers occur, for example under the tail (vent) and on the cheeks. To attempt pointlessly to divide most bulbuls into either 'greenbuls' or 'brownbuls' is a waste of time, and serves little if any purpose.

**1:** *The African Red-eyed Bulbul* (Pycnonotus nigricans) *is readily distinguished by the red wattle around the eye.* (Photo: Charles Barrett)
**2:** *The Black-eyed Bulbul* (P. barbatus) *has no significant wattle around the eye.* (Photo: Geoff McIlleron)
**3:** *Terrestrial Bulbul* (Phyllastrephus terrestris), *a noisy brown bulbul usually found in small groups on the ground, scratching among dry leaves.* (Photo: Geoff McIlleron)

1: *The Sombre Bulbul* (Andropadus importunus) *is basically dull-coloured, but with a striking white iris.*
2: *The Yellow-streaked Bulbul* (Phyllastrephus flavostriatus) *is immediately distinguished by its habit of dropping one wing alternately. The yellow streaks on the underparts are almost indistinguishable.*
3: *The Stripe-cheeked Bulbul* (Andropadus milanjensis) *has a limited distribution in the north-east.*
4: *The Yellow-bellied Bulbul* (Chlorocichla flaviventris) *has a clear yellow belly and underparts.*
(Photos: Geoff McIlleron)

Bulbul (with white eye-wattles) have shown highly limited 'hybridization' with overlap. We have two *Andropadus* species, the Sombre Bulbul with its well-known 'Willie' call, and the Stripe-cheeked with a limited distribution on our east, one *Chlorocichla* bulbul with its bright yellowish belly, and three *Phyllastrephus* bulbuls. Here the Terrestrial Bulbul occurs in small flocks, usually scratching noisily among dead leaves. The Yellow-streaked Bulbul fascinatingly drops one wing at a time continually when feeding, supposedly to scare insects. Our Slender (now Tiny) Bulbul is hardly tiny, but

We have three representatives of the most plentiful and best-known genus, *Pycnonotus*, common in gardens and regularly associated with man or his fruit. Often leading the snake/owl warning chorus (and all 'dark-capped'), the Black-eyed Bulbul, Red-eyed Bulbul and Cape relatively small, and like the Stripe-cheeked is found in north-eastern regions. Lastly we have the Eastern Nicator, one of three aberrant *Nicator* bulbuls, with a relatively heavy hooked bill, long incorrectly classified as a shrike and probably still deserving of study.

# LEAF-WARBLERS, BABBLERS AND WARBLERS
## FAMILY SYLVIIDAE

Three flycatcher-like warblers (*Erythrocercus*, *Stenostira* and *Elminia*) commence this large family of 45 warblers and babblers, and the second genus *Stenostira* (though endemic and still named Fairy Flycatcher) has uncertain affinities. The same applies to the Moustached Warbler *Melocichla*, Cape Grassbird *Sphenoeacus*, Rockrunner *Achaetops*, Broad-tailed Warbler *Schoenicola*, and Victorin's Warbler which was placed in *Bradypterus* but now *Cryptillas*, all monogeneric. Three crombecs are placed in *Sylvietta*, four eremomelas in *Eremomela*, with three *Bradypterus* warblers (African Sedge-Warbler, Knysna Warbler and Barratt's Warbler), eight similar *Acrocephalus* warblers with various name combinations of reed-warbler, marsh-warbler and

1: *Yellow Reed-warbler* (Chloropeta natalensis). (Photo: Peter Ginn)
2: *Mashona (Southern) Hyliota* (Hyliota australis). (Photo: Peter Ginn)
3: *Yellow-bellied Eremomela* (Eremomela icteropygialis). (Photo: Peter Ginn)
4: *Yellow-throated Woodland Warbler* (Phylloscopus ruficapilla). (Photo: Peter Ginn)
5: *Victorin's Warbler* (Cryptillas victorini). (Photo: Geoff McIlleron)
6: *Cape Reed-warbler* (Acrocephalus gracilirostris). (Photo: Cyril Laubscher)
7: *Chestnut-vented Tit-Babbler* (Parisoma subcaeruleum) *at nest*. (Photo: Cyril Laubscher)
8: *Southern Pied Babbler* (Turdoides bicolor). (Photo: Will Nichol)
9: *Arrow-marked Babbler* (T. jardineii). (Photo: Warwick Tarboton)

sedge-warbler (some migratory, some resident) and two *Hippolais* migrant warblers.

We also have one *Chloropeta* warbler, which resembles *Acrocephalus* in reed-warbler head profile, nest and eggs, closely resembling a yellow reed-warbler, and probably deserving of further study. The Willow Warbler *Phylloscopus* is a common migrant, the commonest bird in Sweden, and the Yellow-throated Warbler is now placed in the same genus, but resident here. Two *Hyliota* warblers are readily distinguished by the relative length of their wing-stripes. Five relatively large *Turdoides* babblers are decidedly sociable and noisy. The Bush Blackcap *Lioptilus nigricapillus* is an attractive endemic species, probably a bulbul or babbler with uncertain affinities. There are also two *Parisoma* tit-babblers, one with a white vent and one with a chestnut vent. Finally, there are three migratory *Sylvia* warblers: the Blackcap, Garden Warbler, and Common Whitethroat, which often return to the identical winter quarters they occupied in previous years.

# WHITE-EYES
## FAMILY ZOSTEROPIDAE

Extremely well-known small white-eyes, insectivorous and frugivorous, visit gardens everywhere in southern Africa. They range from the highest forest trees to low shrubs in semi-desert habitat. In the breeding season they form territorial pairs, but in the non-breeding season they are decidedly sociable and form flocks of various sizes, which communicate with each other by soft whistles. The plasticity of white-eye species is remarkable, varying in total from about 70 species to nearly 100 species, extending from Africa to Asia and Australia. The great majority are found in the genus *Zosterops*, with much geographic variation resulting from the restless integration, and relatively few isolated populations on islands or mountain-tops. In this family the tenth primary feather is absent or very reduced, and one isolate has a black eye-ring instead of the usual white eye-ring. Their main diet is insects, also fruit, and nectar for which their short bills puncture flowers from the side. They are considered a major fruit pest in Australia. In one orchard

**1:** *The Cape White-eye complex ranges gradually in colour from largely grey birds to the extreme of largely green birds.*
**2:** *The Yellow White-eye* (Zosterops senegalensis) *is a rather bright yellow bird, reproductively isolated from the Cape White-Eye, and found in the east of South Africa.* (Photos: Geoff McIlleron)

20 000 white-eyes are claimed to have been shot, in another 1 200 in one day.

With such large flocks, high winds blow large numbers out to sea, or with luck to other islands. On Norfolk Island near Australia, three successive waves of white-eye colonists with time for speciation established themselves as species: *Z. albogularis*, *Z. tenuirostris* and *Z. lateralis*. Regrettably *albogularis* appears to have gone extinct in the early 1990s (P. Comben, pers. comm.). New Zealand was colonized in about 1850 by one white-eye species whose Maori name meant 'small stranger'. Apart from various islands around Africa or peaks permitting isolation, the Yellow White-eye and Cape White-eye appear to have established themselves as valid species, but the so-called Orange River White-eye with brown flanks (*pallidus*) intergrades with the adjacent white-eyes. Such restless intergradation cannot result in valid viable species, lacking sufficient isolation and time for the erection of genetic barriers. Also, with many available white-eye nests, we see so few Sharp-billed Honeybird chicks that we are obviously not paying sufficient attention to these little parasites.

# African Warblers
## Family Cisticolidae

Maclean (1993) emphasized that the cisticolas are among the hardest of all small Southern African passerines to identify by sight alone, and that it is especially important here to use distribution, habitat, songs and plumage features in combination for sure identification of the 17 species of cisticolas found in southern Africa. To further complicate identification, cisticolas have both breeding and non-breeding plumage. All birders in Africa can be grateful for the outstanding study of cisticolas carried out by Rear-Admiral Lynes (1930), who laid an excellent foundation for those who followed. Since cisticola calls during the breeding season are one of the outstanding methods of identification, some identifications may have to wait until the following season. The advances in small compact tape-recorders have also been a great advantage. Sometimes there are other clues like the plain glossy brick-red or terracotta eggs of the Croaking Cisticola, or the lack of display flights in the so-called 'Lazy' Cisticola. The Fantail Cisticola with its clinking call has the widest distribution of any of our cisticolas: Africa, southern Europe, southern Asia, and Australia. The top of its nest is open, with living broad green grass-blades glued to the nest for camouflage, and it is the only cisticola nest where I have heard the chicks hissing like a venomous snake for protection. The Neddicky Cisticola reaches Kenya, while the Croaking Cisticola reaches the Sudan and Guinea Bissau.

*The Green-backed Bleating Warbler* (Camaroptera brachyura), *or Bleater, is found in more humid areas, and the similar Grey-backed Bleater in more arid areas. They are clearly conspecific but gradually merge into each other. Also called* camaroptera, *from the scientific name, an unnecessary mouthful. The bleating call is clear; the Afrikaans name* Blêrtinktinkie *is apt.* (Photo: Fanie Hendriks)

Four typical long-tailed prinias are next, then the Karoo and Drakensberg Prinias (formerly lumped together). The Namaqua Warbler was formerly classified as a prinia, as was Roberts's Warbler, due to its long tail, in the eastern highlands of Zimbabwe (such was the dedication of the late Con Benson that he discovered this new species of bird while on honeymoon!) Two other longish-tailed warblers are the much-overlooked Red-winged Warbler and the Rufous-eared Warbler. A further five *Apalis* species are next recorded here. Then come the adjacent Green-backed and Grey-backed Bleating Warblers, then the (Kalahari) Barred Warbler which has both a breeding and non-breeding plumage. The Stierling's Barred Warbler does not appear to have a clear eclipse plumage, though it is a typical 'tailor-bird', sewing green leaves together to camouflage its nest. Last is the Cinnamon-breasted Warbler, apparently with dark coloration, but with bright chestnut if seen close-up, and with a distinctive black tail. Its song is a loud series of whistles.

**1:** *The Desert Cisticola* (Cisticola aridulus) *has a longer tail and nest-entrance near the top.* (Photo: Cyril Laubscher)
**2:** *Wing-snapping (Ayres') Cisticola* (C. ayresii) *at nest. It is easily distinguished by a series of wing-snaps in display.* (Photo: Cyril Laubscher)
**3:** *The Wailing Cisticola* (C. lais) *is easily recognized by its wailing call.* (Photo: Geoff McIlleron)
**4:** *The Fan-tailed Cisticola* (C. juncidis) *has a short tail, gives a 'clinking' call in flight, and is distributed over four continents.* (Photo: Geoff McIlleron)
**5:** *The Black-chested Prinia* (Prinia flavicans) *has an unusually long tail, and black chest-band only seasonally.* (Photo: Geoff McIlleron)

# Larks and Sparrowlarks
## Family Alaudidae

The larks are distinguished from all other passerines on two characteristics. First, the back of the tarsus is rounded and not sharp, and it is covered with scales rather than a solid plate. They also have a primitive syrinx with a cartilage support rather than bone. This well-known family of about 75 species is therefore easily identifiable. They have almost an Old World distribution, 55 species in Africa with 25 species here in southern Africa. Only one lark, the Horned, reached the New World, with a sub-population in Colombia. Another of our larks, the Red-capped, extends from the Cape to Europe and Asia. In one remarkable case a population of Rudd's Lark was found in the Drakensberg range, and to great surprise another small isolated population 4 000 km away in Somalia.

Larks are all small birds that prefer open flats or savanna, none occurring in forest. They eat chiefly seeds and insects, with thick to delicate bills. The Hoopoe-Lark has an extended bill which enables it to dig out locust or grasshopper larvae 5 cm deep. Larks never hop but walk, up to 8 kph. They line hollows to nest in, against grass-tufts or stones for camouflage, except for the *Mirafra* genus which additionally pulls grass over the nest to hide it. Exceptions are the

**1:** *Spike-heeled Lark* (Chersomanes albofasciata): *note the long hind-toe and claw.* (Photo: John Wesson)
**2:** *The Sabota Lark* (Calendulauda sabota) *gives his cheery call from selected calling-posts.* (Photo: Eliot Lyons)
**3:** *The Rufous-naped Lark* (Mirafra africana) *is a truly exceptional mimic.* (Photo: John Wesson)

1: *Grey-backed Sparrowlark* (Eremopterix verticalis).
(Photo: Eliot Lyons)
2: *Dusky Lark* (Pinarocorys nigricans). (Photo: Fanie Hendriks)
3: *Clapper Lark* (Mirafra apiata). (Photo: Geoff McIlleron)

Red Lark and Namib Lark which for nesting take advantage of cool rodent-holes not in use. Larks have truly remarkable adaptations to soil coloration, knowing the importance to them of a matching background, and will if necessary, fly over the head of someone trying to chase them onto dunes of the 'wrong' colour as Prozesky found. This colour-matching is considered to be the best in the bird world.

Larks are some of the most brilliant songsters in the world, and the European Skylark has been introduced elsewhere for this reason – to Vancouver, New Zealand and Hawaii. Also introduced to Long Island, New York, they became extinct in 1913 after about 30 years. As a family, larks are famous for their beautiful songs, and various poets have become lyrical over this. Our best singer is the Melodious Lark, but various other larks sing well, and some are excellent mimics, like the Sabota Lark which is known to incorporate imitations of over 60 other bird species (Maclean 1993). Since the Roman Empire, larks have remained a delicacy in Europe, and literally millions of migrating larks have been harvested for this reason. Precise figures have been kept concealed because of the strong opposition to this practice. One accurate figure is 1 000 255 larks which were marketed for R4 520 at Dieppe in the 1867–1868 winter, and the slaughter was far greater in the south.

# SPOTTED CREEPER

## FAMILY SALPORNITHIDAE

The only creeper in Africa, this beautiful and interesting bird species is classified in a monotypic genus. However, its relationships are not clear, except that it has a sibling relative in India. Various possible links have been suggested, including the stiff rectrices. Here the propping function involves the same delayed moult of central tail-feathers or soft non-propping rectrices. It is clear that the problem is one of a popular niche rather than of closely related birds. Tree bark and to a lesser degree cliffs provide shelter for numerous prey insects and other small animals.

The creepers superficially resemble each other, and climb trees with the same upward spiral search pattern, after which they fly down to the base of the next tree and repeat the upward performance. To complicate the matter more, our Spotted Creeper builds a saucer-shaped nest in a tree-fork like its Australian counterparts. This nest is outstandingly camouflaged with lichens and spider-webs, matching spots and sunlight to further increase the dappling effect of the light under the trees. The incubating female holds her bill at a remarkable 60° in the air, interpreted as resembling a twig for further camouflage. If the female is uneasy, she increases the angle to 75°, but gradually relaxes to the original 60°. If the creeper is nervous and 'freezes' when climbing a tree, it is then observed with difficulty. The first sighting of the Spotted Creeper in Africa was surprisingly recorded when it was climbing up a maize plant in Angola.

*The Spotted Creeper* (Salpornis spilonotus), *the only creeper in Africa, incubating extremely well camouflaged from below.* (Photo: Peter Ginn)

# Thrushes, Robins, Chats and Old World Flycatchers

## Family Muscicapidae

This family includes some of the finest songbirds in South Africa and simultaneously some of the most attractively coloured songsters we have. Furthermore, their tameness and confiding behaviour with regard to humans is often remarkable. For example, the well-named Familiar Chat is named 'Spekvretertjie' in Afrikaans from its habit of eating the animal fat used to grease the hubs of wagon-wheels in the early days of transport. Members of this family are relatively small to medium in size and include nearly 30 genera. Although the many songsters include exceptional singers like the migratory world-class Thrush-Nightingale, the various thrushes and robins together with others make a memorable chorus.

Our four *Monticola* rock-thrushes and two *Zoothera* ground-thrushes are also fine singers. The Groundscraper Thrush's name is derived from its nearly vertical dives which flatten off to skim just above the ground and then shoot up into the branches above again. Although it was earlier thought to form a species-pair with the Song Thrush of Europe, closer examination showed that the latter's mud-walled nest does not match the Groundscraper nest, while the Groundscraper eggs are almost identical with those of the Mistle Thrush (Milstein 1968), quite unlike Song Thrush eggs. However, the Groundscraper also has a fine song.

Although bird-ringers on considerable movement data and its variable belly-vent appearance were the first to cast serious doubts on the validity of the so-called species 'split' between the Olive Thrush and the intergrading 'Karoo Thrush', the corroboratory evidence seems superficial and requiring justification by an in-depth study. Noteworthy taxonomic changes in better-known groups, such as the re-appraisal of the Karoo Scrub-Robin (Oatley 2004) seem increasingly rare.

Our two species of *Cichladusa* palm-thrushes are excellent singers, while chats like our Mocking Chat, *Thamnolaea*, as well as our Ant-eating Chat and Arnot's Chat, *Myrmecochicla*, are all accomplished mimics. To watch at close range a Chorister Robin imitating not one but a whole flock of Red-faced Mousebirds or an exceptional Brown-hooded Kingfisher imitation is memorable, or to stand, as I did at Crook's Corner

(Pafuri) with five Heuglin's Robins spaced around me competing in full crescendo song is unforgettable. For details, Terry Oatley's beautifully illustrated monograph *The Robins of Africa* should be obtained by anyone interested in this exciting group, to which he has devoted most of his life.

1: *Arnot's Chat* (Myrmecocichla arnoti) *is predominantly black with a white crown and shoulder-patch. It is common in mopane woodland.* (Photo: Eliot Lyons)

2: *The Familiar Chat* (Cercomela familiaris) *flicks its wings at rest and trembles its tail. It is known for eating animal fat lubrication from ox-wagon wheels, even when travelling.* (Photo: Cyril Laubscher)

3: *The Mocking Chat* (Thamnolaea cinnamomeiventris) *(male shown here) is one of our best mimics and often nests in old striped swallow nests.* (Photo: Cyril Laubscher)

4: *The Chorister Robin* (Cossypha dichroa) *is easily distinguished by its dark upperparts and orange underparts and is a fine songster.* (Photo: Cyril Laubscher)

5: *The Heuglin's Robin* (C. heuglini) *is distinguished from the Chorister by its clear white eye-stripe.* (Photo: Geoff McIlleron)

6: *The White-throated Robin* (C. humeralis) *is a good singer and mimic.* (Photo: Geoff McIlleron)

7: *The Natal Robin* (C. natalensis), *also an outstanding singer and mimic.* (Photo: Neville Brickell)

1: *Starred Robin* (Pogonocichla stellata): *the white stars on the forehead and throat are usually concealed, but the bright yellow (not orange) tail is particularly conspicuous.* (Photo: Geoff McIlleron)
2: *The Swynnerton's Robin* (Swynnertonia swynnertoni) *is a small rare robin found in our extreme eastern region bordering Mozambique.* (Photo: Geoff McIlleron)
3: *The White-browed Scrub-Robin* (Cercotrichas leucophrys) *is a confiding songster with heavily streaked breast, white wing-bar and prominent white eye-stripe. It regularly cocks its tail as shown.* (Photo: Geoff McIlleron)
4: *The Kalahari Scrub-Robin* (C. paena) *is a relatively pale bird, without the breast-streaks and white wing-bar of the White-browed Scrub-Robin.* (Photo: Geoff McIlleron)
5: *The Brown Scrub-Robin* (C. signata) *is a dull version of the Bearded Scrub-Robin and prefers montane habitat although found at sea level in Zululand. It is a good songster.* (Photo: Geoff McIlleron)
6: *The Bearded Scrub-Robin* (C. quadrivirgata) *is similar to but clearly brighter than the Brown Scrub-Robin, with orange flanks and rump.* (Photo: Fanie Hendriks)

**Far left:** *The Groundscraper Thrush* (Psophocichla litsitsirupa) *is an attractive thrush, characterized by an orange wing-panel, no wing-bars, and is a fine songster.*
**Left:** *The Orange Ground-Thrush is a rather shy forest dweller with a fine song normally uttered from a concealed perch.*
(Photos: Peter Ginn)

*The Spotted Ground-Thrush* (Zoothera gurneyi) *closely resembles the Groundscraper Thrush but has a prone rather than upright posture, with two white wing-bars.* (Photo: Geoff McIlleron)

**Far left:** *The Cape Rock-Thrush* (Monticola rupestris) *is our largest rock-thrush. The male has a brown back and the blue extends to the upper breast.*
(Photo: Cyril Laubscher)
**Left:** *The Sentinel Rock-Thrush* (M. explorator) *is another good songster.*
(Photo: Fanie Hendriks)

**Far left:** *The Black Flycatcher* (Melaenornis pammelaina) *has all-black plumage, a dark brown iris, a squarish tail and gape not noticeable.*
**Left:** *The Dusky Flycatcher* (Muscicapa adusta) *is a typical restless, small flycatcher.*
(Photos: Bob Bloomfield)

**Far left:** *A Pallid Flycatcher* (Bradornis pallidus)*, similar to the Marico Flycatcher but greyish brown.*
(Photo: Cyril Laubscher)
**Left:** *The Marico Flycatcher* (Bradornis mariquensis) *is a warm grey colour with whiter underparts.*
(Photo: Geoff McIlleron)

**Far left:** *The Spotted Flycatcher* (Muscicapa striata) *is a common migrant to South Africa, best identified by its striated forehead.*
**Left:** *The Blue-grey Flycatcher* (Muscicapa caerulescens) *is uniformly blue-grey but with a little black and white coloration in front of the bill.* (Photos: Fanie Hendriks)

THRUSHES, ROBINS, CHATS AND OLD WORLD FLYCATCHERS • FAMILY MUSCICAPIDAE

# Starlings, Mynas and Oxpeckers
## Family Sturnidae

Our attractively plumaged starlings commence with two closely related long-tailed starlings (Pale-winged and Red-winged), seven *Lamprotornis* starlings which are collectively known as 'morning star', and one Plum-coloured Starling species. Then there are two aberrant starling species (Pied and Wattled) and two alien species (one starling of European origin, one a myna of Asiatic origin). The European Starling is the greatest fruit pest in continental North America and similarly in Australia. The Common Myna, however, is not a fruit pest on such a scale, but rather a parasite on man, living in close association with humans and their dwellings.

**1:** *The Lesser Blue-eared Starling* (Lamprotornis elisabeth), *seen here at its nest-hole, is not easily distinguished at a distance in adult plumage from other similar glossy starlings like the Greater. However, its chicks with their chestnut underparts make identification certain.* (Photo: Geoff McIlleron)

**2:** *The Wattled Starling* (Creatophora cinerea), *with the male shown here in full breeding finery, is decidedly aberrant in constructing cup-shaped nests in acacia tree colonies. Thereafter the male rapidly loses his nuptial attire and becomes plain again.* (Photo: Fanie Hendriks)

**3:** *The Pied Starling* (Spreo bicolor) *has a satiny-brown plumage with a striking white iris. It is prepared to excavate its own nest-burrow in vertical earth-bank colonies, but increasingly uses man-made structures for nesting.* (Photo: Eliot Lyons)

**4:** *Two Burchell's Starlings* (Lamprotornis australis) *having a serious territorial argument.* (Photo: Fanie Hendriks)

*The Plum-coloured Starling* (Cinnyricinclus leucogaster) *male (left) has the entire body except belly and vent a spectacular glossy plum-coloured shade of violet approaching amethyst, which varies a bit with wear. The female (right) has a mottled brown head, similar upperparts and white underparts longitudinally streaked with brown.* (Photos: Cyril Laubscher)

Finally we have the two specialized *Buphagus* oxpeckers, which should rather have been classified in their own specialized family. We nearly lost both these two valuable bird species locally to almost universally applied arsenical cattle-dip pesticides. The Red-billed Oxpeckers managed to survive, and have built up to adequate numbers again. Long extinct in the Kruger National Park, the proposal of reintroduction of the Yellow-billed Oxpecker into the Kruger by the Wildlife Society was wisely turned down by the National Parks Board. Vindicated by the first sighting of Yellow-billed Oxpeckers on hippos in the extreme north of the Kruger by Dr Anthony Hall-Martin, a totally natural reintroduction had taken place from Gona-re-Zhou in Zimbabwe instead. This natural reintroduction into their former range from where they had been so blindly eradicated by the compulsory arsenical cattle-dipping programme is obviously preferable.

Few if any commentators have pointed out the anomaly of the ideal host for oxpeckers: the largest terrestrial mammal we have, found in large thriving herds, but where even the large herds have strangely never been recorded to tolerate oxpeckers. This is the African Elephant, where any oxpeckers which alight on elephants receive short shrift, and the elephant's trunk swings unhesitatingly into action to 'swat' such a misguided oxpecker, one which has never realized how ticklish elephants apparently are.

**Above:** *Yellow-billed Oxpecker* (Buphagus africanus). *Although this species and its close relative, the Red-billed Oxpecker, should be classified in their own family, they are here an addendum to the starlings. The Yellow-billed Oxpecker is larger, has a two-tone yellow and red bill, no eye-wattle and a pale rump.* (Photo: Sharon Heald)
**Left:** *The Red-billed Oxpecker* (B. erythrorhynchus) *has a yellow eye-wattle, all-red bill and dark rump.* (Photo: Brendan Ryan)

# Sunbirds
## Family Nectarinidae

The sunbirds are a favourite bird-group due to a combination of their exceptional male coloration and their relative tameness. People are often tolerated extremely close to sunbirds. One example is where a sunbird, then unknown to science, on Central Africa's Ruwenzori peak at 4 000 metres in 1904 actually settled on the shotgun held by a British Museum bird-collector. For obvious reasons, sunbirds are often confused with the hummingbirds of the family Trochilidae.

The hummingbirds are limited to the New World with a peak in South America. Even more important is that the two groups are unrelated, but that the hummingbirds are then related to another group of master-flyers: the swifts and spine-tails. On the other hand, with their long bills, both sunbirds and hummingbirds drink nectar from flowers while hovering in front of them. With relatively weaker legs and feet, the hummingbirds fly continuously, and can actually fly backwards. Sunbirds prefer to feed from a perched position.

There is a similar group to sunbirds found in south-eastern Asia, known as *Arachnothera* or spiderhunters, closely resembling sunbirds, but with much duller males. Although the hummingbirds build cup-shaped nests, and the sunbirds build purse-shaped nests with a porch overhanging the entrance, the spiderhunters build

**Left:** *Male Collared Sunbird* (Hedydipna collaris) *in an elongated threat posture, emphasising his attractive metallic throat.*
**Right:** *Female Collared Sunbird building onto her nest.*
(Photos: Peter Ginn)

**Top:** *Our largest sunbird, the Malachite Sunbird* (Nectarinia famosa), *with both male and female feeding on* Erica *flowers.*
**Bottom:** *Male and female Marico Sunbirds* (Cinnyris mariquensis) *feeding on* Aloe *inflorescences.* (Photos: Cyril Laubscher)

unique cup-shaped nests sewn by means of the rim to the undersides of leaves.

Seven genera and 21 species of sunbird occur in South Africa. Rarest is the Blue-throated Sunbird (Milstein, Bridgefort & Bridgefort 2004). Sunbirds generally stick their long bills well into open flowers, to drink the nectar directly. They drink water extremely rarely. Sunbird females gather all the nest-building material and do all the building. However, the males accompany their females on all their collecting trips.

# Sugarbirds

## Family Promeropidae

The sugarbirds were named most aptly as the 'sugarbush' birds in Afrikaans, as their entire existence is dependent on the well-known *Protea* plants. They are unique because they are the only bird family limited to southern Africa. The family consists of only two closely related species, which are unquestionably classified under the same genus. This uniqueness has given rise to problems with regards to their classification. The father of modern classification, Linnaeus, first classified them with the hoopoe, but soon thereafter with the bee-eaters. Then they were linked to the sunbirds but their nests differed: an open cup compared with a closed purse protected by a porch entrance, and their plumage completely lacks the glossy component of the sunbirds. Despite the considerable distance without any relatives intermediate, they were then classified as a subfamily of the Australian Meliphagidae or honeyeaters. Further research showed that this was not justified. The sugarbird's tongue is unique and differs in various anatomical respects from that of the honeyeater.

The two species of sugarbirds have even been superficially lumped together as one species, but are undoubtedly two: valid even sympatrically in the Pirie Mountains, near King William's Town, in the same patch of proteas. An apparent hybrid is known from this region 100 years ago, but which does not affect their status. The male Cape Sugarbird has a considerably longer tail and is duller coloured than Gurney's. The Cape Sugarbird female also builds a much untidier nest than Gurney's. From above, it looks like a Catherine's wheel as part of a fireworks display. The bill of Gurney's is also stronger. The fourth, fifth and sixth primaries are broader and strangely shaped, and enables a longer display flight. Gurney's steeper display flight causes wing-noises in the

**Top:** *Female Gurney's Sugarbird* (Promerops gurneyi) *incubating on her nest, much neater than that of the Cape Sugarbird.*
(Photo: Peter Steyn)
**Bottom:** *Male Gurney's Sugarbird perched on a look-out post, brighter with tail much shorter than the Cape Sugarbird.*
(Photo: Neels Bothma)

**Far left:** *The much longer tail of the male Cape Sugarbird* (Promerops cafer) *is well shown here, almost disproportionate.*
(Photo: Nico Myburgh)

**Left:** *The tail of the female Cape Sugarbird can be seen here to be about as long as that of the male Gurney's Sugarbird.*
(Photo: Geoff McIlleron)

wind, and singing by the male takes place during the downward dive.

Considerable activity and song by the male warn against mutual enemies like shrikes and mongooses. All territorial males were observed to hide immediately from a Rufous-breasted Sparrowhawk, and remain silent and well hidden for half an hour before resuming normal activities. Breeding coincided with protea flowering, so that Gurney's Sugarbirds nested simultaneously with Cape Sugarbirds. Obvious adjacent breeding in a full-flowering patch of *Protea longifolia* took place. Sugarbirds help to expose and distribute pollen from recently opened protea flowers, but not to the same key role undertaken by the Australian honeyeaters with eucalypts. Although nectar is important to sugarbirds, insects form a most important part of their diet and proteas remain essential.

# Weavers, Queleas and Widows
## Family Ploceidae

Buffalo-weavers are our largest ploceids, with males having red bills, black plumage and white wing-patches, while females and juveniles are brown instead of black. They build untidy linked nests high in trees, often also in every pylon available. Despite this considerable nest-height above ground, Black Mambas have been observed to loop from compartments into adjacent compartments so as to feed on eggs and chicks. White-browed Sparrow-weavers construct a decoy-series of separate double-holed grass-nests usually in the same tree, but select one nest to breed in after sealing one entrance hole. Thick-billed Weavers have powerful bills, capable of cracking large hard seeds and are well-known for leaving barbet-like bite-marks on bird-ringer fingers. Sociable Weavers build enormous communal nests in trees, or if forced to do so on a series of telephone poles. A recent deplorable tendency of local children is setting such nests alight to dine off roast Sociable Weaver chicks.

Weavers, queleas, bishops and widows sometimes nest in large colonies. Our largest widow, the Long-tailed Widow, spends from early morning till dusk with the proverbial daggers-drawn, displaying while patrolling the grassland territory of his nesting females against all other males. Then from dusk the males split off to gather peacefully in dribs and drabs to roost communally together in the same reed-patch. It reminds me precisely of thirsty friends going off to the local pub for a 'last one' after work.

1: *The Spotted-backed Weaver* (Ploceus cucullatus) *shows here the spots from which its name is derived.* (Photo: Eliot Lyons)
2: *The female Red-billed Buffalo-Weaver* (Bubalornis niger) *is brown, whereas the male is black.* (Photo: J.J. Theron)
3: *The untidy nests of the Red-billed Buffalo-Weaver, all divided into apartments.* (Photo: J.J. Theron)
4: *The male Red-headed Weaver* (Anaplectes melanotis) *builds its nest from strong fibrous material. If crushed, it takes up its original form in seconds.* (Photo: Peter Ginn)
5: *Female Thick-billed Weaver* (Amblyospiza albifrons) *at her nest. Thick-billed Weavers build most attractive unique nests.* (Photo: Martin Goetz)
6: *Male Thick-billed Weaver at his nest.* (Photo: Martin Goetz)
7: *The Yellow Weaver* (Ploceus subaureus) *is not a coastal species but has also nested sporadically in the Lowveld on a considerable scale.* (Photo: Geoff McIlleron)
8: *An excited Lesser Masked Weaver* (P. intermedius) *male shows an interested female over his newly constructed nest.* (Photo: Fanie Hendriks)
9: *Male Spectacled Weaver* (P. ocularis). (Photo: Frank Weber)

**1:** *The White-browed Sparrow-weaver* (Plocepasser mahali) *is found in the Lowveld in small numbers.* (Photo: Geoff McIlleron)

**2:** *The Golden Bishop* (Euplectes afer) *is a favourite bird due to the way the male puffs itself into a golden ball and drifts around over the short marshy vegetation it prefers to nest in.* (Photo: Fanie Hendriks)

**3:** *The Southern Red Bishop* (E. orix) *is a common sight in our marshes and reed-beds.* (Photo: Geoff McIlleron)

**4 & 5:** *Similar to the Red Bishop, the Fire-crowned (Black-winged) Bishop* (E. hordeaceus) *(female on left, male on right) has a northerly distribution with us.* (Photos: Cyril Laubscher)

**6:** *The tiny Scaly-feathered Finch* (Sporopipes squamifrons) *builds waxbill-like nests everywhere, some extremely low down.* (Photo: Fanie Hendriks)

**7:** *The impressive display flight of the Long-tailed Widow* (Euplectus progne) *male as he patrols his territory to protect his nesting females.* (Photo: Fanie Hendriks)

# Waxbills, Firefinches and Twinspots
## Family Estrildidae

The waxbills are one of the most strikingly attractive groups of small seed-eating birds, great favourites of aviculturalists. The lovely Locustfinch has a very different call to its relative, the familiar Quailfinch. Our Orange-breasted Waxbill uses old nests like those of bishops and other smallish weavers. The Red-headed and Cut-throat Finches also use such old nests. The Swee Waxbill is possibly a distinct species from the Yellow-bellied Waxbill, but interestingly both lack the diagnostic palate-spots. The Green Twinspot is one of our outstandingly attractive waxbills, and the Red-faced Crimsonwing likewise. The Black-faced, Grey, Cinderella and the Common Waxbill are all close relatives, also the Violet-eared and Blue, and finally the Red-throated and Pink-throated Twinspots. Then there are four *Lagonosticta* firefinches, three *Spermestes* mannikins, two *Pytilias* and the Lesser Seedcracker.

The bright sealing-wax red colour of the Common Waxbill's bill gave its name not only to the well-known Common Waxbill, but indeed to the entire group of waxbills as a whole. The ball-shaped grass nest is carefully built among tufts of grass on the ground to form a typically 'double-storey' structure with the upper-storey placed firmly on the lower level compartment. This extension to the nest reaches from ground level via a ramp to the upper level, the so-called 'cock's nest'. The little white eggs are laid in the lower compartment. I had earlier found such a nest with a clutch of eggs on the edge of a small pan, and it could be clearly seen that the water level was rising.

The entire clutch hatched, but soon the chicks were standing belly-deep in water. Not prepared to see them all drown, I carefully transferred the forlorn chicks into the original 'cock's nest' above. With sufficient dry space available, they were unhesitatingly fed and cared for by their parents in the 'cock's nest', thrived and were soon ready to fledge. The photographs taken after fledging show this rather untidy nest. However, the most fascinating aspect of this nesting was the apparent insistence by the parent pair to build yet a second 'cock's nest', apparently to replace the original 'cock's nest'. Constructed by this unusual Common Waxbill pair, they apparently felt by instinct this to be an essential requirement for their nest. Parasitism by the Pin-tailed Whydah was not noticeable in this particular case, though often recorded in other Common Waxbill and Orange-breasted Waxbill nests. The Black-cheeked Waxbill is also on record as building a 'cock's nest' on top of the main ball.

**Far left:** *Common Waxbill* (Estrilda astrild) *at its nest: ramp and entrance chamber to the nest below the bird, entrance to 'cock's nest' immediately above its head.* (Photo: Cape Bird Club)
**Left:** *The unique 'three-storey' nest of the Common Waxbill (see text above).* (Photo: Peter Milstein)

A final aspect of this interesting family is what appears to be an anti-predator strategy. Predation of arboreal waxbill nests and others by mammals like monkeys (in particular), bushbabies and genets is a serious problem. In one season in my garden I lost nine Collared Sunbird nests to the Samango Monkeys, which roam from tree to tree out of reach of my dogs. These tiny sunbirds and other species, like two species of mannikins, Black Sunbird and Bar-throated Apalis, seem powerless to prevent this raiding, despite nesting right against my house in desperation. However, several times when watching nests being built, I have noticed waxbills deliberately site their little nests in the immediate vicinity of large wasp nests. These waxbill nests seem to survive. I am convinced that this siting is no coincidence, but a deliberate strategy for survival. The observant monkeys appear to be reluctant to infuriate the wasps, which do not hesitate to attack such intruders eagerly.

**1:** *The Violet-eared Waxbill* (Granatina granatina) *is extremely attractive, particularly the male's violet 'ears'.* (Photo: Cyril Laubscher)

**2 and 3:** *The Swee Waxbill* (Coccopygia melanotis) *is decidedly pretty, with a two-tone red and black bill (male shown on left; female on right). A possible sibling species, provisionally named African Swee, is found to our north.* (Photos: Geoff McIlleron)

**4 and 5:** *The male Orange-breasted Waxbill* (Sporaeginthus subflavus) *(right) is much more handsome than most waxbills. The duller female (left) does not usually make her own nest but uses old nests of bishops, etc.* (Photos: Geoff McIlleron)

**6:** *The Blue Waxbill* (Uraeginthus angolensis) *is probably our commonest waxbill with sibling species in East and West Africa.* (Photo: Geoff McIlleron)

**7:** *The Red-faced Crimsonwing* (Cryptospiza reichenovii) *(male shown) is a beauty with a more north-eastern distribution.* (Photo: Geoff McIlleron)

**8:** *Another most attractive waxbill is the Green Twinspot* (Mandingoa nitidula), *where males have red faces and females yellow faces.* (Photo: Cyril Laubscher)

**1:** *The Red-billed Firefinch* (Lagonosticta senegala), *our smallest firefinch.* (Photo: Fanie Hendriks)

**2:** *Jameson's Firefinch* (L. rhodopareia). *I once found an adult entangled by the thighs in a Golden Orb spider's web, spinning around, unable to escape.* (Photo: Cyril Laubscher)

**3:** *The Blue-billed Firefinch* (L. rubricata) *is parasitised by the Black Widow-finch.* (Photo: Neville Brickell)

**4:** *Green-winged Melba* (Pytilia melba), *prettier than the Orange-winged Melba.* (Photo: Cyril Laubscher)

**5:** *The African Quailfinch* (Ortygospiza atricollis) *allows people to approach closely, then suddenly flies up with a characteristic tinkling call.* (Photo: Cyril Laubscher)

**6:** *The Red-headed Finch* (Amadina erythrocephala) *is mostly a western species, nesting in old nests of suitable species. However, it has recently extended into the Lowveld using old buffalo-weaver nests.* (Photo: Geoff McIlleron)

**7:** *The Cut-throat Finch* (A. fasciata), *named for its obvious 'cut-throat' is basically an eastern species, also using old nests.* (Photo: Geoff McIlleron)

**8:** *The Bronze Mannikin* (Spermestes cucullatus) *is our commonest mannikin.* (Photo: Geoff McIlleron)

**9:** *The larger Magpie Mannikin* (S. fringilloides) *is relatively rare with a restricted distribution here.* (Photo: Fanie Hendriks)

**10:** *The Red-backed Mannikin* (S. bicolor) *is easily the most attractive of our three mannikins, but a less common forest-dweller.* (Photo: Geoff McIlleron)

# Whydahs, Widow-finches and Cuckoo-finch

## Family Viduidae

In this family we find our seven *Vidua* whydahs and widow-finches (indigobirds), as well as the even more unusual Cuckoo-finch. Although birders tend to get the impression of a more prolific disproportionate number of parasitic cuckoos and other such parasites, this is not the case. An estimate has even been made that fewer than 3% of hosts in South Africa are parasitized. Apart from habitual deliberate parasitism, there are various possible causes for such apparent egg-placing behaviour, which should also be taken into consideration.

With the problem of 'dumped' eggs, where the nest of a specific female might for example have been destroyed during her egg-laying, the egg concerned can possibly simply have not been conveniently retained by the female in her oviduct. Then she may simply 'dump' it, lain without any semblance of a nest, on a sandbar for example. Alternatively, such an unwanted egg may be laid in a

**Left:** *The Sharp-tailed Paradise Whydah* (Vidua paradisaea) *male is easily distinguished from the Broad-tailed by their different tails.*
**Top right:** *The Sharp-tailed Paradise Whydah female, in dull plumage but identifiable.*
**Bottom right:** *The Shaft-tailed Whydah* (V. regia) *male and female. The male is particularly attractive.* (Photos: Cyril Laubscher)

conspecific nest with eggs, or even in the nest of a different species. Such eggs may hatch, with the chick then possibly becoming imprinted on the host species. Cases are known where such imprinted chicks may later mate successfully with a member of the host species. This is the known origin for example of small-scale hybridization between Yellow-billed Ducks and Red-billed Teals (Milstein 1979, 2000).

Particularly with the viduine parasites, where a number of suitable species are theoretically available for parasitization, some aspects of their main hosts may possibly be linked and favoured. Obviously it is generally necessary to globally balance 'clever' individual hosts, which are not fooled, with those which are readily fooled. Of the viduine parasites, only the Cuckoo-finch (perhaps significantly) lays non-white eggs. With the others, some little immaculate white eggs of similar appearance, shape and size can only be distinguished with relative difficulty in many cases, if at all.

However, another safeguard appears to have evolved here. Identification spots in specific patterns are found on the chick palates of at least some of the estrildine host species, clearly visible in begging chicks. Remarkably this clear identification is precisely duplicated by evolution in at least some of the viduine parasite chicks on a host-specific basis. In an Orange-breasted Waxbill nest I was monitoring, two eggs distinguished from the host eggs by their size and shape were laid on the same day. They were clearly laid there by two different Pin-tailed Whydah females. Therefore at least some of the parasite eggs can be visually identified.

However, it appears that here the host female is either not capable of distinguishing the parasite egg(s) from her own eggs, or that she simply does not care. Contrary to the *Cuculus* cuckoos and the *Indicator* honeyguides, where the parasitizing female may fly off with a host egg in her bill to ensure space for her future chick, the estrildine host chicks and the parasite chicks with their matching palate markings appear to co-exist amicably throughout, even after fledging. They totally lack the murderous hooks of the honeyguide hatchlings. The parasitic viduine female must optimally parasitize nests well before the host chicks hatch. The host female identifies chicks, whether her own or a parasite, by the species-specific palate spots in begging open mouths.

One wonders whether chicks with the 'wrong' palate spots or none at all are allowed to starve, otherwise why would such a system be developed? The viduine parasite chicks in particular seem to match their hosts with some accuracy. They seem to thrive with their selected hosts. Once a careful simultaneous count at my bird table included 49 mostly young Black Widow-finches, but interestingly only one Steel-blue Widow-finch. There are a number of cases observed where supposedly aloof adult cuckoos and other birds have fed soliciting fledged but still dependent parasite chicks, particularly if the chick is calling loudly.

The parasites do not always have it their own way. For example I once found a typical nest of the Fan-tailed Cisticola which a Cuckoo-finch had unsuccessfully attempted to parasitize. The Cuckoo-finch egg was larger

**1:** *The male Pin-tailed Whydah* (Vidua macroura), *an aggressive species well known for chasing other birds from feeding-tables.* (Photo: John Wesson)
**2:** *The Black Widow-finch* (V. funerea) *(male shown) parasitizes the Blue-billed Firefinch, palate spots and calls match the firefinch chicks.* (Photo: Peter Ginn)
**3:** *The Purple Widow-finch* (V. purpurascens) *(male shown) parasitizes the Jameson's Firefinch.* (Photo: Cyril Laubscher)
**4:** *Note the thick bill of the Cuckoo-finch* (Anomalospiza imberbis) *(male shown), which seems to parasitize several host species.* (Photo: Peter Ginn)

and differently coloured, but had been smashed with the unavoidable fall down from the entrance, situated as usual right at the top of the nest. There was also damage to the tiny cisticola eggs, and the nest had been recently abandoned. However, the system is by no means static, with continual progression by the contenders. The Sharp-tailed Paradise Whydah chicks definitely make use of the Green-winged Melba call in their deception, while the Broad-tailed Paradise Whydah is rare with me, and parasitizes the Orange-winged Melba, not Green-winged. Compared to parasitic cuckoos, our knowledge of viduine parasites leaves much to be desired. For this reason, a combined account is preferable rather than attempting to present accuracy when such data is largely lacking.

# SPARROWS AND PETRONIAS
## FAMILY PASSERIDAE

From the earliest references to sparrows, those in the Bible, the impression is given of commonness and low value. Yet, they as a group are cheerful and cheeky, often associated with man and his habitations. The House Sparrow was one of the English bird species introduced by Rhodes to remind him of 'home'. However, they did not 'take over' from the Cape Peninsula. This resulted from the similar Indian introduction into Durban, responsible for irreversible proliferation in southern Africa and far beyond. It is consequently disturbing to note the present puzzling decline of the House Sparrow in Britain, whence English friends told me recently of birders who come to their coastal home to see House Sparrows!

Our handsome Cape Sparrows build large domed nests of soft vegetation, as does the Great Sparrow, but the Grey-headed Sparrow, common in the Lowveld, nests in holes and crannies like the House Sparrow. Grey-headed Sparrows would in time have filled the niche here now usurped by the House Sparrows.

Known for generations in Europe incorrectly as Hedge Sparrows and also Dunnocks, the petronias are not sparrows, and our sole representative of this group, the Yellow-throated Petronia, nests in holes as shown.

**1:** *The Cape Sparrow* (Passer melanurus) *male, the only sparrow to have so much black on its head.* (Photo: John Wesson)
**2:** *The Great Sparrow* (Passer motitensis) *male with a slight resemblance to the House Sparrow.* (Photo: Cyril Laubscher)
**3:** *The Grey-headed Sparrow* (Passer diffusus) *shows its plain grey head and clear white wing-bar.* (Photo: Charles Barrett)
**4:** *The Yellow-throated Petronia* (Petronia superciliaris) *with its heavy white eye-stripe feeding a chick; yellow spot on throat not visible.* (Photo: Peter Ginn)

# Wagtails, Longclaws and Pipits
## Family Motacillidae

We have three resident wagtail species: the Cape, African Pied and Mountain; then the migratory Grey and Yellow together with another recent migrant, the Citrine Wagtail from the Eastern Cape. Recently, Alström & Odeen (2002) have emphasized incongruence between mitochondrial DNA, nuclear DNA and non-molecular data in the avian genus *Motacilla*. Clearly too much emphasis has been placed on mitochondrial DNA which apparently has been overrated as an oracle by itself, and is not the sole answer as we have been led to believe. The unchallenged estimations of species phylogenies, species limits and systematics in some passerine birds may clearly not be what they seem when properly evaluated in the face of some objective opposition. A rethink and more objective approach seem overdue instead of kow-towing to the proponents of this very expensive technique whatever their findings.

Pipits are a difficult group, but there are a few easy ones. The migratory Golden Pipit is very bright, smaller ones like ones like Bushveld and Short-tailed identifiable, and the Striped Pipit is boldly striped with yellow feather edging.

Three longclaw species occur with us: the Orange-throated, Yellow-throated and Pink-throated, easily distinguished by their throat-colours (see next page). While photographing Yellow-throated Longclaws from a hide, Ginn (1989) came to realize that the long toes and claws enable easier walking on the grass-tufts.

**1:** *The dapper black, grey and white Mountain Wagtail* (Motacilla clara) *would follow the mountain streams down after rains in Hoedspruit district, wagging its long tail.* (Photo: Peter Steyn)
**2:** *The African Pied Wagtail* (M. aguimp) *replaces the Cape Wagtail in our hotter areas, often as a garden bird.* (Photo: Geoff McIlleron)
**3:** *The Cape Wagtail* (M. capensis) *is a common and confiding bird, which suffered considerable mortality by gardeners unwittingly using dieldrin on their lawns.* (Photo: Fanie Hendriks)
**4:** *The Striped Pipit* (Anthus lineiventris) *is both handsome and easy to identify, unusual for a pipit. This was a regular winter visitor in Hoedspruit district.* (Photo: Peter Ginn)

**Left:** *The Pink-throated Longclaw* (Macronyx ameliae) *is the most beautiful, rarest and shyest of the group, found with us only in our hot north-eastern corner.* (Photo: Warwick Tarboton)
**Centre:** *The Orange-throated Longclaw* (M. capensis) *is the common Highveld longclaw, and its mewing call while flying away is well known.* (Photo: Peter Ginn)
**Right:** *The Yellow-throated Longclaw* (M. croceus) *is the common longclaw of the Lowveld, usually found near water, and when flushed tends to perch on top of a convenient tree to watch the intruder.* (Photo: Peter Ginn)

# CANARIES, BUNTINGS AND CHAFFINCHES
## FAMILY FRINGILLIDAE

Our canaries are more popular for their songs in Japan than here, and the Yellow-eyed Canary is for example a favourite there, where it is known as 'Green Singing Finch'. The overlooked Lemon-breasted Canary was one of the last bird species to be described in South Africa, where it had been long confused with the plainer Black-throated Canary, but which was clearly a good species. The Yellow Canary, Bully Canary and Cape Canary are also relatively bright yellow, while our Forest Canary is attractive but heavily streaked. Some of our duller canaries like the Streaky-headed Canary and the Cape and Drakensberg Siskins are rather unattractive, but the handsome Black-headed Canary makes up for them. However, more research is still required with the closely related Damara Canary where there have been disputes over its validity for years. The Chaffinch, introduced by Rhodes, is still found in a limited area on the eastern slopes of Table Mountain and may yet survive. We have five bunting species with their typical angled bills, and of them the extremely dull Lark-like Bunting is easily the most difficult to identify.

1: *The Lemon-breasted Canary* (Crithagra citrinipectus), *long overlooked as a distinct species.* (Photo: Cyril Laubscher)
2: *The Forest Canary* (C. scotops) *is darkish green and heavily striated, inclined towards a forest habitat.* (Photo: Fanie Hendriks)
3: *The Black-headed Canary* (Serinus alario) *has an unusual colour pattern, but its link to the Damara Canary still requires clarity.* (Photo: Fanie Hendriks)
4: *The Yellow Canary* (C. flaviventris) *is an attractive bird and sings well.* (Photo: Fanie Hendriks)
5: *This Lark-like Bunting* (Emberiza impetuani) *pair is so plain as to be readily overlooked.* (Photo: Cyril Laubscher)
6: *The Cape Bunting* (Emberiza capensis) *is rather plain, apart from its head-markings.* (Photo: Geoff McIlleron)
7: *The Golden-breasted Bunting* (E. flaviventris) *is our handsomest bunting and has a sweet song.* (Photo: Fanie Hendriks)
8: *The Cinnamon-breasted Bunting* (E. tahapisi) *often matches its substrate well.* (Photo: Fanie Hendriks)

CANARIES, BUNTINGS AND CHAFFINCHES • FAMILY FRINGILLIDAE • 197

# Epilogue

In this book I have attempted to give birders and would-be birders some insights into our fascinating birdlife which may not be readily available to them. To me there is little point in ticking the birds each birder sees on a life-list like a stamp collection without having some inkling about where they fit into God's great plan for the subcontinent and the remarkable avifauna we have been blessed with. As tragic, is not making use of such data, simply accumulating it to gather dust in a cupboard. There may be some serious conservation worker or interested person who would love to know what you have observed, but which you may consider is well known to others or inconsequential.

Never forget the ornithologist who with true humbleness wrote that he wondered how many great bird experts had lived and died before a schoolboy saw a starling 'anting'. Mrs Margaret Morse Nice was apparently an ordinary housewife when she decided untaught to study the song-sparrows around her home. These common American birds led her with her keen insight to become a world authority on the group and behaviour.

Here bird clubs and the right attitude can play an incredible role. Not by looking down one's nose at the mistakes all beginners make, causing confusion by foisting unjustified foolish names on the public, or jealously denying a remarkable sighting was possible because they have not seen it themselves.

To conclude a decidedly personal view of the South African avifauna, I would simply like to state my belief that in this view, despite the high level of development which has taken place in our country, and despite some serious mistakes which are not over, the picture as I see it is very far from the doom and gloom found in many other parts of the world. Because southern Africa is a subcontinent, I believe we have no birds here in danger of total extinction. Local extinctions with blind habitat destruction yes, but with wise management the stocks are replenished or the niche taken by another similar species. The Bateleur Eagle for example seems to be staging a comeback because many farmers have realized the harm they are doing to such non-target species by blanket treatment of their veld with strychnine-injected meat-pills before the calving or lambing season.

*A skein of Greater Flamingoes flighting past, with the intensive development of Walvis Bay in the background, reminding us that co-existence is possible.* (Photo: Tony Heald)

# Bibliography

ALSTRÖM, P. & ÖDEEN, A. 2002. Incongruence between mitochondrial DNA, nuclear DNA and non-molecular data in the avian genus *Motacilla*: implications for estimates of species phylogenies. Summarised in Alström, P. & Zetterström, B. 2003. *Pipits and wagtails of Europe, Asia and North America: identification and systematics*. Christopher Helm / A. Black: Princeton University Press.

ALVAREZ DEL TORO, M. 1971. On the breeding biology of the American Finfoot in southern Mexico. *Living Bird* 10: 79–88.

ANDERSON, M. 2000a. Letter: Sandgrouse shooting in the Northern Cape. *Africa Birds & Birding* 5 (5): 8–10.

ANDERSON, M.D. 2000b. Sandgrouse hide opens at Witsand Nature Reserve. *Africa Birds & Birding* 5 (2): 23.

ANONYMOUS. 2000. White-winged Flufftails at Wakkerstroom. *Africa Birds & Birding* 5 (3): 87.

AUSTIN, O.L. 1962. *Birds of the world*. London: Hamlyn.

BALFOUR, D. 2001. Flamingos dying at Lake Bogoria. *Africa Birds & Birding* 6 (5): 16.

BENSON, C.W., BROOKE, R.K. & IRWIN, M.P.S. 1971. The Slaty Egret is a good species. *Bull. Brit. Orn. Club* 91: 131–133.

BOCK, W.J. 1958. A generic review of the plovers (Charadiinae, Aves). *Bulletin Museum Comparative Zoology, Harvard* 118 (2): 27–97.

BROWN, L. 1965. *Africa. A natural history*. London: Hamish Hamilton.

BROWN, L. 1972. *African birds of prey*. 2nd ed. London: Collins.

BROWN, L. 1976. *Birds of prey: their biology and ecology*. London: Hamlyn.

BROWN, L. 1980. *The African Fish Eagle*. Cape Town: Purnell.

BROWN, L. & AMADON, D. 1968. *Eagles, hawks and falcons of the world*. Feltham: Country Life Books.

BROWN, L.H., URBAN, E.K. & NEWMAN, K. (eds.) 1982. *The birds of Africa. 1*. London: Academic Press.

CADE, T.J. & MACLEAN, G.L. 1967. Transport of water by adult sandgrouse to their young. *Condor* 69: 323–343.

CHITTENDEN, H. & MYBURGH, N. 1996. Vultures in the village. *Africa Birds & Birding* 1 (1): 20–27.

CLANCEY, P.A. 1952. On the status of *Tauraco reichenowi* (Fisher), and its relationship to the other South African forms of the genus *Tauraco* Kluk. *Durban Mus. Novit.* 4 (3): 31–39.

CLANCEY, P.A. 1994. Combined biogeographic role of river valleys and aridity in Southern African bird distribution. *Durban Museum Novitates* 19: 13–29.

COETZEE, D. 1999. Letter: White-winged Flufftails. *Africa Birds & Birding* 4 (5): 10–11.

COOPER, J. 2004. Are mice killing the albatrosses of Gough? *Africa Birds & Birding* 9 (1): 46–50.

CRAMP, S., SIMMONS, K.E.L., FERGUSON-LEES, I.J., GILLMOR, R., HOLLOM, P.A.D., HUDSON, R., NICHOLSON, E.M., OGILVIE, M.A., OLNEY, P.J.S., VOOUS, K.H. & WATTEL, J. 1977. *Handbook of the birds of Europe, the Middle East and North Africa: the birds of the Western Palearctic. 1*. Oxford: Oxford University Press.

CROWE, T. 2000. Gamebirds in southern Africa. *Africa Birds & Birding* 5 (2): 68–74.

CYRUS, D.P. 1989. White Pelican *Pelecanus onocrotalus*. In Ginn, P.J., McIlleron, W.G. & Milstein, P. le S. (eds.) *The complete book of southern African birds*. Cape Town: Struik Winchester.

DELACOUR, J. & MAYR, E. 1945. The family Anatidae. *Wilson Bull.* 57 (1): 3–55.

DODMAN, T., KATANEKWA, V., ASPINALL, D. & STJERNSTEDT, R. 2000. Status and distribution of the Black-cheeked Lovebird, Zambia. *Ostrich* 71 (1&2): 228–234.

EYTON, T.C. 1838. *A monograph of the Anatidae, or duck tribe*. London.

FREITAG, S. & ROBINSON, T.J. 1993. Phylogeographic patterns in mitochondrial DNA of the Ostrich (*Struthio camelus*). *Auk* 110 (3): 614–622.

FRY, C.H. 1975. Wings over the Sahara. In *The second bird-watchers' book*: (ed.) J. Gooders. Newton Abbot: David & Charles.

FRY, C.H. 1984. *The bee-eaters*. Calton: Poyser.

FRY, C.H., KEITH, S. & URBAN, E.K. (eds.) 1988. *Birds of Africa. 3*. London: Academic Press.

GARGETT, V. 1990. *The Black Eagle. A study*. Randburg: Acorn Books.

GENTIS, S. 1976. Co-operative nest building by Hamerkops. *Honeyguide* 88: 48.

GILL, E.L. 1945. *A first guide to South African birds*. 3rd ed. Cape Town: Maskew Miller.

GINN, P.J. 1989a. Pinkbacked Pelican *Pelecanus rufescens*. In Ginn, P.J., McIlleron, W.G. & Milstein, P. le S. (eds.) *The complete book of southern African birds*. Cape Town: Struik Winchester.

GINN, P.J. 1989b. African Broadbill *Smithornis capensis*. In Ginn, P.J., McIlleron, W.G. & Milstein, P. le S. (eds.) *The complete book of southern African birds*. Cape Town: Struik Winchester.

GINN, P.J. 1989c. Common Scimitarbill *Rhinopomastus cyanomelas*. In Ginn, P.J., McIlleron, W.G. & Milstein, P. le S. (eds.) *The complete book of southern African birds*. Cape Town: Struik Winchester.

GURNEY, J.H. 1871. Note in Ayres, T. (1871). Additional notes on birds of the territory of the Trans-Vaal Republic. *Ibis Ser.* 3, 1: 253–270.

HAAGNER, A. & IVY, R.H. 1923. *Sketches of South African bird-life*. 3rd ed. Cape Town: Maskew Miller.

HALL, B.P. 1963. The francolins, a study in speciation. *Bull. Br. Mus. Nat. Hist. Zool.* 10: 107–204.

HALLIDAY, T. 1978. *Vanishing birds*. London: Sidgwick & Jackson.

HANCOCK, P. 2001. Lesser Jacana. Toeing the line? *Africa Birds & Birding* 6: 46–53.

HARRIS, T. & ARNOTT, G. 1988. *Shrikes of southern Africa*. Cape Town: Struik Winchester.

HARRISON, J.H., ALLAN, D.G., UNDERHILL, L.G., HERREMANS, M., TREE, A.J., PARKER, V. & BROWN, C.J. (eds.) 1997. *The atlas of southern African birds. Volume 1: Non-passerines*. Johannesburg: BirdLife South Africa.

HARRISON, P. 1983. *Seabirds: an identification guide*. London: Croom Helm.

HOCKEY, P. 1997. African Black Oystercatcher. Between the tides. *Africa Birds & Birding* 2 (5): 28–34.

HOCKEY, P. & ASPINALL, S.J. 1996. The Crab Plover. Enigmatic wader of the desert coasts. *Africa Birds & Birding* 1 (1): 60–67.

HUXLEY, J.S. 1914. The courtship-habits of the Great Crested Grebe (*Podiceps cristatus*); with an addition to the theory of sexual selection. *Proc. Zool. Soc. Lond.* 1914: 491–562.

INGOLD, J.L., GUTMAN, S.I. & OSBORNE, D.R. 1987. Biochemical systematics of the crowned cranes. *Proc. Int. Crane Workshop, Bharatpur*. (Feb. 1983): 317–322.

JENKINS, A. 2003. On a wing and a prayer. *Africa Birds & Birding* 8 (4): 34–41.

JENSEN, R.A.C. 1966. Genetics of Cuckoo Egg Polymorphism. *Nature* 209: 827.

JOHNSGARD, P.A. 1967. Observations on the behaviour and relationships of the White-backed Duck and the Stiff-tailed Ducks. *Wildfowl* 18: 98–107.

JOHNSON, D. 2002. Letter: The non-riddle of flamingo deaths. *Africa Birds & Birding* 7 (2): 9.

KAHL, M.P. 1967. Observations on the behaviour of the Hamerkop *Scopus umbretta* in Uganda. *Ibis* 109: 25–32.

KEITH, S., BENSON, C.W. & IRWIN, M.P.S. 1970. The genus *Sarothrura* (Aves, Rallidae). *Bull. Am. Mus. Nat. Hist.* 143 (1): 1–84.

KEMP, A.C. & KEMP, M.I. 1980. The biology of the southern ground hornbill *Bucorvus leadbeateri* (Vigors) (Aves: Bucerotidae). *Ann. Tvl. Mus.* 32: 65–100.

KEMP, A.C. & MACLEAN, G.L. 1973a. Neonatal plumage patterns of Three-banded and Temminck's Coursers and their bearing on courser genera. *Ostrich* 44: 80–81.

KEMP, A.C. & MACLEAN, G.L. 1973b. Nesting of the Three-banded Courser. *Ostrich* 44: 82–83.

KEMP, A.C. & TARBOTON, W. 1976. Small South African bustards. *Bokmakierie* 28: 40–43.

LACK, D. 1956. Swifts in a tower. London: Chapman & Hall.

LIVERSIDGE, R. 1963. The nesting of the Hamerkop *Scopus umbretta*. *Ostrich* 34: 55–62.

LLOYD, P. 1997. Desert nomad extraordinaire. *Africa Birds & Birding* 1 (5): 26–32.

LOCKLEY, R.M. 1971. Non-stop flight and migration in the Common Swift *Apus apus*. *Proc. 3rd Pan-Afr. orn. Congr.:* 265–269.

LORBER, P. 1985. What makes a Hamerkop's nest? *Honeyguide* 31 (1): 48.

LÖTTER, W.J. 1975. Is kraanvoëls ware landlewende voëls? (with English summary). *Bokmakierie* 27: 75–78.

LYDEKKER, R. (ed.) 1895. The royal natural history. 4. *Birds*. London: Warne.

LYNES, H. 1930. Review of the genus *Cisticola*. *Ibis* Twelfth Series, Vol. 6. *Cisticola* Supplement.

MACKWORTH-PRAED, C.W. 1964. Article 'Pitta' in Thomson, A.L. (ed.) *New Dict. Birds*. London: Nelson.

MACLEAN, G.L. 1967. The breeding biology and behavior of the Double-banded Courser *Rhinoptilus africanus* (Temminck). *Ibis* 109: 556–569.

MACLEAN, G.L. 1970. The neonatal plumage pattern of the Double-banded Courser. *Ostrich* 41: 215–216.

MACLEAN, G.L. 1993. *Roberts' birds of South Africa*. 6th ed. Cape Town: Trustees of the John Voelcker Bird Book Fund.

MALAN, G. 1998. Letter: Spider webs in nest. *Africa Birds & Birding* 3 (3): 13–14.

MASTERSON, A.N.B. 1989a. Openbilled Stork *Anastomus lamelligerus*. In Ginn, P.J., McIlleron, W.G. & Milstein, P. le S. (eds.) *The complete book of southern African birds*. Cape Town: Struik Winchester.

MASTERSON, A.N.B. 1989b. Abdim's Stork *Ciconia abdimii*. In Ginn, P.J., McIlleron, W.G. & Milstein, P. le S. (eds.) *The complete book of southern African birds*. Cape Town: Struik Winchester.

MASTERSON, A.N.B. 1989c. Woollynecked Stork *Ciconia episcopus*. In Ginn, P.J., McIlleron, W.G. & Milstein, P. le S. (eds.) *The complete book of southern African birds*. Cape Town: Struik Winchester.

MASTERSON, A.N.B. 1989d. White Stork *Ciconia ciconia*. In Ginn, P.J., McIlleron, W.G. & Milstein, P. le S. (eds.) *The complete book of southern African birds*. Cape Town: Struik Winchester.

MATHEWS, N.J.C. 1979. Observation of the Shoebill in the Okavango swamps. *Ostrich* 50: 185.

McLACHLAN, G.R. & LIVERSIDGE, R. 1957. *Roberts' Birds of South Africa*. (2nd ed.). No place: Trustees of the South African Bird Book Fund.

McLACHLAN, G.R. & LIVERSIDGE, R. 1978. *Roberts' Birds of South Africa* (4th ed.) Cape Town: Trustees of the John Voelcker Bird Book Fund.

MEINERTZHAGEN, R. 1964. Article 'Sandgrouse' in Thomson, A.L. (ed.) *New Dict. Birds*. London: Nelson.

MENDELSOHN, J.M., SINCLAIR, J.C. & TARBOTON, W.R. 1983. Flushing flufftails out of vleis. *Bokmakierie* 35: 9–11.

MILSTEIN, P. 1995. Tinkering around at Mariepskop. *Birding in southern Africa* 47 (2): 36–39.

MILSTEIN, P. le S. 1962. The Angola Kingfisher *Halcyon senegalensis*. Part 1: Biology. *Ostrich* 33: 2–12.

MILSTEIN, P. le S. 1967. Authentic egg of Greater Honeyguide. *Ostrich* 37: 57.

MILSTEIN P. le S. 1968. Affinity of *Turdus litsitsirupa*. *Bull. Brit. Orn. Cl.* 88: 1.

MILSTEIN, P. le S. 1973. Buttons and Bald Ibises. *Bokmakierie* 25: 57–60.

MILSTEIN, P. le S. 1974. More Bald Ibis buttons. *Bokmakierie* 26: 88.

MILSTEIN, P. le S. 1975a. How baby Egyptian geese leave a high nest. *Bokmakierie* 27: 47–51.

MILSTEIN, P. le S. 1975b. The biology of Barberspan with special reference to the avifauna. *Ostrich* Suppl. 10: 1–74.

MILSTEIN, P. le S. 1975c. Observations on penduline tit nest structure. *Bokmakierie* 27 (2): 8–9.

MILSTEIN, P. le S. 1979. The evolutionary significance of wild hybridization in South African Highveld ducks. *Ostrich* Suppl. 13: 1–48.

MILSTEIN, P. le S. 1983. *Uit die natuur. Ons Voëls*. Roodepoort: Cumboeke.

MILSTEIN P. le S. 1993. A study of the Egyptian Goose *Alopochen aegyptiacus*. Unpubl. Ph.D thesis, University of Pretoria.

MILSTEIN, P. le S. 1999. The Lowveld. *Africa Birds & Birding* 4 (4): 62–66.

MILSTEIN, P. le S. 2000a. Letter: White-winged Flufftail. *Africa Birds & Birding* 5 (1): 9–10.

MILSTEIN, P. le S. 2000b. Survival aspects of the Yellow-billed Duck. *Pelea* 19: 116–121. 21st Anniversary Scientific Edition.

MILSTEIN, P. le S., BRIDGEFORT, M.A. & BRIDGEFORT, C.M. 2004. Bluethroated Sunbirds in the Limpopo-Mpumalanga Lowveld. *Hornbill* 74: 39–49.

MILSTEIN, P. le S. & HUNTER, H.C. 1974. The spectacular Black Heron. *Bokmakierie* 26 (4): 93–97.

MILSTEIN, P. le S., JONES, C.C. & STEYN, D.J. 2000. Sooty Falcons in the Central Lowveld. *Hornbill* 58: 39–47.

MILSTEIN, P. le S., PRESTT, I. & BELL, A.A. 1970. The breeding cycle of the Grey Heron. *Ardea* 58: 171–257.

MILSTEIN, P. le S. & WOLFF, S.W. 1987. The over-simplification of our "francolins". *S. Afr. J. Wild. Res.* Suppl. 1: 58–65.

MITCHELL, S. 1977. Apparent atypical habitat and behaviour of Peters' Finfoot. *Honeyguide* 92: 43.

MOREAU, R.E. 1966. *The bird faunas of Africa and its islands*. London: Academic Press.

OATLEY, T. 2003. Going to ground. The life of a terrestrial woodpecker. *Africa Birds & Birding* 8 (5): 28–33.

OATLEY, T.B. 2004. A re-appraisal of the taxonomic status of the Karoo Scrub-Robin. *Ostrich* 75: 156–158.

OLSON, S.R. & FEDUCCIA, A. 1980. Relationships and evolution of flamingoes (Aves: Phoenicopteridae). *Smithsonian Contrib. Zool.* 316: 73.

OWINO, A. 2002. Letter: Flamingos in Kenya: the true story. *Africa Birds & Birding* 7 (1): 10.

PARKER, V. 1999. *The atlas of the birds of Sul do Save, southern Mozambique*. Cape Town & Johannesburg: Avian Demography Unit and the Endangered Wildlife Trust.

PETERSEN, S. 2003. Hooked towards extinction. *Africa Birds & Birding* 8 (6): 74–75.

PITMAN, C.R.S. 1964. Article 'Painted Snipe' in Thomson, A.L. (ed.) *New Dict. Birds*. London: Nelson.

RADFORD, A. 2003. Co-operative breeding and competitive feeding. *Africa Birds & Birding* 8 (5): 13.

ROBINSON, T.J. & MATTHEE, C.A. 1999. Molecular genetic relationships of the extinct ostrich, *Struthio camelus syriacus*: consequences for ostrich introductions into Saudi Arabia. *Animal Conservation* 2: 165–171.

ROWAN, M.K. 1983. *The Doves, Parrots, Louries and Cuckoos of Southern Africa*. Cape Town & Johannesburg: David Philip.

RUSHWORTH, D. 2005. Occurrence of Mottled Swifts along eastern escarpment. *Hornbill* 77: 32.
RYAN, P. 1999. The fastest bird? *Africa Birds & Birding* 4 (2): 17.
RYAN, P. 2001. Chatham Albatross. *Africa Birds & Birding* 6 (4): 18.
RYAN, P. 2002. Relatively speaking ... *Africa Birds & Birding* 7 (1): 38–39.
RYAN, P. 2004. Conserving albatrosses. *Africa Birds & Birding* 9 (1): 36–45.
RYAN, P. & SINCLAIR, I. 2001. The great skua debate. *Africa Birds & Birding* 6 (4): 16–17.
SCHMITT, M. 1971. Black Heron breeding at Westdene. *Witwatersrand Bird Club News Sheet* No. 74: 6.
SEARS, H.F., MOSELY, L.J. & MUELLER, H.C. 1976. Behavioral evidence on skimmers' evolutionary relationships. *Auk* 93: 170–174.
SIEGFRIED, W.R. 1968. Non-breeding plumage in the adult male Maccoa Duck. *Ostrich* 39: 91–93.
SIEGFRIED, W.R. 1975. On the nest of the Hamerkop. *Ostrich* 46: 267.
SIMS, R.W. 1959. The *Ceyx erithacus* and *rufidorsus* species problem. *J. Linn. Soc. (Zool.)* 44: 212–221.
SIMMONS, K.E.L. 1964. Article 'Grebe' in Thomson, A.L. (ed.) *New Dict. Birds*. London: Nelson.
SIMMONS, R. 2002. Letter: Reviving the dead flamingos. *Africa Birds & Birding* 7 (3): 9.
SIMMONS, R. 2004. Blood brothers. *Africa Birds & Birding* 9 (3): 43–48.
SINCLAIR, J.C. 1989. Redtailed Tropicbird *Phaethon rubricauda*. In Ginn, P.J., McIlleron, W.G. & Milstein, P. le S. (eds.) *The complete book of southern African birds*. Cape Town: Struik Winchester.
SINCLAIR, I., HOCKEY, P. & TARBOTON, W. 2002. *Sasol birds of southern Africa*. 3rd ed. Cape Town: Struik.
SINCLAIR, I. & RYAN, P. 2003. *Birds of Africa south of the Sahara*. Cape Town: Struik.
STOKES, T. 1968. *Birds of the Atlantic Ocean*. Feltham: Country Life.
SOUTH AFRICAN ORNITHOLOGICAL SOCIETY LIST COMMITTEE. 1969. *Check list of the Birds of South Africa*. No place: no publisher.
STEYN, P. 1996. *Nesting birds*. Vlaeberg: Fernwood Press.
STEYN, P. 2000. Herculean Hamerkops. *Africa Birds & Birding* 5 (2): 76–81.
STONEHOUSE, B. 1964a. Article 'Sheathbill' in Thomson, A.L. (ed.) *New Dict. Birds*. London: Nelson.
STONEHOUSE, B. 1964b. Article 'Tropicbird' in Thomson, A.L. (ed.) *New Dict. Birds*. London: Nelson.
STONEHOUSE, B. 1964c. Article 'Frigatebird' in Thomson, A.L. (ed.) *New Dict. Birds*. London: Nelson.
TALJAARD, F. 2003. Kestrels in the Karoo. *Africa Birds & Birding* 8 (4): 44.
TARBOTON, W. 1989a. Sacred Ibis *Threskiornis aethiopicus*. In Ginn, P.J., McIlleron, W.G. & Milstein, P. le S. (eds.) *The complete book of southern African birds*. Cape Town: Struik Winchester.
TARBOTON, W. 1989b. African Jacana *Actophilornis africanus*. In Ginn, P.J., McIlleron, W.G. & Milstein P. le S. (eds.) *The complete book of southern African birds*. Cape Town: Struik Winchester.
TARBOTON W. 1989c. Black Stork *Ciconia nigra*. In Ginn, P.J., McIlleron, W.G. & Milstein, P. le S. (eds.) *The complete book of southern African birds*. Cape Town: Struik Winchester.
TARBOTON, W. 1996. The bird that walks on water. *Africa Birds & Birding* 1 (3): 22–30.
TARBOTON, W. 1997. Gabar Goshawk. *Africa Birds & Birding* 2 (6): 26–28.
TARBOTON, W. 2001. *A guide to the nests & eggs of southern African birds*. Cape Town: Struik.
TARBOTON, W. 2004. Woodland Kingfisher. *Africa Birds & Birding* 9 (2): 28–33.
TARBOTON, W. & ERASMUS, R. 1998. *Owls and owling in southern Africa*. Cape Town: Struik.
TARBOTON, W., KEMP, M.I. & KEMP, A.C. 1987. *Birds of the Transvaal*. Pretoria: Transvaal Museum.
THERON, G. 2001. Mangrove Kingfisher in the Durban Aquarium. *Hornbill* 61: 44–45.
THOMSON, A.L. 1964. Article 'Hammerhead' in Thomson, A.L. (ed.) *New Dict. Birds*. London: Nelson.
TREE, A.J. 1989a. Painted Snipe *Rostratula benghalensis*. In Ginn, P.J., McIlleron, W.G. & Milstein, P. le S. (eds.) *The complete book of southern African birds*. Cape Town: Struik Winchester.
TREE, A.J. 1989b. Lesser Jacana *Microparra capensis*. In Ginn, P.J., McIlleron, W.G. & Milstein, P. le S. (eds.) *The complete book of southern African birds*. Cape Town: Struik Winchester.
TREE, A.J. 1989c. Crab Plover *Dromas ardeola*. In Ginn, P.J., McIlleron, W.G. & Milstein, P. le S. (eds.) *The complete book of southern African birds*. Cape Town: Struik Winchester.
TREE, A.J. 1989d. Redwinged Pratincole *Glareola pratincola*. In Ginn, P.J., McIlleron, W.G. & Milstein, P. le S. (eds.) *The complete book of southern African birds*. Cape Town: Struik Winchester.
TREE, A.J. 1989e. Rock Pratincole *Glareola nuchalis*. In Ginn, P.J., McIlleron, W.G. & Milstein, P. le S. (eds.) *The complete book of southern African birds*. Cape Town: Struik Winchester.
URBAN, E.K., FRY, C.H. & KEITH, S. (eds.) 1986. *Birds of Africa*. 2. London: Academic Press.
URBAN, E.K., FRY, C.H. & KEITH, S. (eds.) 1997. *Birds of Africa*. 5. London: Academic Press.
VAN PERLO, B. 1999. *Birds of southern Africa*. London: Harper Collins.
VAN REENEN, A. 2004. *For the love of birds*. Tzaneen: Loretta Farm Publications.
VERDOORN, G. & VAN ZYL, N. 2003. Poisoning: the bane of birds' lives. *Africa Birds & Birding* 8 (1): 20.
VERNON, C.J. 1971. Notes on the biology of the Black Coucal. *Ostrich* 42: 242–258.
VERNON, C.J. 1984. The breeding biology of the Thickbilled Cuckoo. *Proc. V Pan-Afr. orn. Congr.*: 825–840.
WANLESS, R. 2001. Preening power. *Africa Birds & Birding* 6 (1): 55–59.
WANLESS, R. 2002. Frigatebirds aerial attitude. *Africa Birds & Birding* 7 (1): 36–41.
WARBURTON, L. 2002. Black-cheeked Lovebird: Africa's most threatened lovebird. *Africa Birds & Birding* 7 (1): 52–59.
WEAVING, A.J.S. 1989. Lesser Flamingo *Phoeniconaias minor*. In Ginn, P.J., McIlleron, W.G. & Milstein, P. le S. (eds.) *The complete book of southern African birds*. Cape Town: Struik Winchester.
WHATELEY, A. 1982. Anting in the African Finfoot. *Ostrich* 53: 177.
WILSON, R.T. & WILSON, M.P. 1984. Breeding biology of the Hamerkop in central Mali. *Proc. V Pan-Afr. orn. Congr.*: 855–865.
WILSON, R.T. & WILSON, M.P. 1986. Nest building in the Hamerkop *Scopus umbretta*. *Ostrich* 57: 224–232.
WINTERBOTTOM, J.M. 1951. *Common birds of the Cape*. Cape Town: Longmans Green.
WINTERBOTTOM, J.M. 1952. *Common birds of the waterways*. Cape Town: Longmans Green.
WIRMINGHAUS, O. 1995. Colour variation and anomalies in South African parrots. *Birding in southern Africa* 47: 76–77.
WIRMINGHAUS, J.O., DOWNS, C.T., PERRIN, M.R. & SYMES, C.T. 2002. Taxonomic relationships of the subspecies of the Cape Parrot *Poicephalus robustus* (Gmelin). *Journal of Natural History* 36: 361–378.
WOLFF, S.W. & MILSTEIN, P. le S. 1976. Rediscovery of the White-winged Flufftail in South Africa. *Bokmakierie* 28: 33–36.
ZALOUMIS, E.A. & MILSTEIN, P. le S. 1975. The conservation of wetland habitats for waterfowl in Southern Africa. *Afr. Wildl.* Suppl. to Vol. 29: 1–12.

# Index

Aardvark 83
*Accipiter rufiventris* 109
Accipitridae 108, 114
*Achaetops* 170
*Achatina immaculata* 29
*Acrocephalus* 170, 172
    *A. gracilirostris* 171
*Actophilornis africanus* 87
*Aegypius occipitalis* 110
African barbets 25
African warblers 173
*Afrotis afra* 73
*Agapornis* 57
    *A. roseicollis* 55
Alaudidae 175
Albatross, Black-browed 150
    Chatham 149
    Laysan 149
    Short-tailed 151
    Wandering 149, 150
    Yellow-nosed 150
albatrosses 149
alcedinid kingfishers 40
Alcedinidae 40, 42, 44
*Alcedo atthis* 40
    *A. cristata* 41
    *A. semitorquata* 41
Alcidae 100, 149
*Alle alle* 149
*Alopochen aegyptiaca* 18
*Amadina erythrocephala* 191
    *A. fasciata* 191
*Amaurornis* 79
    *A. flavirostris* 79
*Amblyospiza albifrons* 187
*Anaplectes melanotis* 187
*Anastomus lamelligerus* 141
Anatidae 17
Anatinae 18
Anatini 18
*Andropadus* 170
    *A. importunus* 170
    *A. milanjensis* 170
*Anhinga rufa* 122
Anhingidae 122
*Anomalospiza imberbis* 193
*Anous* 108
Anseriformes 15
Anserinae 18
Anserini 18
*Anthoscopus* 166
    *A. caroli* 166
    *A. minutus* 166
*Anthropoides paradiseus* 75
*Anthus lineiventris* 195
*Apalis* 174
Apalis, Bar-throated 190
*Apaloderma narina* 37
*Aplopelia larvata* 71
Apodidae 58
Apodiformes 58
Apodinae 58
*Aptenodytes* 146
Apterygidae 10
*Apus apus* 59

*Aquila* 112
    *A. spilogaster* 109
*Arachnothera* 184
*Archaeopteryx lithographica* 9, 61
*Ardea* 127
    *A. cinerea* 127
    *A. goliath* 127
Ardeidae 125
*Ardeola* 128
    *A. ralloides* 127
    *A. rufiventris* 127
*Ardeotis kori* 73
*Asio capensis* 65
Auk, Little 149
auks 100
Avocet, American 95
    Chilean 96
    Pied 95
    Red-necked 95
avocets 95
Aythini 18

Babbler, Arrow-marked 151, 171
    Southern Pied 171
babblers 15, 165, 170
baboons 15
*Balearica regulorum* 76
Barbet, Acacia Pied 26
    Black-collared 22, 26
    Crested 25, 26
barbets 25
barn owls 63
Bathawk 111
*Batis capensis* 160
    *B. molitor* 160
Batis, Cape 160
    Chinspot 160
batises 159, 160
Bay Owl, Congo 64
    Oriental 64
bay owls 63
Bee-eater, Blue-cheeked 47, 48
    European 46, 47, 48
    Little 47
    Madagascar 48
    Northern Carmine 48
    Olive 48
    Southern Carmine 47, 48
    Swallow-tailed 46, 47
    White-fronted 47
bee-eaters 46, 59
*Bias musicus* 160
birds' nest soup 59
Bishop, Black-winged 188
    Fire-crowned 188
    Golden 188
    Southern Red 22, 188
bishopbirds 27
bishops 51, 187
Bittern, Dwarf 128
    Great 129
    Little 128
bitterns 125
Black Mamba 186
Blackcap 172

Bush 172
Blêrtinktinkie 173
bo'sun birds 120
Bokmakierie 159
boobies 120, 121
Booby, Brown 121, 122
    Masked 121
    Red-footed 121
*Bostrychia hagedash* 135
Boubou, Southern 52, 160
    Tropical 52
boubous 159
Brachypteraciinae 38
*Bradornis mariquensis* 181
    *B. pallidus* 181
*Bradypterus* 170
Broadbill, African 52, 154
    African Green 154
    Grey-headed 154
    Rufous-sided 154
broadbills 154
brownbuls 169
*Bubalornis niger* 187
*Bubo capensis* 65
Bucerotidae 27
Bucerotiformes 27
Bucorvidae 29
*Bucorvus leadbeateri* 30
Buffalo-Weaver, Red-billed 115, 187
    White-headed 115
buffalo-weavers 186
*Bugeranus carunculatus* 74
Bulbul, African Red-eyed 169
    Black-eyed 169, 170
    Cape 170
    Red-eyed 170
    Slender 170
    Sombre 170
    Stripe-cheeked 170
    Terrestrial 169, 170
    Tiny 170
    Yellow-bellied 170
    Yellow-streaked 170
bulbuls 51, 169
Bunting, Cape 197
    Cinnamon-breasted 197
    Golden-breasted 197
    Lark-like 196, 197
buntings 196
*Buphagus africanus* 183
    *B. erythrorhynchus* 183
Burhinidae 91, 100
*Burhinus* 91
    *B. capensis* 91
    *B. vermiculatus* 92
bushbabies 190
Bush-Shrike, Gorgeous 159
    Grey-headed 159
    Olive 160
bush-shrikes 159, 162
Bustard, Australian 73
    Black-bellied 72
    Denham's 72
    Great 73
    Hartlaub's 72

Kori 48, 72, 73
Long-legged 72
Ludwig's 72
Stanley's 72
bustardquails 19
bustards 71, 72
*Butorides striata* 128
Buttonquail, Black-rumped 20, 21
    Hottentot 21
    Kurrichane 20, 21
buttonquails 19, 20, 21
Buzzard, Augur 111
    Forest 111
    Honey 108
    Jackal 111
    Lizard 111
    Long-legged 111
    Steppe 111
buzzards 108
*Bycanistes* 29
    *B. bucinator* 28

Cairini 18
*Calendulauda sabota* 175
*Calonectris* 152
*Camaroptera brachyura* 173
*Campephaga flava* 164
Campephagidae 163
*Campethera bennettii* 24
canaries 196
Canary, Black-headed 196, 197
    Black-throated 196
    Bully 196
    Cape 196
    Damara 196, 197
    Forest 196, 197
    Lemon-breasted 196, 197
    Streaky-headed 196
    Yellow 196, 197
    Yellow-eyed 196
Capitoniidae 25
Caprimulgidae 67
Caprimulgiformes 67
*Caprimulgus natalensis* 68
    *C. rufigena* 68
Casuariidae 10
*Catharacta* 106
Cathartidae 113
Centropodidae 53
*Centropus benghalensis* 54
    *C. burchellii* 53
    *C. cupreicaudus* 53
    *C. grilli* 53
    *C. toulou* 54
*Cercococcyx* 52
*Cercomela familiaris* 178
*Cercotrichas leucophrys* 179
    *C. paena* 179
    *C. quadrivirgata* 179
    *C. signata* 179
*Ceryle* 44
    *C. rudis* 45
cerylid kingfishers 44
Cerylidae 44
*Ceyx* 41

Chaetopidae 165
*Chaetops aurantius* 165
    *C. frenatus* 165
*Chaetorhynchus* 156
Chaeturinae 58
Chaffinch 196
Charadriidae 83, 96
Charadriiformes 81
Charadriinae 97
*Charadrius dubius* 100
    *C. pecuarius* 98
Chat, Ant-eating 177
    Arnot's 177, 178
    Familiar 177, 178
    Mocking 177, 178
chats 177
*Chersomanes albofasciata* 175
chickadees 166
Chionidae 89
*Chionis albus* 90
    *C. minor* 90
*Chlidonias* 108
    *C. hybrida* 108
*Chloroceryle* 44
*Chlorocichla* 170
    *C. flaviventris* 170
*Chloropeta* 172
    *C. natalensis* 171
*Chrysococcyx* 52
    *C. caprius* 51
    *C. cupreus* 51
    *C. klaas* 51
*Ciccaba* 67
*Cichladusa* 177
*Ciconia ciconia* 139
    *C. episcopus* 140
    *C. nigra* 140
Ciconiidae 139
Ciconiiformes 117
*Cinnyricinclus leucogaster* 183
*Cinnyris mariquensis* 184
*Cisticola aridulus* 174
    *C. ayresii* 174
    *C. juncidis* 174
    *C. lais* 174
Cisticola, Ayres' 174
    Croaking 173
    Desert 174
    Fan-tailed 173, 174, 194
    Lazy 173
    Neddicky 173
    Wailing 174
    Wing-snapping 174
cisticolas 173
Cisticolidae 173
*Cladorhynchus leucocephalus* 95
*Clamator* 51
    *C. glandarius* 51
*Coccopygia melanotis* 190
Coliidae 48
Coliiformes 48
*Colius* 48
    *C. colius* 50
    *C. striatus* 50
*Collocalia* 59
*Columba arquatrix* 70
    *C. delegorguei* 70
Columbidae 69
Columbiformes 55, 69, 81
Coot, Eurasian 80

    Red-knobbed 80
coots 78, 80
*Coracias* 38, 39
    *C. caudatus* 38
    *C. cyanogaster* 39
    *C. garrulus* 39
    *C. naevius* 39
    *C. spatulatus* 39
Coraciidae 38
Coraciiformes 38
*Coracina* 164
    *C. pectoralis* 164
Cormorant, Bank 124
    Cape 124
    Crowned 124
    Galapagos 124
    Guanay 123
    Reed 124
    White-breasted 124
cormorants 17, 123
Corvidae 161
corvids 161
*Corvinella aequatorialis* 162
    *C. melanoleuca* 162, 163
*Corvus* 161
    *C. albicollis* 161
    *C. albus* 161
    *C. capensis* 161
*Corythaixoides concolor* 62
*Cossypha dichroa* 178
    *C. heuglini* 178
    *C. humeralis* 178
    *C. natalensis* 178
*Coturnix adansonii* 13
    *C. delegorguei* 13
Coucal, Black 53, 54
    Burchell's 53, 54
    Coppery-tailed 53, 54
    Green 51
    Senegal 54
    White-browed 54
coucals 53
Courser, Bronze-winged 103
    Burchell's 103
    Cream-coloured 103
    Double-banded 103, 104
    Temminck's 103
    Three-banded 103
coursers 100, 103
Crake, African 79
    Baillon's 79
    Black 79
    Corn 79
    Little 79
    Spotted 79
    Striped 79
crakes 78
Crane, Black Crowned 75
    Blue 75, 76
    Common 74
    Demoiselle 74, 76
    Grey Crowned 75, 76
    Wattled 74, 75
    Whooping 74
cranes 74, 81, 125
*Creatophora cinerea* 182
*Crecopsis egregia* 79
Creeper, Spotted 36, 176, 177
Crested-Flycatcher, Blue-mantled 157

*Crex* 79
Crimsonwing, Red-faced 189, 190
*Crithagra citrinipectus* 197
    *C. flaviventris* 197
    *C. scotops* 197
crombecs 170
Crow, American 162
    Black 135, 161, 162
    House 161
    Pied 161
crowned pigeons 70
crows 51, 161
*Cryptillas* 170
    *C. victorini* 171
*Cryptospiza reichenovii* 190
Cuckoo, African 51, 52
    African Emerald 51, 52
    Barred Long-tailed 52, 154
    Black 52
    Common 51, 52
    Diderick 51, 52
    European 51, 52
    Great Spotted 51
    Jacobin 51
    Klaas's 51, 52
    Lesser 52
    Levaillant's 51
    Madagascar 52
    Red-chested 51, 52
    Striped 51
    Thick-billed 51
Cuckoo-finch 192, 193, 194
Cuckoo-Hawk, African 108
cuckoo-roller 38
cuckoos 50, 193, 194
Cuckooshrike, Black 164
    Grey 164
    White-breasted 164
cuckooshrikes 163
Cuculidae 50, 53
Cuculiformes 50, 55, 60
*Cuculus* 52, 193
    *C. gularis* 51
    *C. solitarius* 51
Curlew, Eurasian 84
    Hudsonian 84
Cursorinae 103
*Cursorius* 103
    *C. rufus* 103
    *C. temminckii* 103
*Cypsiurus parvus* 59

Dabchick 118
*Dacelo* 42
dacelonid kingfishers 42
Dacelonidae 42
Darter, African 122
darters 122
Death-bird 64
*Dendrocygna* 16
    *D. bicolor* 16
    *D. viduata* 16
Dendrocygnidae 15
*Dendroperdix* 12
    *D. sephaena* 12
*Dendropicos griseocephalus* 25
    *D. namaquus* 25
Dicruridae 156
*Dicrurus* 156
    *D. adsimilis* 157

    *D. ludwigii* 157
Dikkop, Cape 91
    Eurasian 91
    Senegal 91, 92
    Spotted 91, 92
    Water 91, 92
dikkops 91, 100, 102
dinosaurs 8
*Diomedea* 149
    *D. exulans* 149
Diomedeidae 149
divers 117
Diving-petrel, Common 148
Doodsvogel 64
Dove, African Mourning 70
    Cape Turtle 67
    Cinnamon 70, 71
    Diamond 70
    European Rock 69
    Laughing 67
    Lemon 70, 71
    Namaqua 69, 70
    Tambourine 70, 71
doves 69, 81
Dowitcher, Asiatic 85
drietoonkwartel 20
Dromadidae 10, 100
*Dromas ardeola* 101
Drongo, Fork-tailed 51, 52, 156, 157
    Square-tailed 156, 157
drongos 156
*Dryoscopus cubla* 160
Duck, Comb 18
    Eider 19
    Fulvous 16, 17
    Knob-billed 18
    Maccoa 17, 19
    White-backed 16, 17
    White-faced 16, 17
    Yellow-billed 18
ducks 17
Duculinae 71
Dunnock 194

Eagle, African Fish 108, 109, 112
    American Bald 108
    Bateleur 109, 198
    Black 108, 111, 112
    Booted 112
    Crowned 109, 112, 156
    Indian Black 111
    Lesser-Spotted 111
    Long-crested 112
    Martial 15, 112, 156
    Steppe 111
    Tawny 111, 142
    Verreaux's 111
    Wahlberg's 112
Eagle-Owl, Cape 65, 66
    Eurasian 66
    Giant 66, 67
    Milky 66
    Spotted 66
    Verreaux's 66, 67
eagle-owls 66
eagles 108
Egret, Cattle 128
    Great 127
    Little 127
    Reddish 127

Slaty 125, 126, 127
Snowy 127
Yellow-billed 127
egrets 125
*Egretta* 127
  *E. alba* 127
  *E. ardesiaca* 126
  *E. vinaceigula* 126
*Elanus* 108
*Elminia* 170
*Emberiza capensis* 197
  *E. flaviventris* 197
  *E. impetuani* 197
  *E. tahapisi* 197
*Ephippiorhynchus senegalensis* 139
*Eremomela* 170
  *E. icteropygialis* 171
Eremomela, Yellow-bellied 171
eremomelas 170
*Eremopterix verticalis* 176
*Erythrocercus* 170
*Esacus* 91
*Estrilda astrild* 189
Estrildidae 189
*Eudyptes* 146
*Euplectes afer* 188
  *E. hordeaceus* 188
  *E. orix* 188
  *E. progne* 188
*Eurocephalus anguitimens* 162, 163
  *E. rueppelli* 163
Eurylaimidae 154
*Eurystomus* 38, 39
  *E. glaucurus* 39

*Falco* 114
  *F. fasciinucha* 116
  *F. naumanni* 115
  *F. peregrinus* 116
  *F. rupicoloides* 115
  *F. vespertinus* 115
Falcon, African Hobby 116
  Eleonora's 116
  Eurasian Hobby 116
  Gyr 116
  Lanner 116
  Peregrine 70, 116
  Pygmy 114, 115
  Red-necked 116
  Sooty 47, 116
  Taita 116
Falconidae 114
Falconiformes 108
Falconinae 114
feral pigeons 70
fig-eaters 155
Finch, Cut-throat 189, 191
  Red-headed 189, 191
  Scaly-feathered 188
Finfoot, African 9, 77
  American 77
finfoots 76
Firefinch, Blue-billed 191, 193
  Jameson's 191, 193
  Red-billed 191
firefinches 189, 193
fisante 12
fishing owls 67
fishing kingfishers 40
Flamingo, Andean 133
  Chilean 133
  Greater 132, 133, 134, 198
  James' 133
  Lesser 132, 133, 134
flamingoes 95, 132
Flufftail, Buff-spotted 80
  White-winged 80, 81
flufftails 78, 79
Flycatcher, African Paradise 158
  Black 181
  Blue-grey 52, 181
  Blue-mantled 157, 158
  Dusky 181
  Fairy 170
  Marico 181
  Pallid 181
  Spotted 181
forest kingfishers 40
Francolin, Hartlaub's 13
  Natal 13
  Red-billed 13
  Swainson's 13
francolins 12, 13
*Francolinus* 12
*Fregata minor* 143
Fregatidae 142
*Fregatta* 147
Frigatebird 143, 144
frigatebirds 142
Fringillidae 196
*Fulica* 80
Fulmar, Northern 151
  Southern 151

gadfly petrels 151
Galliformes 12
*Gallinago media* 84
  *G. nigripennis* 84
*Gallinula* 80
*Gallinula chloropus* 79
Gallinule, African Purple 79, 80
  Allen's 79
  American Purple 79
  Lesser 79
gallinules 78
*Gallirex* 62
  *G. porphyreolophus* 62
Gannet, Australasian 120, 121
  Cape 120, 121
  Northern 120, 121, 122
gannets 119, 120
Garganey 18
*Garrodia* 147
Gaviidae 117
geese 17
genets 190
*Geochelidon* 108
*Geocolaptes olivaceus* 23
*Geronticus calvus* 135
Giant-Petrel, Southern 152
giant-petrels 151
*Glareola nordmanni* 104
  *G. nuchalis* 105
  *G. pratincola* 104
Glareolidae 100, 103
Glareolinae 103
*Glaucidium* 67
  *G. capense* 66
  *G. perlatum* 66
Go'way-bird, Grey 61, 62
go-away-bird 61
Godwit, Bar-tailed 84
goi heron 128
golden plovers 98
Goose, African Pygmy 18
  Egyptian 18
  Magpie 18
  Spur-winged 18, 19
*Gorsachius leuconotus* 128
Goshawk, African 111
  Dark Chanting 111
  Gabar 111
  Little-banded 111
  Pale Chanting 111
  Shikra 111
*Granatina granatina* 190
Grassbird, Cape 170
Grebe, Black-necked 117, 118
  Great Crested 118
  Little 118
  Western 117
grebes 17, 117
Green Singing Finch 196
greenbuls 169
Ground-Hornbill, Northern 30
  Southern 29, 30
ground-hornbills 28, 29, 30, 113
ground-rollers 38
Ground-Thrush, Spotted 180
ground-thrushes 177
Gruidae 71, 74, 85
Gruiformes 71, 81
*Grus* 74
Guineafowl, Black 14
  Crested 14, 15
  Helmeted 14, 15
  Vulturine 14
  White-breasted 14
guineafowls 14
Gull, Cape 107
  Grey-headed 107
  Kelp 107
  Sabine's 107
  Southern Black-backed 107
gulls 100, 105, 107
*Guttera edouardi* 14
*Gygis* 108
Gymnogene, Banded 36
*Gypaetus barbatus* 110
*Gypohierax angolensis* 111
*Gyps coprotheres* 111

Haematopodidae 93
*Haematopus moquini* 93
*Halcyon albiventris* 42
  *H. chelicuti* 43
  *H. leucocephala* 42
  *H. senegalensis* 43
  *H. senegaloides* 43
*Haliaeetus vocifer* 109
*Halocyptema* 147
Hamerkop 129–131
Harrier, African Marsh 111
  Black 111
  Montagu's 111
  Pallid 111
  Western Marsh 111
harriers 109
Hawk, Bat 108
Hawk-eagle, African 109, 112
Ayres' 112
hawks 108
hedgehogs 66
*Hedydipna collaris* 184
Heliornithidae 71, 76
Helmet-Shrike, Black 160
  Red-billed 160
  Retz's 51, 159, 160
  White 159
helmet-shrikes 159, 162
*Hemiparra* 97
hemipodes 19
Heron, Black 126, 127, 129
  Black-headed 127
  Common Squacco 127, 128
  Goliath 127, 128
  Green-backed 128
  Grey 127
  Little Blue 127
  Madagascar Squacco 128
  Rufous-bellied 127, 128
  Western Reef 127
herons 125
*Himantopus* 95
  *H. himantopus* 95
  *H. h. leucocephalus* 95
*Hippolais* 172
Hirundinidae 58, 167
*Hirundo abyssinica* 168
  *H. albigularis* 168
  *H. atrocaerulea* 167
  *H. cucullata* 168
  *H. dimidiata* 168
  *H. smithii* 168
Hoatzin 9
homing pigeons 69
Honey Badger 22
honeybees 22, 46, 47, 59
Honeybird, Cassin's 21
  Sharp-billed 21, 173
  Slender-billed 21
honeybirds 21
honeyeaters 185
Honeyguide, Greater 22
  Lesser 22, 23
  Scaly-throated 22
honeyguides 21, 193
Hoopoe, African 31, 32, 33
  Eurasian 32, 33
Hoopoe-Lark 175
hoopoes 31, 32, 35
*Hoploxypterus* 97
hornbill ivory 27, 28
Hornbill, African Grey 29
  Helmeted 27
  Red-billed 29
  Trumpeter 28
  White-crested 29
  Yellow-billed 28, 29
hornbills 27
houtkapper 25
hummingbirds 58, 184
*Hydrobates* 147
Hydrobatidae 147
*Hyliota* 172
  *H. australis* 171
Hyliota, Mashona 171
  Southern 171
hymenopterans 47

*Ibidorhynchus struthersii* 95
Ibis, Bald 135, 136
   Glossy 135
   Hadeda 135
   Hermit 136
   Sacred 136, 137
   Scarlet 137
Ibisbill 95
ibises 135
imperial pigeons 71
*Indicator* 21, 193
   *I. indicator* 22
   *I. minor* 22
   *I. variegatus* 22
Indicatoridae 21
indigobirds 192
*Ispidina picta* 41
*Ixobrychus sturmii* 128

Jacana, African 87, 88
   Lesser 87, 88, 89
   Pheasant-tailed 87
jacanas 87
Jacanidae 85, 87
jackdaws 161
jaegers 106
Jay, Common 162
jays 161
*Jynx ruficollis* 23

Kaiservögel 160
Kestrel, Dickinson's 116
   Eastern Red-footed 115
   Greater 115
   Grey 115
   Lesser 115
   Rock 115
   Western Red-footed 115
kestrels 115
Kingfisher, Belted 44, 45
   Brown-hooded 42, 43, 177
   Common 40, 41, 44
   Crested 44
   Dwarf 40
   Earthworm-eating 42
   Giant 44, 45
   Grey-headed 43
   Grey-hooded 42, 43
   Half-collared 41
   Malachite 41, 42
   Malachite Crested 42
   Mangrove 43, 44
   Pied 44, 45
   Pygmy 40, 41
   Ringed 44
   Shovel-billed 42
   Striped 43, 44
   Woodland 43, 44
kingfishers 40, 42, 44
Kite, Black 108
   Black-shouldered 108
   Yellow-billed 108, 110
kites 108
Kittiwake, Black-legged 107
Kittlitz's Plover 98
Kookaburra 42
Korhaan, Barrow's 72
   Black 72, 73
   Blue 72, 73
   Buff-crested 72

Karoo, 72
   Red-crested 72
   Rüppell's 72
   Savile's 72
   White-bellied 72
korhaans 71, 72
kwarteltjie 20

*Lagonosticta* 189
   *L. rhodopareia* 191
   *L. rubricata* 191
   *L. senegala* 191
lake terns 108
Lammergeier 109, 110, 114
*Lamprotornis* 182
   *L. australis* 182
   *L. elisabeth* 182
land-snail, giant 29
*Laniarius* 159
   *L. aethiopicus* 160
   *L. atrococcineus* 160
Laniidae 162
*Lanius* 162
   *L. collurio* 163
   *L. minor* 163
Lapwing 97
lapwings 97
Laridae 100, 105
Lark, Clapper 176
   Dusky 176
   Horned 175
   Melodious 176
   Namib 176
   Red 176
   Rudd's 81, 175
   Rufous-naped 175
   Sabota 175, 176
   Spike-heeled 175
larks 175
*Larosterna* 108
Laughing Jackass 42
leaf-warblers 170
*Leptoptilos crumeniferus* 140
Leptosomatinae 38
*Lepus* hares 65
*Limnodromus semipalmatus* 85
*Limosa* 84
*Lioptilus nigricapillus* 172
*Lissotis melanogaster* 72
litany bird 69
Locustfinch 189
Loggerhead Shrike 163
Longclaw, Orange-throated 195, 196
   Pink-throated 195, 196
   Yellow-throated 195, 196
longclaws 195
loons 117
Loriinae 55
Lourie, Knysna 9, 61
louries 48, 60
Lovebird, Black-cheeked 57
   Fischer's 57
   Lilian's 57
   Masked 57
   Rosy-faced 55, 57
   Yellow-collared 57
lovebirds 57
*Lugensa* 151
Lybiidae 25
*Lybius torquatus* 26

Macaw, Hyacinth 56
*Macheiramphus alcinus* 111
*Macrodipteryx* 69
   *M. vexillarius* 68
*Macronectes giganteus* 152
*Macronyx ameliae* 196
   *M. capensis* 196
   *M. croceus* 196
Magpie, European 163
magpies 161
Malaconotidae 159
*Malaconotus blanchoti* 159
Malkoha, Green 51
*Mandingoa nitidula* 190
Mannikin, Bronze 191
   Magpie 191
   Red-backed 191
mannikins 189, 190
marsh-warbler 170
Martin, Banded 168
   Brown-throated 168
   Congo River 167
   House 168, 169
   Mascarene 168
   Rock 169
   Sand 168
martins 167
*Megaceryle* 44
   *M. maximus* 45
*Melaenornis pammelaina* 181
Melba, Green-winged 191, 193
   Orange-winged 193
*Melichneutes* 21
*Melierax* 111
*Melignomon* 21
Meliphagidae 185
*Melocichla* 170
Mergini 19
Meropidae 46
*Merops* 46
   *M. apiaster* 46
   *M. bullockoides* 47
   *M. hirundineus* 46
   *M. nubicoides* 47
   *M. persicus* 47
   *M. pusillus* 47
*Micrococcus cerolyticus* 22
*Micronisus* 111
*Milvus* 108
   *M. aegyptius* 110
*Mirafra* 175
   *M. africana* 175
   *M. apiata* 176
mollymawks 149
monarch flycatchers 157
Monarchidae 157
monkeys 15, 29, 190
   Samango 190
*Monticola* 177
   *M. explorator* 180
   *M. rupestris* 180
Moorhen, Common 79, 80
   Lesser 80
moorhens 79
*Morus* 120
   *M. capensis* 121
*Motacilla* 195
   *M. aguimp* 195
   *M. capensis* 195

   *M. clara* 195
Motacillidae 195
Mousebird, Red-faced 49, 50, 177
   Speckled 49, 50
   White-backed 49, 50
mousebirds 48, 49, 60
*Muscicapa adusta* 181
   *M. caerulescens* 181
   *M. striata* 181
Muscicapidae 177
*Musophaga* 62
Musophagidae 60
Musophagiformes 60
Muttonbird 152
*Mycteria ibis* 141
Myna, Common 182
   Hill 56
mynas 182
*Myrmecochicla* 177
   *M. arnoti* 178

*Nectarinia famosa* 184
Nectariniidae 184
*Neophron percnopterus* 110
*Nesofregatta* 147
*Netta erythrophthalma* 19
*Nettapus auritus* 19
New World vultures 108, 113
*Nicator* 170
Nicator, Eastern 170
nicators 169
nighthawks 67, 69
Night-heron, Black-crowned 128
   White-backed 128
Nightjar, European 68
   Fiery-necked 69
   Freckled 68
   Natal 68
   Pennant-winged 68, 69
   Rufous-cheeked 68
   Standard-winged 69
   Swamp 68
nightjars 67
Noddy, Brown 108
   Grey 108
   Lesser 108
*Numida meleagris* 14
Numididae 14

*Oceanites* 147
   *O. oceanicus* 147
Oceanitidae 147
*Oceanodroma* 147
*Oena capensis* 69
Oilbird 67
Old World cuckoos 50
Old World flycatchers 177
Old World orioles 155
Old World vultures 108
*Opisthocomus hoazin* 9
Oriole, African Golden 155, 156
   Black 155
   Black-headed 155, 156
   Eurasian Golden 155
   Green-headed 155
Oriolidae 155
*Oriolus* 155
   *O. auratus* 156
   *O. larvatus* 155
*Ortygospiza atricollis* 191

Oscines 167
Osprey 67, 108
Ostrich 10, 27, 29
Otidae 71
*Otus* 66
   *O. senegalensis* 66
Owl, Barn 63, 64, 66, 67
   Barred 67
   Elf 66
   Grass 63, 64, 65, 67
   Great Horned 66
   Marsh 63, 64, 65, 67
   Pel's Fishing 65, 67
   Snowy 64, 66
   White-faced 65, 66
   Wood 65
Owlet, Barred 66
   Pearl-spotted 66, 67, 157
Oxpecker, Red-billed 183
   Yellow-billed 183
oxpeckers 182
*Oxyura maccoa* 19
Oxyurini 19
Oystercatcher, African Black 93, 94
   Eurasian 94
oystercatchers 93

*Pachycoccyx* 51
*Pachyptila* 151
Painted-snipe, American 86
   Greater 85, 86, 87
   Lesser 86, 87
painted-snipes 85
palm-thrushes 177
paradise kingfishers 42
Parakeet, Carolina 55
   Ring-necked 57
   Rose-ringed 55
Paridae 166
*Parisoma* 172
*Parisoma subcaeruleum* 171
Parrot, Brown-headed 56
   Cape 56, 57
   Grey-headed 56, 57
   Ground 55
   Meyer's 56, 57
   Night 55
   Owl 55
   Rüppell's 57
parrots 48, 55
Partridge, Coqui 12
   Crested 12
   Shelley's 12
partridges 12, 13
*Parus* 166
   *P. niger* 167
*Passer diffusus* 194
   *P. melanurus* 194
   *P. motitensis* 194
Passeridae 194
Passeriformes 58, 153
patryse 12
Peacock, Blue 12
   Green 12
*Pelagodroma* 147
*Pelecanoides urinatrix* 148
Pelecanoididae 148
*Pelecanus occidentalis thagus* 137
   *P. onocrotalus* 138
   *P. rufescens* 138

Pelican, Brown 137
   Dalmatian 137
   Great White 137, 138, 150
   Pink-backed 137, 138
Pelicanidae 137
pelicans 137
*Peliperdix* 12
   *P. coqui* 12
Penduline-Tit, Cape 166
   European 166
   Grey 166
penduline-tits 166
Penguin, Adèlie 144, 145, 146
   African 146
   Emperor 144, 146
   Galapagos 146
   Gentoo 146
   Jackass 145, 146
   King 146
   Macaroni 146
   Magellan 146
   Magellanic 146
   Rockhopper 146
penguins 117, 144
Petrel, Antarctic 151
   Balearic 152
   Blue 151
   Gould's 151
   Grey 152
   Kerguelen 151
   Pintado 151
   Snow 151
   Spectacled 152
   White-chinned 152
   White-winged 151
petrels 151
*Petronia superciliaris* 194
Petronia, Yellow-throated 194
petronias 194
*Phaethon rubricauda* 119
Phaethontidae 118
*Phaetusa* 108
Phalacrocoracidae 123
*Phalacrocorax* 124
   *P. africanus* 124
   *P. lucidus* 124
phalaropes 85
Phasianidae 12, 14
Pheasant, Crested Argus 12
*Philomachus pugnax* 85
*Phodilus* 63
   *P. badius* 64
   *P. prigoginei* 64
*Phoebastria* 149
*Phoebetria* 149
*Phoeniconaias* 133
*Phoenicoparrus* 133
Phoenicopteridae 95, 132
*Phoenicopterus* 133
   *P. minor* 132
   *P. ruber* 132
Phoeniculidae 33, 35
*Phoeniculus purpureus* 33
*Phyllastrephus* 170
   *P. flavostriatus* 170
   *P. terrestris* 169
*Phylloscopus* 172
   *P. ruficapilla* 171
Picidae 23
Piciformes 21

Piet-my-Vrou 51
Pigeon, African Green 70, 71
   Eastern Bronze-naped 70
   Passenger 70, 71
   Rameron 70
   Speckled 70
pigeons 69
*Pinarocorys nigricans* 176
Pintail, Northern 18
Pipit, Bushveld 195
   Golden 195
   Meadow 52
   Short-tailed 195
   Striped 195
pipits 195
*Pitta angolensis* 153
Pitta, Angola 153
   Green-breasted 154
pittas 153
Pittidae 153
Plains Wanderer 19
*Platalea alba* 136
*Platysteira peltata* 160
Ploceidae 186
*Plocepasser mahali* 188
*Ploceus cucullatus* 187
   *P. intermedius* 187
   *P. ocularis* 187
   *P. subaureus* 187
Plover, Black-bellied 96
   Blacksmith 98, 99
   Black-winged 98
   Caspian 98
   Chestnut-banded 98
   Common Ringed 98
   Crab 100, 101, 102
   Crowned 66, 98, 99, 100
   Egyptian 103
   Greater Sand 98
   Grey 96, 98
   Kentish 98
   Lesser Black-winged 98, 100
   Lesser Sand 98
   Little Ringed 98, 100
   Long-toed 97
   Mongolian 98
   Quail 19
   Spur-winged 98
   Three-banded 98
   Wattled 98, 99
   White-crowned 97, 98
   White-fronted 100
plovers 96
*Pluvialis* 98
   *P. dominica* 98
   *P. fulva* 98
*Pluvianus aegypticus* 103
Pochard, Southern 18
*Podica senegalensis* 77
*Podiceps nigricollis* 117
Podicipedidae 117
*Pogoniulus bilineatus* 27
   *P. chrysoconus* 26
   *P. pusillus* 26
*Pogonocichla stellata* 179
*Poicephalus* 56
   *P. cryptoxanthus* 56
   *P. fuscicollis* 57
   *P. meyeri* 56

   *P. robustus* 56
   *P. robustus fusicollis* 57
   *P. robustus suahelicus* 57
   *P. suahelicus* 56
*Polihierax* 114
   *P. semitorquatus* 115
*Porphyrio* 79
   *P. madagascariensis* 79
   *P. mantelli* 79
*Porzana* 79
Pratincole, Australian 103, 104
   Black-winged 104, 105
   Collared 104
   Grey 104
   Madagascar 105
   Red-winged 104, 105
   Rock 105
pratincoles 100, 103, 104
*Prinia flavicans* 174
Prinia, Black-chested 174
   Drakensberg 174
   Karoo 174
prinias 52, 174
*Prionops caniceps* 160
   *P. plumatus* 159
   *P. retzii* 159
prions 151
*Procellaria* 152
Procellariidae 151
Procellariiformes 147
*Procelsterna* 108
Prodoticsidae 21
*Prodotiscus* 21
Promeropidae 185
*Promerops cafer* 186
   *P. gurneyi* 185
Psittacidae 55
Psittaciformes 55
Psittacinae 55
*Psittacula* 55
   *P. krameri* 55
*Psophocichla litsitsirupa* 180
ptarmigans 91
*Pternistis* 12, 13
*Pternistis adspersus* 13
   *P. natalensis* 13
   *P. swainsonii* 13
*Pterocles* 81, 82
   *P. bicinctus* 82
   *P. burchelli* 81
   *P. namaqua* 82
Pteroclidae 81
*Pterodroma* 151
*Ptilopsis* 66
   *P. granti* 65
Puffback, Black-backed 159, 160
   Southern 159, 160
puffbacks 159
*Puffinus* 152
Pycnonotidae 169
*Pycnonotus* 170
   *P. barbatus* 169
   *P. nigricans* 169
*Pygoscelis* 146
*Pytilia melba* 191
pytilias 189

Quail, Blue 13, 54
   Common 13
   Harlequin 13

Lark 19
Painted 13
Quailfinch, African 163, 189, 191
quails 12
Quelea, Red-billed 15
queleas 186, 187
Quetzal, Resplendent 37

Rail, African 79
rails 78
Rallidae 71, 78, 79, 80
*Rallus* 79
Ramphastidae 27
Raven, White-necked 161, 162
ravens 114, 161
*Recurvirostra* 95
  *R. avosetta* 95
Recurvirostridae 95
Red Rock-rabbit 65
reed-warblers 170
Reed-Warbler, Cape 171
  Yellow 171
Reeve 84
Reichsvögel 160
Rheidae 10
Rhinopomastidae 35
*Rhinopomastus* 35
  *R. cyanomelas* 35
*Rhinoptilus* 103
  *R. chalcopterus* 103
  *R. cinctus* 103
ringed plovers 97
Ringneck, African 55
*Riparia paludicola* 168
*Rissa* 107
Robin, Chorister 177, 178
  Heuglin's 178
  Natal 178
  Starred 52, 179
  Swynnerton's 179
  White-throated 178
robins 52, 177
Rockjumper, Cape 165
  Drakensberg 165
rockjumpers 165
Rockrunner 170
Rock-Thrush, Cape 180
  Sentinel 180
rock-thrushes 177
Roller, Blue-bellied 38, 39
  Broad-billed 39
  Eurasian 39
  European 39, 40
  Lilac-breasted 38, 39, 40
  Purple 39, 40
  Racket-tailed 39, 40
rollers 38
*Rostratula benghalensis* 86
Rostratulidae 85
Ruff 84, 85
Rynchopidae 105
*Rynchops flavirostris* 106

Sagittariidae 112
*Salpornis spilonotus* 177
Salpornithidae 176
Sanderling 84
sandgrouse 81
Sandgrouse, Burchell's 81, 82, 83
  Double-banded 82, 83

Namaqua 82, 83
Yellow-throated 83
Sandpiper, Curlew 85
  Terek 84
*Sarkidiornis melanotos* 19
*Sarothrura elegans* 80
Saw-wing, Black 169
  Eastern 169
  White-headed 169
*Schoenicola* 170
Scimitarbill, Abyssinian 35
  Black 35
  Common 35, 36
scimitarbills 35
*Scleroptila* 12
  *S. shelleyi* 12
Scolopacidae 83, 96
Scopidae 129
Scops-Owl, African 66
*Scopus umbretta* 129
*Scotopelia* 67
  *S. peli* 65
screech-owls 66
Scrub-Robin, Bearded 179
  Brown 179
  Kalahari 179
  Karoo 177
  White-browed 179
seagulls 107
Secretarybird 112–114
Sedge-warbler, African 170
sedge-warblers 172
Seedcracker, Lesser 189
seed-snipes 82
*Serinus alario* 197
Shearwater, Manx 152
  Short-tailed 152
shearwaters 151, 152
Sheathbill, Greater 89, 90
  Lesser 90
sheathbills 89
Shelduck, South African 18
*Sheppardia* 52
Shoveler, Northern 18
Shrike, Brubru 159
  Crimson-breasted 52, 159, 160
  Fiscal 51
  Great Grey 163
  Lesser Grey 163
  Long-tailed 162
  Magpie 162
  Northern 163
  Red-backed 163
  Vanga 160
  White-crowned 162, 163
  White-tailed 160
  Woodchat 163
Siskin, Cape 196
  Drakensberg 196
Skimmer, African 106
skimmers 105
Skua, Antarctic 106
  Arctic 106
  Long-tailed 106
  Pomarine 106
  South Polar 106
skuas 105
Skylark, European 176
*Smithornis capensis* 154
*Smutsornis* 103

Snake-eagle, Black-chested 109
  Brown 109
  Southern Banded 109
  Western Banded 109
snake-eagles 109
Snipe, African 83, 84
  Great 83, 84
social wasps 46, 47
Somateriini 19
Sparrow, Cape 52, 194
  Great 194
  Grey-headed 194
  Hedge 194
  House 194
Sparrowhawk, Black 111
  Little 111
  Ovambo 111
  Rufous-breasted 109, 111, 186
Sparrowlark, Grey-backed 176
sparrowlarks 175
sparrows 51, 194
Sparrow-Weaver, White-browed 186, 188
speg 25
Spekvretertjie 177
*Spermestes* 189
  *S. bicolor* 191
  *S. cucullatus* 191
  *S. fringilloides* 191
*Sphecotheres* 155
Spheniscidae 144
*Spheniscus* 146
  *S. demersus* 145
*Sphenoeacus* 170
spiderhunters 184
Spinetail, Batlike 58
  Böhm's 58
  Mottled 58
spinetails 58
Spoonbill, African 136, 137
  Roseate 137
spoonbills 135
*Sporaeginthus subflavus* 190
*Sporopipes squamifrons* 188
*Spreo bicolor* 182
spurfowl 13
Squirrel, Bush 36
Starling, Burchell's 51, 182
  European 182
  Greater Blue-eared 182
  Lesser Blue-eared 182
  Pale-winged 182
  Pied 51, 182
  Plum-coloured 182, 183
  Red-winged 182
  Wattled 182
starlings 51, 182
*Steatornis caripensis* 67
*Stenostira* 170
*Stephanoaetus coronatus* 109
Stercorariidae 105
*Stercorarius* 106
*Sterna* 108
  *S. balaenarum* 107
  *S. caspia* 107
Sternidae 105
Stilt, Banded 95
  Black-winged 95
*Stiltia isabella* 103
stilts 95

Stork, Abdim's 15, 141
  African Open-billed 140, 141
  Black 140, 141
  Black-necked 142
  Marabou 140, 142
  Saddle-bill 139, 142
  Shoebill 140, 142
  White 15, 139, 141, 142
  Woolly-necked 140, 141
  Yellow-billed 140, 141
storks 125, 139
Storm-petrel, Wilson's 147, 148
storm-petrels 147
*Streptopelia decipiens* 70
Strigidae 63, 64
Strigiformes 63
*Strix* 67
  *S. woodfordii* 65
*Struthio camelus* 10
  *S. c. massaicus* 10
Struthionidae 10
Sturnidae 182
Sugarbird, Cape 185, 186
  Gurney's 185, 186
sugarbirds 185
*Sula* 120
Sulidae 120
Sunbird, Black 190
  Blue-throated 185
  Collared 184, 190
  Malachite 184
  Marico 184
sunbirds 52, 184
Swallow, Angolan 168
  Barn 168
  Blue 167, 168
  European 168
  Greater 168
  Greater Striped 168
  Grey-rumped 168
  Lesser 168
  Lesser Striped 168
  Mosque 168
  Pearl-breasted 168
  Red-breasted 168
  Red-rumped 168
  South African Cliff 167
  White-throated 168
  Wire-tailed 168
swallows 58, 167
swamphen 8
Swan, Coscoroba 15, 16
  Mute 18
Swee, African 190
Swift, Alpine 58, 59
  Common 59, 60
  Horus 59
  Little 59
  Palm 59
  White-rumped 168
swifts 58
*Swynnertonia swynnertoni* 179
*Sylvia* warblers 172
*Sylvietta* 170
Sylviidae 170
*Syrrhaptes* 81
  *S. tibetanus* 82

Tadornini 18
Takahe 79, 80

*Tanysiptera* 42
*Tauraco* 60, 62
   *T. corythaix* 61, 62
      *T. c. corythaix* 61
      *T. c. livingstonii* 61, 62
      *T. c. phoebus* 61, 62
      *T. c. reichenowi* 61, 62
      *T. c. schalowi* 62
   *T. fischeri* 61
   *T. livingstonii* 61
   *T. persa* 61, 62
   *T. schuetti* 61
*Tchagra australis* 160
   *T. minuta* 159
Tchagra, Black-crowned 159, 160
   Brown-crowned 159
   Marsh 159
   Southern 159
tchagras 159
Teal, Cape 18
   Red-billed 18
*Telacanthura ussheri* 58
*Telephorus* 159
   *T. olivaceus* 160
   *T. viridis* 159
*Terathopius ecaudatus* 109
Tern, Arctic 108
   Caspian 107, 108
   Damara 107, 108
   Fairy 108
   Gull-billed 108
   Inca 108
   Large-billed 108
   Whiskered 108
   White 108
terns 105, 107
*Terpsiphone viridis* 158
*Thalassarche* 149
*Thalassornis leuconotus* 16, 17
*Thamnolaea* 177
   *T. cinnamomeiventris* 178
thick-knees 91
*Thinocoridae* 82
*Threskiornis aethiopicus* 136
Threskiornithidae 135
Thrush, Groundscraper 177, 180
   Karoo 177
   Mistle 177
   Olive 177
   Orange 180
   Song 177
thrushes 165, 177
Thrush-Nightingale 177
Tinker, Green 27
   Red-fronted 26, 27
   Yellow-fronted 26, 27
   Yellow-rumped 27
Tit, Southern Black 167
Tit-Babbler, Chestnut-vented 171
tit-babblers 172
tits 166
*Tockus* 29
   *T. erythrorhynchus* 29
   *T. leucomelas* 28

   *T. nasutus* 29
toucans 27
*Trachyphonus vaillantii* 26
*Treron calvus* 70
*Tricholaema leucomelas* 26
Trochilidae 58, 184
*Trochocercus cyanomelas* 158
Trogon, Bare-cheeked 36, 37
   Bar-tailed 36
   Narina 36, 37, 38
Trogonidae 36
Trogoniformes 36
trogons 36
Tropicbird, Red-billed 119, 120
   Red-tailed 119, 120
   White-tailed 119, 120
tropicbirds 118
true crows 161
true eagles 111
true falcons 114
true owls 64
true quails 13
true shrikes 162
true snipes 86
true rollers 38
tubenoses 148
Turaco 9
   Knysna 61, 62
   Purple-crested 62
   Ross's 62
turacos 48, 60
*Turdoides* 172
   *T. bicolor* 171
   *T. jardineii* 171
Turnicidae 19
Turniciformes 19
*Turnix* 20
   *T. nanus* 20
   *T. sylvaticus* 20
Turnstone, Ruddy 84
Turtle-Doves, Eurasian 71
*Turtur afer* 71
   *T. tympanistria* 71
Twinspot, Green 189, 190
   Pink-throated 189
   Red-throated 189
twinspots 189
typical hornbills 27
*Tyto* 63, 64
   *T. alba* 63
   *T. capensis* 63
Tytonidae 63, 64, 67

*Upupa* 35
   *U. africana* 31
Upupidae 31, 35
Upupiformes 31
*Uraeginthus angolensis* 190
*Urocolius* 48
   *U. indicus* 49

Vanellinae 97
*Vanellus* 97
   *V. albiceps* 97

   *V. armatus* 99
   *V. coronatus* 99
   *V. crassirostris* 97
   *V. lugubris* 100
   *V. senegallus* 99
   *V. vanellus* 97
Verdin 166
*Vidua* 192
   *V. funerea* 193
   *V. macroura* 193
   *V. paradisaea* 192
   *V. purpurascens* 193
   *V. regia* 192
Viduidae 192
Vulture, Bearded 109
   Cape 111
   Egyptian 109, 110
   Hooded 109
   Lappet-faced 109, 142
   Palmnut 109, 111
   Rüppell's 109
   White-backed 109
   White-headed 109, 110
vultures 108

waders 81, 83, 96
Wagtail, African Pied 195
   Cape 195
   Citrine 195
   Grey 195
   Mountain 195
   Yellow 195
wagtails 195
Waldrapp 136
Warbler, Barratt's 170
   Barred 174
   Bleating 52
   Broad-tailed 170
   Cinnamon-breasted 174
   Garden 172
   Green-backed Bleating 51, 173, 174
   Grey-backed Bleating 173, 174
   Kalahari Barred 174
   Knysna 170
   Moustached 170
   Namaqua 174
   Red-winged 174
   Roberts's 174
   Rufous-eared 174
   Stierling's Barred 174
   Victorin's 170, 171
   Willow 172
   Yellow-throated 172
   Yellow-throated Woodland 171
warblers 170
watertrapper 77
wattled hornbills 28
Wattle-eye, Black-throated 160
wattle-eyes 159, 160
Waxbill, Black-faced 189
   Blue 189, 190
   Cinderella 189
   Common 189
   Grey 189

   Orange-breasted 189, 190, 193
   Swee 189, 190
   Violet-eared 189, 190
   Yellow-bellied 189
waxbills 189
Weaver, Lesser Masked 187
   Masked 52
   Red-headed 187
   Sociable 115, 186
   Spectacled 187
   Spotted-backed 187
   Thick-billed 186, 187
   Yellow 187
weavers 51, 186, 187
whale-birds 151
Whimbrel 84
whistling ducks 15
White-eye, Cape 172, 173
   Orange River 173
   Yellow 172, 173
white-eyes 172
Whitethroat, Common 172
Whydah, Broad-tailed Paradise 193
   Pin-tailed 189, 193
   Shaft-tailed 192, 193
   Sharp-tailed Paradise 192, 193
whydahs 192
Widow, Long-tailed 187, 188
Widow-finch, Black 191, 193
   Purple 193
   Steel-blue 193
widow-finches 192
widows 186, 187
Wood-Dove, Blue-spotted 71
Wood-Hoopoe, Black-billed 34
   Forest 34
   Grant's 34
   Green 33, 34, 35
   Red-billed 33, 34
   Violet 34
   White-headed 34
wood-hoopoes 33, 35
Wood-Owl, African 67
Woodpecker, Bearded 24, 25
   Bennett's 24
   Cardinal 24
   Ground 23, 24, 25
   Olive 25
woodpeckers 23, 24, 25
Woolly Mammoth 8
Wryneck, Northern 23
   Red-breasted 23
wrynecks 23, 24

*Xema* 107

*Zoothera* 177
   *Z. gurneyi* 180
Zosteropidae 172
*Zosterops albogularis* 173
   *Z. lateralis* 173
   *Z. pallidus* 173
   *Z. senegalensis* 172, 173
   *Z. tenuirostris* 173